DATE DUE

Demco, Inc. 38-293

FOOLS' PLAYS

A study of satire in the *sottie*

FOOLS' PLAYS

A study of satire in the *sottie*

HEATHER ARDEN

Assistant Professor, Department of
Romance Languages and Literatures
University of Cincinnati

CAMBRIDGE UNIVERSITY PRESS

CAMBRIDGE

LONDON   NEW YORK   NEW ROCHELLE
MELBOURNE   SYDNEY

Published by the Press Syndicate of the University of Cambridge
The Pitt Building, Trumpington Street, Cambridge CB2 1RP
32 East 57th Street, New York, NY 10022, USA
296 Beaconsfield Parade, Middle Park, Melbourne 3206, Australia

First published 1980

Printed in Great Britain by
Western Printing Services Ltd, Bristol

Library of Congress Cataloging in Publication Data
Arden, Heather, 1943–
Fools' plays.
Bibliography: p.
Includes index.
1. French drama – To 1500 – History and criticism.
2. French farces – History and criticism. 3. Satire,
French – History and criticism. 4. Fools and jesters
in literature. I. Title.
PQ514.A7   842'.052   78–73603
ISBN 0 521 22513 2

To the memory of my father

Contents

Preface

I want to thank the members of the Department of French and Italian of New York University for their help and guidance in the research for this study and in the writing of the original manuscript: in particular, thanks go to Jindrich Zezula, Evelyn Birge-Vitz, Aram Vartanian, and Nancy Regalado. My deepest thanks also go to Alan Schaffer, who has been a crucial influence on my intellectual development, and whose encouragement and advice helped me over many rough spots. A number of research grants from Wilkes College aided in the completion of this work, as did the efforts of the librarians at the Farley Library, in particular Fred Krohle. Finally, I thank Bruce Craddock for his unlimited patience with this 'fooling', his perceptive editorial comments, and his unfailing willingness to help with all phases of the preparation of this work.

Introduction

Qu'aujourd'uy Toult le Monde est fol.

Tout le Monde, l. *292*

The idea of *folie*[1] fascinated the late Middle Ages. Medieval people, whether learned or barely literate, not only believed the number of fools in the world to be infinite, but they greatly enjoyed repeated illustrations of this belief. For this reason interminable enumerations of fools of all kinds are found in medieval literature, from the monologue of the popular entertainer to the mock-serious treatise of the moralist. Such lists were so appreciated that they could become the subject of an entire *sermon joyeux*, monologue, or *cri*: the *Cry pour la Sottie du Prince des Sotz* opens with a call to all

> Sotz lunatiques, Sotz estourdis, Sotz sages,
> Sotz de villes, de chasteaulx, de villages,
> Sotz rassotz, Sotz nyais, Sotz Subtils...

and continues through 57 different kinds of *sots* and *sottes*. *Le Monologue des nouveaulx sotz de la joyeuse bende* enumerates 'sotz' for 49 lines; *Le Monologue des sotz joyeulx* comes up with 68 lines. The *sermon joyeux* entitled 'A tous les foulx qui sont dessoubz la nue' goes into great and amusing detail concerning the 'foulx' of the various nations of the world and in particular of the provinces of France:

> Les Picquars ilz sont trop eureux;
> Et que sont-ilz! foulx amoureux:
> Si une chièvre portoit coiffète,
> Ilz en feroient leur amyète.
> Foulx de Paris sont si grant nombre
> Que aux autres foulx portent encombre.[2]

Ll. 225–30: The Picards are very happy; And what are they? Fools in love:
If a nanny-goat were wearing a bonnet, They would make her their girl-
friend. The fools of Paris are in such great supply That of the other fools
they get in the way.

No level of society escapes the touch of *folie*, for 'L'on a bien
veu, par plusieurs foys, / De sotz papes et de sotz roys' (ll. 280–1).
Rabelais undoubtedly heard such enumerations recited at fairs
and festivals, at the crossroads of Montpellier and of Paris, and
on the *tréteaux* of dramatic performances, for he has Pantagruel
and Panurge pass in review various 'fols' (in the guise of a *blason*
for the fool Triboulet): 207 kinds in all, including 'Fol Mercurial',
'Fol prædestiné', 'Fol buliste', 'conclaviste', and 'doctoral';
'Fol talmudicque', 'abréviateur', and 'couilart'.[3]

The *fou* and *folie* fascinated not only the less educated but also
writers and artists; for books, paintings, and engravings were
produced on the subject. *Das Narrenschiff* of Sebastian Brant, the
best known of a number of German works, was translated,
adapted, and imitated. The humanist printer Badius Ascensius
composed two studies of *folie* inspired by Brant; and in 1509
Alexander Barclay contributed his own adaptation of Brant,
under the title *Ship of Folys*. The masterpiece of 'fool-literature'
of the fifteenth and sixteenth centuries is of course Erasmus's
Moriae encomium. Painters joined the writers in the ranks of those
who, if not themselves fools, were nonetheless fascinated by them:
Bosch has given us the *Extraction of the Stone of Madness* and the
Ship of Fools; Brueghel, *Mad Meg*; and Dürer, imaginative
illustrations of the *Ship of Fools*.

Fools both natural and artificial were everywhere in the fifteenth
and sixteenth centuries. They were of course to be seen in the
dumb shows, and they performed with mountebanks and
bateleurs at fairs and festivals; they were also entertainers and
servants in taverns and brothels.[4] One of the earliest examples of
French secular theater, *Le Jeu de la feuillée*, contains a fool in a
scene set in a tavern, a scene which anticipates the later development of the *sottie*. Thus, if one went to a fair, a tavern, a brothel,
or the playing of a dramatic *jeu*, there were fools; similarly, if
one went to the serious, uplifting performance of a *mystère*,
there were fools: in *La Passion de Troyes* (1490), for instance, and

in the mystery plays about various saints (see below, p. 16). The moralities also frequently put on stage a *fou* or *sot*. A character named Folie appears in *Bien Avisé, Mal Avisé*, and the best of the moralities, *La Condamnation de Banquet*, has an *intermède de fou*.

Not only had the theater its fools, but so too had the 'stage' that was the nobleman's castle or the manor of the well-to-do bourgeois.[5] The account books of noblemen, in particular those of the Dukes of Burgundy, show how valued were fools at court: thirty-one *sots* and *sottes*, *fous* and *folles*, *nains* and *géants* are mentioned in the accounts of the Dukes.[6] Triboulet, the fool of Louis XII and François I, was so famous that Rabelais, as we have seen, composed a *blason* for him. These domestic fools were evidently prized by their masters, for, according to the *sots* of *Les Sobres Sots*, 'Ils sont traictés humainement / Par le commandement du maistre.'[7] So important was the idea of *folie* that at times it merged with another dominant obsession of the late Middle Ages, the obsession with death. Not only is there usually a fool in the Danse Macabre, but Douce has found a drawing of the Danse in which Death itself is closely associated with the fool (p. 331).

The omnipresent fool – in castles, courts, and country fairs, in the theater, in philosophy and theology, in painting and engraving – was the visual manifestation of what Michel Foucault has so succinctly called 'la montée de la folie sur l'horizon de la Renaissance'.[8] Therefore, Enid Welsford was correct when she pointed out that 'the folly of writing about fools is more apparent than real'.[9] It is indeed worthwhile to try to understand this fascination with the seemingly illogical patter of the *fou*, a fascination which existed simultaneously, and often in the same person, with the desire for classical clarity and reason.

So important was the concept at this time that it was acted out in its own dramatic genre, the *sottie*. Short comic plays performed by *sots* (actors dressed like jesters), these plays put on stage various kinds of folly or madness: 'Car en soties n'a que follye' ('For in *sotties* there is only foolishness'); thus ends the *sottie Les Sotz nouveaulx*. This type of play was the most important literary expression in France of the idea of *folie*.[10] Yet, whereas other kinds of medieval comic plays, the farce in particular, have been analyzed in detail, until recently little study had been given to the *sottie*. Most existing studies are superficial or incomplete (that is, they do not consider all extant plays), and frequently they are contradictory. The earliest monograph on the *sottie*, written by Emile Picot a century ago, is based on no more than half of the *sotties* known today, for since his study two additional collections have been turned up, thus adding greatly to our knowledge of the genre.[11]

Renewed interest in the *sottie* has recently led to several studies that are more systematic,[12] but which neglect one of the most vital aspects of the genre, the attitudes expressed or implied through its particular use of satire. I will show that the *sotties*, or at least a significant group of them, express certain attitudes toward the social hierarchy of their time and toward key ideas such as *ordre* and *tromperie*; and that these *sotties* reflect a certain view of the class conflict that was developing in the late Middle Ages. Finally, I will return to the question of the theatrical use of Dame Folie and her fools as means for acting out lower-class attitudes.[13] Such popular attitudes in the *sottie* have never before been analyzed, though these plays can tell us much about medieval popular thinking, about class conflict at the end of the Middle Ages, and about the nature of satire and its social function.

The following analysis of the *sottie* will not deal at length with questions of literary history, as historical allusions in the plays and the history of the various troupes have already been studied to a much greater extent than has the nature of satire in the *sottie*. However, certain types of information do help to clarify the satirical techniques and goals of the plays: in particular, I will discuss the possible differences between the *sottie* and the farce; the dates, sources, and origins of the plays; and the men that wrote and acted them, their repertories, and their relations with the authorities. After a summary look at these questions, I will turn to the texts themselves, for they ultimately have the most to tell us about popular attitudes in the late Middle Ages.

I

The plays

What is a *sottie*?[1] That question seems to have a simple answer: a *sottie* is a type of comic play which flourished in the late Middle Ages, and which attempts to amuse through broad stage business (slapstick), a whimsical use of language, or a satiric view of society. More specifically, a *sottie* is a short comic play in verse, generally less than 400 lines long, usually with five characters, most of whom are *sots*, 'fols', or an equivalent ('suppost', 'esbahy', 'gallant', 'nouveau', or 'compagnon'). But the simplicity of these definitions is deceptive. The major problem in defining the *sottie* is the question of how it differs from the farce and the *moralité*. One of the first modern critics of the medieval theater, Petit de Julleville, believed that the *sottie* was nothing more than a farce played by *sots*.[2] And Gustave Cohen, in his *Recueil de farces françaises inédites du XVe siècle*, gave up entirely the idea of dividing the plays into genres.[3]

It is easy to understand his decision, for even the titles of the plays are confusing: what is to be made of the fact that many of the plays that are by all indications *sotties* are entitled 'farce' in their earliest versions? Although many of the plays considered today to be *sotties* are so entitled,[4] enough are called 'farce', or even 'moralité', to indicate that the playwrights (or perhaps the copyists and printers) did not carefully restrict the various terms to one type of play. According to L. C. Porter, even the critics of the time did not distinguish between them: 'A partir déjà de Sebillet, nous ne trouverons guère de critique qui ose prendre l'initiative de distinguer nettement entre ces deux genres.'[5]

If the title will not provide the basis of selection, what else will? As the *sotties* were plays performed by actors wearing the

5

costume of the *sot*, this costume seems to offer a possible criterion: Barbara Swain argues that if any play bears in its text signs of 'requiring the fool's costume – that play, whatever denominated by the printer or scribe, may legitimately be included among the *sotties*'.[6] Unfortunately, most plays do not indicate the costume in which they were to be played. Other critics, however, accept this basis of selection, at least implicitly, as does Cohen: 'La sottie ne diffère de la farce que par ses origines, la qualité et surtout le costume de ses acteurs.'[7]

Some critics have attempted to determine the repertory of a particular troupe, on the supposition that *sotties* were played by the Enfants-sans-souci of Paris, or by one of the similar provincial *compagnies joyeuses*, and that farces were played by the Basoche, or society of law clerks (see below, pp. 24ff.). But the plays tell us even less about which troupe performed them than they do about the costumes. Furthermore, it seems likely that a particular troupe put on several types of plays.[8] *Les Coppieurs* gives us evidence of this: a group of *sots* are looking for a new play to put on; they consider *Pathelin*, *Poitrasse*, *Le Povre Jouhan*, *La Fillerie*, and *Les Troys Coquins* – in other words, a variety of farces and *sotties*. Thus, we must either consider all these plays, including *Pathelin*,[9] as *sotties*, or recognize that a troupe could do either farces or *sotties*, with only a change of costume.[10]

This is not to say that a particular play was *both* farce and *sottie*: I cannot agree with Droz about the 'mixed' nature of every play, that it could be one day *sottie*, the next farce, 'qu'un même texte pouvait, au gré des acteurs, être farce ou sottie'.[11] This interpretation is put into question by a passage in another *sottie*, *Les Vigilles de Triboullet* (a *sottie* probably played by the troupe which performed *Les Coppieurs*). The late master *sot* Triboulet could recite a variety of works, including *Pathelin*, *La Farce des amoureux*, and *La Belle dame sans merci* (hardly a *sottie*!). We should not confuse 'repertory' and 'genre': to use a modern example, though the repertory of the Comédie Française includes both tragedies and comedies, it does not play *Phèdre* either as a tragedy or as a comedy, according to its wish and its costumes.

Emile Picot, in his introduction to the *Recueil général* (p. ix), has suggested various criteria for recognizing a *sottie*: 'Les sotties se reconnaissent d'abord à leur titre, puis à leurs personnages désignés sous les noms de sots, de fous, de galants, de compagnons, de pèlerins, d'ermites; elles se reconnaissent enfin à leur dialogue, dans lequel nous trouvons toujours des traces de la fatrasie.' I cannot agree with the 'fatrasic' view of the origins of the *sottie* (which will be discussed below, pp. 21–3), and as for the title, it is, as we have seen, often misleading. The designation of the characters as *galants*, or *fous*, is hardly less so. Several medieval plays have a *fol* in a different sort of role than that of the *sotties* (e.g., in *Le Fol, le mari, la femme, et le curé*); and although *galant* is sometimes synonymous with *sot* (the terms are interchanged in *Les Sobres Sots*), plays with *galants* are sometimes farces (*Troys Galans et Phlipot*).

Several critics have tried to gain a better view of the differences between these two types of plays by comparing a *sottie* and a farce that deal with similar subjects. Barbara Cannings (now Barbara C. Bowen) suggested that the answer to the question 'What is this play about?' is the key to distinguishing a *sottie* from a farce.[12] She compares a *sottie* and a farce whose subjects she considers very similar, but whose points of view and purposes are divergent. If the play is about 'people', Bowen would class it as a farce. If, on the other hand, it is about 'political, historical, or religious ideas', if its significance is symbolic rather than personal, then it is a *sottie*. Porter, after comparing two plays with the same theme, reaches similar conclusions: 'Bref, si la farce est le portrait que le peuple a fait de lui-même et de ses mœurs, la sotie reflète fidèlement ce que le peuple pensait de la noblesse et de la hiérarchie ecclésiastique.'[13] This distinction is correct but incomplete, for the *sottie* reflects what the people thought not only of the nobility and the Church hierarchy, as we shall see, but also of social hierarchy in general and of those who hold power in it specifically.

Slowly the idea has come to be more and more accepted by scholars of the medieval theater that, in the words of Ian Maxwell, 'However confused the frontier, farce and *sottie* form separate kingdoms.'[14] For it was not simply a 'stage device', when performing a *sottie*, to change to the cap and robe of the *sot*, to take in hand the *marotte* of the fool. This metamorphosis would be an act expressive of all the significance of *folie* at the end of the Middle Ages, so we must ask why the actors chose to transform themselves into *sots* for certain plays and not for others. One's view of the differences between the farce and the *sottie* is a function of one's conception of the meaning of *folie* in this period, for if *folie* is only a costume, accompanied by a style of dramatic interpretation, then the two genres are not very different. If, on the other hand, the 'fol' is seen as not simply a source of amusement but as a major element in man's view of himself, then the fool's cap indicates that a difference does exist between those plays in which it is worn and those for which it is doffed.

To my knowledge, only Grace Frank, in her excellent history of medieval French drama, has observed that the texts themselves indicate that a difference exists. Gringore, for example, in his *Jeu du Prince des Sotz*, writes this *explicit*: 'Fin du Cry, Sottie, Moralité et Farce composez par Pierre Gringore, dit Mère Sotte, et imprimé pour icelui'. 'Cry, Sottie, Moralité et Farce': Gringore is stating what is generally believed to have been the order of theatrical performances observed in his day.[15] To place a *sottie* at the beginning and a farce at the end would indicate that the two genres were distinguishable and distinctive.

Finally, it is possible that some of the confusion in the terminology of the titles is a result of the use of the term 'farce' in two senses. The term of course referred to a type of play of the kind that Bowen has delineated, or that Gaston Paris has called a humorous portrayal of the dupery of women and rogues.[16] But the term also seems to have been used to designate any short comic play. In this sense, therefore, there would be no contradiction if a manuscript or printed text called a *sottie* a 'farce'. As the term *comédie* was not generally used until the Renaissance (nor was the word 'satire'[17]), the term 'farce' served to indicate a short comic play. This is probably the reason that 'farces' frequently turn out to be *sotties*, but that no *sottie* (so called in the title) has yet turned out to be a farce in the more limited sense. This is also probably the reason that the three *sots* of *Les Coppieurs*, in the passage cited above (see p. 6), ask for and receive what they refer to as 'farces', but which include *sotties*, as the titles offered by the *coppieur* indeed indicate. Finally, in the *Sottie jouée a Geneve en la Place du Molard* (*Les Béguins*), the *sots enfarinés* (that is, made up as *sots*) are ready to play a 'farce' (l. 294).[18]

If there is growing agreement about the ways in which farces differ from *sotties*, there has been little discussion of the distinction between *sotties* and *moralités*. Both types have certain characteristics in common: both have allegorical characters and both offer a moral 'lesson' that sums up the values embodied in the characters. In general, however, the *sotties* are less abstract, more humorous, more concerned with political satire (based on what are considered to be the proper principles for structuring and governing society) than with individual vices and virtues, and they generally indicate in some way that their characters are *sots*. There are some plays, however, that combine the characteristics of two or more types, for the medieval comic theater was not a series of discrete categories, but a continuum. The farce, for example, shows the greatest individualization of characters; the *moralité*, the least; and the *sottie* usually falls in between. The existence of 'mixed' plays does not obscure the fact that about sixty plays of a 'pure' type are also be to found, and it is with those plays, which are almost certainly *sotties*, that an analysis of the genre must begin.

Thus, when looking for *sotties*, we cannot rely solely on the title, or on the presence or absence of characters explicitly called *sots*. Each play must be analyzed from the point of view of certain general characteristics: abstract or symbolic characters (whether called 'sots', 'gens nouveaulx', or something similar); satiric themes that deal with broad social questions, not with individual manners as does the farce; a dramatic structure based on a conflict between the *sots* and one or more antagonists; and, finally, an imaginative, uncommon use of language (as in *Les Menus Propos*). These characteristics of the *sottie* were developed, as we shall see, in order to fulfill a certain social function, a symbolic reaffirmation of group values and rejection of a threatening force. It is because of this unique social function and the means used to achieve it that the *sottie* differs from both the farce and the *moralité*.

These criteria have led to the exclusion from this study of

some plays that have previously been considered to be *sotties* (such as *Le Povre Jouhan*, which was included by Droz in the *Trepperel* volume of *sotties*, and *Troy Galans et Phlipot*, in Picot's *Recueil général*, vol. III). It has meant making a selection of probable *sotties* from Cohen's *Recueil*, and it has meant including plays that have not previously been included in a collection of *sotties* (*Mestier et Marchandise*, *Pou d'Acquest*, and *Les Povres Deables*, for example). Finally, I have limited the plays considered to those with more than one character, thereby eliminating the monologues and *sermons joyeux*.

Le Povre Jouhan and *Troys Galans et Phlipot* are not 'true' (or 'pure'), but mixed *sotties*; that is, they have *sots* or *galants* but the situation, plot, and other characters are farcical. The question of *Les Povres Deables* is more complicated. There remains today much disparity of opinion concerning the nature of this play: Picot believes it to be a morality; Maxwell, while continuing to class it as a farce, calls it a 'satiric examination rather than a play'; and Harvey attempts a synthesis by describing it as 'a *sottie* with farce characters in place of *sots* and with much of the tone of the morality play'.[19] Maxwell has sufficiently demonstrated, however, that *Les Povres Deables* could not have been the morality that was played with the *sottie La Reformeresse*, as Picot has claimed, because the two plays are basically of the same type, with the same subject. The similarity between them is indeed striking, and it can be argued that they are both *sotties*.

Mestier et Marchandise and *Pou d'Acquest* are included because they act out symbolic conflicts of a broad social nature similar to the conflicts of other *sotties;* they each have three main characters that resemble *sots*, and these characters are referred to as 'povres sos' or by terms equivalent to *sot;* and they include characters that appear in other *sotties* (Le Temps, Les Gens, Pou d'Acquest).

The *sotties* analyzed in this study probably represent only a fraction of the popular theatrical production of the fifteenth and sixteenth centuries.[20] The account books of towns and of noblemen mention subsidies for the production of comic plays which have since been lost.[21] In addition, we have other records of productions of plays that were probably *sotties*, such as *Le Monde qui tourne le dos à Chacun*, in 1538. (This is most likely a *sottie*, although Petit de Julleville calls it a 'moralité'.[22]) But the clearest evidence comes from the fact that two-thirds of the remaining *sotties* are found in only four collections, all of which have survived not because of the value placed on them by their owners, or because of the beauty of their bindings or illuminations, but by accident. For example, the well-known collection now in the British Library (*Le Recueil de Londres*) was discovered in a German attic in 1845: it contains no fewer than 64 plays, 55 of which were formerly unknown, including eight *sotties*: *Les Cris de Paris*; *Folle Bobance*; *Le Gaudisseur et le Sot*; *Les Gens nouveaulx*; *Pou d'Acquest*; *Le Roy des Sotz*; *Tout, Rien, et Chascun*; and *Les Trompeurs*. The *sotties* in this *recueil*, which were printed in Paris, Lyon, and Rouen, and later collected and bound together, are reprinted in the largest modern collection of *sotties*, the *Recueil général des sotties*, edited by Emile Picot (1902–12). This edition contains all the *sotties* mentioned in the *Répertoire* of Petit de Julleville, as well as a play discovered by Picot, *L'Astrologue*, two fragments of *sotties*, and the *Satyre* of Roger de Collerye.

Most of the *sotties* in the famous 'La Vallière' manuscript are also included in the *Recueil général*. Written in Normandy about 1575, this manuscript contains 74 dramatic works, among which are 15 *sotties*: *Les Brus*; *Chascun, Plusieurs*; *Deulx Gallans et Sancté*; *Les Veaulx*; *Le Jeu du Capifol*; *Mestier et Marchandise*; *Les Povres Deables*; *Le Pelerinage*; *La Mère de Ville*; *La Reformeresse*; *Les Sobres Sots*; *Tout le Monde*; *Les Troys Galans et un Badin*; *Troys Galans et Monde*; and *Troys Pelerins et Malice*.

About 1928 another important discovery was made: in the library of a Florentine historian, the collection now known as the *Recueil Trepperel* was discovered by an Italian bookseller. It had belonged to English and French collectors, who had offered it in turn to the Bibliothèque Nationale, to the Arsenal, and to important Parisian bibliophiles. All refused it, although it represented the greatest addition to the *sottie* since the *Recueil de Londres*.[23] Thanks to careful and scholarly editing by Eugénie Droz, the 16 *sotties* of this collection were published in 1935 in a well-annotated, corrected edition. Fourteen of these plays were previously unknown.

The most recent additions to our collection of *sotties* are the

plays published by Gustave Cohen in 1949, in the *Recueil de
farces françaises inédites du XVe siècle*. Cohen believes that most
of the 53 plays in the collection were written and performed in
Paris or its surroundings, in the years 1480 to 1492.[24] The editor
deduces from these dates that Paris enjoyed, in this period of
relative peace, 'une remarquable efflorescence de notre théâtre
comique' (p. xxi). At least six of the plays in this theatrical out-
burst are, I believe, *sotties*. These plays, with the 14 additional
sotties of the *Recueil Trepperel*, double the number of *sotties* that
have survived – that is, twice the number on which Picot based
his study in 1878.

Some of these collections seem to have constituted the repertories of particular troupes. The *Recueil Trepperel*, for example, is
probably not a number of disparate plays bound randomly
together, but rather groups of plays each performed by a particular
troupe. In *Les Sotz qui corrigent*, for instance, the *sots* mention the
characters in another play in the collection.[25] Bowen has remarked
that many of the La Vallière plays end with the formula 'Une
chanson pour dire adieu',[26] while no play of the Cohen collection
ends in this manner. This suggests that a troupe had a favorite
closing formula, or *envoi*, and, consequently, that these two
collections represent the repertories of two different companies.

Neither the medieval printers and scribes nor the modern
editors adhered to a uniform system of entitling the plays. Few
have a 'proper' title: *Les Sobres Sots* and *Les Menus Propos* are
exceptions. For practicality, therefore, I have given each *sottie* a
short working title, based on the principal characters, when no
real title exists, but preserving the original spelling.

The dating of medieval plays is one of the most vexing problems
for literary historians. The manuscripts and early printed editions
can frequently give us a *date limite* for the plays they contain, but
the plays themselves may be reworkings of older works. Cohen's
collection, as we have seen, was printed about 1540, but the plays,
according to the editor, date from the years 1480–92.[27] Halina
Lewicka has suggested the following latest dates for the three
other collections: *Recueil Trepperel*: 1520; *Recueil de Londres*:
1550; 'La Vallière' manuscript: 1575.[28] Attempts to date the

plays from internal evidence, however, have suggested much earlier dates for the majority of them. Consequently, Lewicka is probably correct, not only with regard to the Cohen collection, but for the others as well, when she remarks: 'L'impression générale qui se dégage du recueil est que l'on a affaire à des pièces tardives, à des remaniements ou des rajeunissements de versions plus anciennes.'[29]

If only more of the plays did what *Le Cry de la Bazoche* has done – it gives its date, 1548, in the title itself! Most of them, however, must be dated by internal evidence, in particular by textual allusions to specific events. For example, an allusion to an accident that occurred during royal jousts gives the date of *L'Astrologue*. Similarity of language or theme can suggest that two plays date from the same period, as Picot believes to be the case for *Les Gens nouveaulx* and *La Folie des Gorriers*.[30] The dates that have been suggested for most of the *sotties*, though, are hesitant and approximate, if not in actual dispute. Sometimes a scholar has been able to give more precision to a conjectural date, as Philipot has clarified Droz's suggested date of 'avant 1488' for *Les Sotz qui corrigent*, by discovering the mention of a performance in 1455.[31] The extent of the difficulties can be seen from the fact that one play, *Les Trompeurs*, has been dated by Picot as 1530, but by Droz as 1470 – a discrepancy of 60 years.[32]

The problems encountered in dating the *sotties* contribute to the larger problem of dating the period of the genre itself. It is not known with any certainty when the *sottie* began to be popular, or when its vogue faded away. All extant *sotties* date from the fifteenth century or later, but our knowledge of the preceding century is admittedly incomplete. Few examples of non-religious plays of that period have survived, and the dramatic nature of the works by Eustache Deschamps is doubtful.[33] Nonetheless, there is evidence that the *sottie* is older than its earliest remaining examples. We know, for instance, that dramatic productions were taking place in Paris as early as 1380, since Antoine Thomas has found a 'lettre de rémission' to perform the mystery of the Passion at that date.[34] Since the secular theater developed concurrently with the religious, it is likely that 'jeux de personnages par manière de farces' existed at this time also.[35]

Perhaps it was for a *sottie* that Louis d'Orléans gave, in 1385, 8 *livres tournois* to the Gallans sans Soulcy of Rouen, to pay them for having 'joué et chanté devant luy par plusieurs fois'.[36]

All but one of the *sotties* that have come down to us were written before 1560, but that date certainly does not mark the death of the *sottie*. Although the Basoche of Paris stopped performing about 1580[37] (partly as the result of censorship), the Confrérie des Sots did not. Picot believes that 'Au commencement du XVIIe siècle, la Confrérie des Sots était toujours en fonctions au milieu de Paris, à l'Hôtel de Bourgogne.... En 1616, la sottie n'avait pas disparu de l'Hôtel de Bourgogne.'[38] The last appearance of the *sots*, as far as Harvey has been able to determine, was in court ballets given in 1620 and 1636.[39] It is likely that the theatrical role of the *sots* at this date was in effect reduced to ballets, buffooneries like those of modern clowns, and the ceremonial use of a permanent *loge* at the Hôtel de Bourgogne. We have no evidence of the performance or the composition of true *sotties* after the beginning of the seventeenth century.

What, then, do the plays themselves tell us about the period of the *sottie*? An analysis of the dates – certain or projected – of the remaining *sotties* reveals that, in the second half of the fifteenth century, the genre was in its heyday. One-third of the 61 plays appear to have been written between 1480 and 1500. Three-quarters (43 of 61 plays) were written between 1460 and 1540. Only four *sotties* are dated before 1460, and six are believed to fall in the period after 1540. Thus, although there is evidence that *sotties* were being performed before 1440 – Gilles de Rais was then organizing theatrical performances for which he commissioned *sotties*[40] – the great majority of the *sotties* fall between 1440 and 1560, the limits of the period covered by this study.

2

The origins and players of the *sottie*

The origins of the *sottie* must of course be considered in the context of the origins of the medieval comic theater as a whole. In addition, however, questions arise that relate to the peculiar characteristics of the *sottie*, for the development of a type of play as distinctive as the *sottie*, with its Mère Sotte and Prince des Sots, accompanied by their *suppôts* in their strange but traditional costume, cannot be entirely accounted for by a general theory of the origins of the comic theater. In particular the idea of an individual genius as the originator of a comic genre (a theory suggested by Joseph Bédier for the two plays of Adam de la Halle)[1] does not apply to the *sottie*, as this type of play was not a unique invention but a constituent of a range of phenomena that extended from the court fool to the *Moriae encomium*, as we have seen. In addition the existence of a great diversity of structures and themes in the *sotties* runs counter to the theory of an individual creator. Nor is there substantial evidence for the theory that the comic theater, and therefore the *sottie*, developed from the dramatic tradition of Latin drama. The author of one *sottie*, *Les Sotz escornez*, mentions in passing the Roman playwright, Terence (l. 118), but there is no other indication that a knowledge of Latin drama was common among *sots*. Furthermore, the *sottie* differs fundamentally in tone and technique from the Latin writings of French schools, such as the ones at Orléans and Fleury-sur-Loire, in the thirteenth century.[2]

A third theory, the one most frequently proposed, claims that the comic theater developed from the religious. This would mean that 'la sottie s'était développée de parades de fous dans les mystères', as Gaston Paris, among others, has claimed.[3] Several scholars have maintained instead that the contrary was true, that is, that the comic elements in the medieval religious theater came from popular drama outside the Church.[4] This question becomes more complex in the *sottie* than in the other non-religious genres, since the *sottie* was closely tied to a particular Church festival, the Fête des Fous. It should be pointed out that a *sot* or *fol* frequently has a role in the mystery plays; in *Le Mystère de Sainte Barbe*, for example, and in those of Saint Bernard de Menthon, Saint Christophe (by Chevalet), Saint Didier (by Guillaume Flamancy, 1482), Saint Sébastien, and Saint Quentin. *La Passion de Troyes* also includes the role of a *sot*. Thus the religious theater is another witness to the widespread preoccupation with *folie* in the late Middle Ages. But this fascination with the *sot* does not seem to grow naturally from the serious religious subject of the *mystères* – it is rather lodged there like a fragment from a foreign object.[5] Thus, Edmond Faral's statement with regard to the comic theater in general is also applicable to the origins of the *sottie*:

> n'est-il pas vraisemblable, autant et plus, que l'esprit comique a agi comme une influence extérieure, de plus en plus sensible, sur un genre que tout destinait à la gravité? Plusieurs raisons... portent à croire que les scènes plaisantes, naturellement étrangères au théâtre sérieux, y furent un emprunt, assez inattendu et d'ailleurs précoce, à une forme d'art voisine et prospère (*Jongleurs*, p. 227).

This related art-form offers the first substantial theory of the origins of the *sottie*. As Faral has demonstrated, the origins of the popular theater are most likely to be found in the performances of the popular entertainer, 'dans l'antique tradition mimique, dont les jongleurs étaient les dépositaires' (p. 228). Although, according to Petit de Julleville,[6] no texts can be attributed with certainty to the *jongleurs*, Faral offers a list of comic plays of the thirteenth century which he believes to have been written by *jongleurs* (p. 213). In any case, what the *jongleurs* inherited from the ancient mimic tradition, and what they in turn passed on to the players of *sotties* and farces, was not so much a repertory as a certain 'esprit mimique, esprit fort riche, qui s'exprime de manières très diverses' (p. 248). Late medieval actors are consequently the successors of the *jongleurs*.

Faral's study of the *jongleur* offers two circumstantial indications of the complex connection between the *jongleur* and the sottie, and two other indications of a more dramatic nature. He demonstrates first of all that *jongleurs* participated in all popular festivals, and especially in the Fête des Fous, where it is probable that they joined in 'toutes les joyeuses abominations, danses, chants, représentations, festins, auxquelles on se livrait dans l'église même et qui scandalisaient si fort les gens graves' (p. 88). It is likely that one of the consequences of this relation of the Church to the *jongleurs* was to be the parody of the liturgy and of the cult that is sometimes found in the *sotties*. Another possible connection between the *jongleur* and the *sot* can be seen in the fact that the former occasionally disguised himself as a *fou*, as indicated by certain miniatures where the *jongleur* appears in the 'bonnet de folie, à longues oreilles, garnies de grelots' (p. 88, n. 3). In a *miserere* from the first half of the thirteenth century, the author writes: 'Mais au fol cui je voi joglant' (Appendix III, p. 209). Thus the *jongleur* seems at times to have 'played the fool', and the fool, the *jongleur*.

Dramatic evidence of the legacy of the *jongleur* is to be found in the texts of the *sotties* themselves. A number of plays require of their performers 'exercices athlétiques' that are similar to the repertory of one type of *jongleur*, the acrobat and funambulist. The *Tombeur de Notre Dame* gives a touching example of this skill when the prayer to the Virgin of the simple, uneducated *jongleur* takes the form of leaps and somersaults:

> Lors li commence a faire saus
> Bas et petis et grans et haus...
> Lors tume et saut et fait par feste
> Le tor de Mes entor la teste...
> Apres li fait le tor françois
> Et puis le tor de Champenois (ll. 163ff.).[7]

Finally, the kind of dialogue that is found in *Le Gaudisseur et le Sot* seems to have been part of the stock-in-trade of the *jongleur*, for he recited a little drama that was called in the thirteenth century 'le jeu de l'Ivre et le jeu du Sot' (Faral, *Jongleurs*, p. 236, n. 5).

The importance of the *jongleur* for the later development of the *sottie* lies not only in his acrobatics and his stock characters, but more especially in the use of masks and disguises, and above all in his understanding of what amused the common people. For only by entertaining the crowds at fairs and festivals could the ordinary *jongleur*, as opposed to his courtly cousin, the *menestrel*, earn his pay. Since his goal was to amuse and move 'le menu peuple', the *jongleur* had to be able to express the concerns of his audience. Therefore, the theory of the 'jongleresque' origins of the *sotties* will prove to be helpful to our understanding of popular attitudes revealed in the plays.

In addition to the *jongleur*, the celebrations of the lower clergy in the Fête des Fous also contributed to the development of the *sottie*. Unlike the farce and the morality, the *sottie* (and the *sermon joyeux*) may reasonably be regarded, in the words of Chambers, 'as the definite contribution of the Feast of Fools to the types of comedy'.[8] The *compagnies des fous* can be traced quite directly to the Fête des Fous.[9] Thus an investigation of the relation of the Feast to the play should provide information about the nature and origins of the *sottie*.

The Fête des Fous was a predominantly French phenomenon, which apparently arose in northern France about the twelfth century and died out four centuries later.[10] When the *sots* of *La Folie des Gorriers* talk about the undertakings of their imaginary valets 'pour passer ces festes' (l. 5), they are probably referring to the Fête des Fous.[11] This celebration was called variously *festum stultorum*, *festum fatuorum*, or even *asinaria festa*, *festum subdiaconorum*, or *festum baculi*,[12] and it was usually celebrated on Innocents' Day (December 28), or the Feast of the Circumcision (January 1), or on other days, such as the feast of Saint Nicholas (December 6). Young would restrict it to the octave of Epiphany.[13] In any case, the Feast fell during the period of ancient Roman celebrations, whether it be the Saturnalia of December (according to Cohen), or the January Kalends (according to Chambers).[14] The latter feast in particular was the occasion on which 'paganism made its most startling and persistent recoil into Christianity'. As we shall see, the rites and revelries of the *festum stultorum* are an unmistakable (some would say outrageous) persistence of paganism in the medieval Church.[15]

In spite of some differences in detail from town to town and from cathedral to cathedral, the spirit of the Fête des Fous was everywhere basically the same. Its underlying principles were the parody of the liturgy and the satiric raising up of the lowly to the places of the powerful. The best analysis of what actually took place during this Feast is given in Chambers's study, *The Mediaeval Stage*. He cites, among other documents, a curious letter of March 12, 1445 from the Faculté de Théologie de Paris to the bishops and chapters of France, which describes, in horrified detail, what was certainly one of the more extreme examples of the Feast: priests and clerics wore masks at the hours of office, danced in the choir dressed as women, panders, or minstrels, and sang wanton songs; they ate black puddings while the celebrant was saying the Mass, and played at dice on the altar. Furthermore, they censed with stinking smoke from the soles of old shoes and ran and leaped through the church. Finally, they drove about the town and its theaters in shabby traps and carts, and provoked the laughter of their fellows and the bystanders with 'infamous performances' (*infamia spectacula*).[16]

The thirteenth-century name for the Feast at Sens was the *asinaria festa*, 'La Fête de l'Ane', for the ceremonial included bringing an ass into church at the singing of the Prose of the Ass (and ending certain liturgical pieces with a bray). An allusion to this widespread custom reappears in the ass's ears of the fool's bonnet. The festivities also included the transference of a staff (*baculus*) to the *dominus festi*. The election of a 'bishop', 'archbishop', 'dean', or even 'pope' of fools from the lower clergy was one of the traditional elements of the festival.[17] (The Ritual of St Omer describes such a ceremony.) The inversion of the usual order of things was sanctified, as it were, in the verse of the Magnificat which was sung fervently and repeatedly at the end of the Fête: *Deposuit potentes de sede et exaltavit humiles*.[18] Consequently, when *ludi theatrales* and *personagiorum ludi* were performed, this theme of the fall of the powerful and the raising up of *le menu peuple* naturally permeated them.

The Church hierarchy tried continually to suppress the revelries and rites of the *festum stultorum*. As early as 1207, Pope Innocent III simultaneously called attention to the wearing of masks by the deacons, priests, and subdeacons and to the playing of *theatrales*

ludi in the churches, and demanded an end to these practices.[19]
Similar prohibitions were handed down by the Council of Paris
in 1212, and by Odo of Tusculum in 1245. Although these
attempts failed, two centuries later they were nonetheless repeated.
No less a clergyman than Jean-Charlier de Gerson, the famous
theologian and rector of the University of Paris, crusaded for the
abolition of the Feast, 'ritus ille impiissimus et insanus qui regnat
per totam Franciam'.[20] Some years after his death, the Great
Council of Basle included a prohibition of the Feast, which was
made ecclesiastical law in France by the Pragmatic Sanction of
1438.[21] But so popular was the Feast of Fools, not only with the
clergy but with the lay public, that the chapters obstinately
continued to celebrate it for another century and a half.

In the spirit of Gerson, some modern scholars have also heaped
anathema on the Feast. Fabre marvels that such an 'orgie sacrilège
. . . enfantée par l'ignorance et la superstition, nourrie par la
grossièreté et la corruption des mœurs'[22] could resist the opposition of 'prélats et rois' for nearly ten centuries. Instead of railing
against the 'abuses' of the Feast, it will increase our knowledge of
popular medieval attitudes to try to understand what these
festivals meant to the people who were determined not to give
them up, even on the injunctions of their rulers. In the literature
of this period, the *sottie* offers one of the best opportunities to
explore this popular feeling, for there is little doubt that the joy
in criticizing the powerful and in raising up the lowly mounted
the *tréteaux* and became theater in the *sotties*. And although some
scholars, Young in particular, minimize the theatrical spirit of
the revelries[23], this spirit can be clearly seen in a festival like that
at Troyes in 1445, where the satire of ecclesiastical hierarchy (no
less than a bishop and two canons) took the form of a play entitled
Hypocrisie, Feintise et Faux Semblant[24]. Just as the Fêtes des Fous
were dying out, the *sociétés burlesques* were developing, and the
irreverent, topsyturvy attitudes of the celebrants of the Feast
passed to the *sots* of the *sottie*.

Both of these theories concerning the origins of the *sottie*,
that of the role of the *jongleur* and that of the Feast of Fools, help
to clarify certain fundamental aspects of the *sottie*: its *jeux de
scène* and acrobatics, its fool's costume and its *confréries* with an

estimated at about 10,000 at the end of the fifteenth century.[46] Similar corporations of law clerks, designated by the same name, existed in most of the large towns of France. Whether or not it can be maintained that the Basoche of Paris had, as Harvey claims (p. 14), 'the more or less exclusive privilege of staging comic plays' in that city, its dramatic activity was nevertheless considerable.

In 1442 the theatrical element of the Basoche was invited by the Confrères de la Passion to join them in the Hôpital de la Trinité, in particular to give comic interludes between the *journées* of the mysteries.[47] A third group of actors then shared the Hôpital de la Trinité: the Enfants-sans-souci.[48] From the time of Charles VI the Enfants are generally believed to have been the principal players of *sotties* in Paris, while the Basoche performed mainly farces and moralities.[49] This is all that is known for sure – the origins and development of this organization are unclear. It would be particularly helpful to know the nature of their relation to the Basoche. Magnin claimed that the two companies were rivals.[50] Harvey, however, has made a strong case for considering the Enfants-sans-souci as subordinate to the Basoche and made up of a select group of its members. For one thing, as both Fabre and Harvey point out, the numerous *arrêts* of the Parlement of Paris, which regulated the drama of the city, mention exclusively the Basoche; no order exists which concerns directly the Enfants-sans-souci.[51] It is difficult to believe that the Enfants, playing satiric political plays, never deserved a reprimand (for the *sots* themselves were sometimes imprisoned). This silence suggests that the Enfants were seen as subordinate to the Basoche and under its legal jurisdiction.

Moreover, the clerks were forbidden to play not only moralities and farces without the consent of Parlement, but also *sotties*:

La cour…a defendu et defend à tous clers et serviteurs, tant du Palais que du Chastelet de Paris, de quelque estat qu'ils soient, que doresnavant ils ne jouent publiquement audit Palais et Chastelet, ni ailleurs en lieux publics, farces, sotties, moralités ne autres jeux à convocation de peuple, sur peine de banissement de ce royaume, et de confiscation de tous leurs biens.[52]

This relation of the Enfants-sans-souci to the Basoche would explain the reference to a *palais* or *salle* in the *sotties* – it would be the Grand'Salle in the Palais de Justice, where the Basochiens held their entertainments.[53] Therefore, Marot probably knows of what he speaks when he says:

> Attache moy une sonnette
> Sur le front d'un moyne crotté,
> Une oreille à chasque costé
> Du capuchon de sa caboche:
> Voyla *un sot de la Bazoche*
> Aussi bien painct qu'il est possible.[54]

Primarily for these reasons, most scholars would agree with Petit de Julleville that the Enfants-sans-souci 'n'étaient... pour ainsi dire, que la Basoche en costume de Sots'.[55]

In addition to the Basoche and the Enfants-sans-souci, a group known as the Pois Pillés seems to have been associated with the Parisian comic stage. The nature and history of this troupe are shrouded in mystery. Odet de Tournebu, in 1580, implies that it is similar to, or even part of, the Basoche, when he says: 'on me jouera aux pois pillez et à la bazoche'.[56] Brantôme speaks of 'jeux de poix pillez' at the Hôtel de Bourgogne,[57] and *Les Menus Propos*, a century earlier, remarks that when the *pois* have sprouted, 'Les folz commencent a monter' (ll. 471–2). Cohen, on the other hand, attributes to Rabelais the earliest mention of the Pois Pillés (see *Quart Livre*, Ch. XXXII). In any case, the last reference to them is by Malherbe, in 1625.[58] And that is almost all that is known of this troupe. It is even doubtful whether we are dealing with a specific troupe or with another name for the Enfants-sans-souci or the Basoche. Perhaps the *jeu de pois pillés* was not even a troupe, but a style of acting, or type of play. (More research is needed on this problem in medieval theatrical history.)

The relationship of the Basoche to the Enfants-sans-souci is potentially an important source of information about the social background of the men who acted in the *sotties*. Who, after all, were the Enfants-sans-souci? The *Histoire* of F. and C. Parfaict maintained that the troupe was 'quelques jeunes gens de famille, qui joignoient à beaucoup d'éducation un grand amour pour les plaisirs, et les moyens de se les procurer'.[59] This opinion was generally accepted until the end of the nineteenth century. Sainte-Beuve, for example, repeats that the *sots* were 'jeunes gens de famille spirituels et dissipés', who found amusement in the 'défauts et ridicules du genre humain'.[60] Petit de Julleville states, at different times, that 'La plupart des Enfants-sans-souci apparte-naient, au moins d'origine, à ces rangs déshérités de la cléricature' (Marot after all does say 'moyne'), or that they were the 'beatniks' ('la bohème') of the fifteenth century.[61] It was not until Gaston Paris that the Basoche origin of the Enfants began to be recog-nized.[62] Today, literary historians generally accept Harvey's well-documented position that the Enfants-sans-souci were a group of law clerks of the Basoche, 'some of the boldest and best-trained intellects of the day'.[63] Why else, one might ask, are nearly all the known writers of *sotties* connected with the Basoche?

Young men of good family, defrocked monks, beatniks, or law clerks – whatever the nature and origin of the Enfants-sans-souci – the question remains as to whether or not they mono-polized the production of *sotties*. Most scholars, in opposition to Harvey's views, say no. Magnin is referring to the oldest dramatic profession when he speaks of 'dicteurs' and 'ménestrels de bouche', that is, *bateleurs*, as players of *sotties*.[64] (There is in fact one *sottie* entitled *Le Bateleur*.) But his opinion seems to be based on a personal reaction rather than on firm historical evidence, for he claims that one can recognize these plays of lowly professional comedians by their 'platitude, obscénité et excessif désordre'. Fabre, one of the two principal historians of the Basoche, does not attribute to the Basochiens the monopoly of comic theatrical productions, as does Harvey: 'les écoliers de l'Université, les collégiens donnaient aussi des représentations théatrales'.[65] Grace Frank makes the clearest statement of the 'anti-monopolist' case when she writes: 'Though many of our comic pieces of this time can plausibly be attributed to the law clerks, we know that students, ecclesiastics (many prohibitions show they took part), artisans (we hear of a shoemaker writing a farce for a legate), and professional jongleurs were also concerned in both their authorship and their performance.'[66]

Two elements in the text of certain *sotties* indicate that profes-sional actors performed many of the plays. First, there is what Picot calls 'une raison physique'.[67] It would take an agile, trained acrobat to perform many of the leaps, somersaults, and other 'exercices athlétiques' that the *sots* are sometimes called upon to perform. The best example of these acrobatics is to be found in *Le Bateleur*, where master drills apprentice in the art of the *badin*:

> Sus! faictes le sault! Hault! Deboult!
> Le demy tour, le souple sault,
> Le faict, le defaict. Sus, j'ay chault,
> J'ey froid. Est il pas bien apris?
> En effect nous aurons le pris
> De badinage, somme toute.

Ll. 15–20: Hup! Make a leap! Up! On your feet! The half-turn, the supple leap, Forward, reverse. Hup, I'm hot, I'm cold. Doesn't he know his stuff? Truly we will have the prize For 'badinage', that's sure. (Cf. also *Les Cris de Paris*, l. 252, and *Troys Galans et Monde*, ll. 93–100.)

It is indeed difficult to imagine a law clerk going through these paces. The second element that suggests professional actors rather than law clerks is the request for money that is made at the end of several *sotties*. In *Les Brus*, for instance, the 'lead' hopes that the absence of music in the play will not diminish the generosity of the audience:

> Pour tant, s'on n'avon poinct musique,
> Pas ne diminues vostre don (ll. 298–9).

And the 'sots nouveaulx farcez, couvez' have told us quite explicitly: 'Baillez argent ilz seront voz.' There is thus some evidence to support the thesis that professional actors, heirs to the skill of the *jongleur*, performed many of the *sotties*. In fact, Faral would give most of the credit for the comic theater of this period to the professionals: 'il ne faut pas douter qu'ici les professionnels aient fait beaucoup plus que les amateurs, et les joueurs de sotties et de farces ne doivent pas, en général, être considérés autrement que comme les successeurs des anciens jongleurs'.[68]

Do the plays give other, more intrinsic indications of the origin of their authors and actors? Bowen believes she can distinguish a farce written by a member of the Basoche from the other farces 'par le manque d'obscénité, par la satire joyeuse de tout ce qui est pédantisme, bêtise de prétendus savants, enseignement en latin, etc., et par la fidélité et le manque de satire dans leur peinture des cours de justice'.[69] It remains to be seen to what extent these traits are found in the *sottie*, and whether or not they are an indisputable indication of Basoche origin. Other scholars, who maintain that law clerks in the guise of Enfants-sans-souci dominated the production of *sotties*, point to 'the complex arrangements in the forms of rondeau, ballade, and quatrain' as sufficient evidence that the authors were men of letters, not 'mountebanks, *bohémiens*, or professional comedians'.[70] But the question has never been answered as to the frequency in the *sottie* of these poetic forms or their significance for this particular genre, over and above the desire of certain poets to show off their virtuosity. In addition, there is evidence that some of the poetic segments existed before the *sottie* in which they are found and were incorporated into it during the composition of the play.

Too often in the past a scholar's rather subjective evaluation of the quality of the *sotties* has influenced his or her view of the social background of the playwrights. Harvey believes that the plays were written with such skill that the learned background of their authors is apparent, whereas Magnin, as we have seen, would make them out to be the work of uneducated itinerant vaudeville performers, since he sees the plays as unstructured, banal, and obscene. Therefore, only a close analysis of the texts of the plays, such as proposed in this study, will give us more information about the type of person who wrote and played them. If, for example, the playwrights came, not from bourgeois families, but from the lower classes, as certain scholars believe (Mikhail Bakhtine, in particular), then the plays should express the attitudes and preoccupations of those classes. Documents tell us only a little about the *joueurs de sotties*. Whether their authors and actors were learned or uneducated, nobles or commoners, clergy or lay, professional actors or law clerks – concerning the answers to these questions, the *sotties* themselves will give us more clues.

The *joueurs de sotties* seem to have acted not solely for payment, but from an intense desire for carnival, for their life as actors was often difficult, even dangerous. They were frequently punished by a thrashing, imprisonment, or defenestration in a sack (as in the case of the unfortunate Maître Cruche, in April 1515).[71] In fact, the oldest judgment dealing with the Basoche details the punishment of the Basochiens in 1442, who played in spite of the prohibition of Parlement.[72] In the case of Henri Baude 44 years later, the accused himself has described what happened after his performance of a satiric play:

> BAUDE, après brisement de portes,
> En effet, a mynuict fut pris
> Et au petit Chastellet mis.[73]

For he had played what was undoubtedly a *sottie*, since the play loudly attacked men close to Charles VIII. A *sottie* inserted in a *mystère* of Saint Eloi led to a criminal trial, due to its 'folle et oultrageuse parole'.[74] A 'roy de la Basoche' was imprisoned in 1516, according to the *Journal d'un bourgeois de Paris, sous le règne de François Ier (1515–36)* (p. 44), for having done something which would admittedly be considered very audacious, even today: he had impersonated the king's mother. About the same time, the famous poet and a member of the Basoche, Clément Marot, composed his 'Epistre pour la Bazoche' to implore the mercy of François I, prompted probably by the scandal caused by the *sot* Pont-Alais and his comrades.[75]

Although the *arrêts* of Parlement mention farces and moralities, it was most likely the *sottie* type of play that the Provost and the Parlement most objected to. The attempts by Parlement to control the Basoche and the *sots* in particular – records of these attempts exist for 1443, 1473, 1474, 1475, 1476, 1477, and 1540[76] – made them more cautious, but not less critical.

Theatrical freedom varied considerably from king to king. It was probably under Louis XII that the *sots* enjoyed their greatest freedom from censorship.[77] He allowed the *sots* to make fun of him and his court, as long as they stayed away from the subject of the Queen. Otherwise, he threatened to have them all hanged.[78] According to Jehan Bouchet, the king's encouragement of the *sots* was the result of clear-headed political principle – the *sottie* was used as his source of information about the abuses and corruption of his ministers:

Qui [la sottie] est permis par les princes et roys
A cette fin qu'ils sçachent les derroys
De leur conseil, qu'on ne leur ause dire,
Desquelz ils sont advertis par satire.
Le roys Loys douzième desiroit
Qu'on les jouast à Paris; et disoit
Que par tels jeux il sçavoit maintes faultes
Qu'on luy celoit par surprinses trop caultes.[79]

Under François I, royal encouragement was more tangible, for the king would sometimes grant money to the Basoche players.[80] Toward the end of his reign, however, François I evidently became less tolerant of the *sots* and their *jeux*.[81]

The *sots* had seen how frequently a king or a parliament could change its mind, and they usually remained on guard. Several *sotties* allude to the danger, for a *sot*, of speaking his mind. One entire play is based on the fear of censorship: *Les Béguins*, 'jouée à Genève en la Place du Molard, le dimanche des Bordes, l'an 1523' (February 22, 1523). This play alludes to four years of civil strife, during which one man associated with the *sots* had been tried and executed, and the Enfants de Bon Temps condemned to silence. When, in 1522, their principal enemy died, the troupe hoped to be allowed their former freedom, and so they performed once more a *sottie*.[82] Those who had tried to 'abolish' folly (l. 51) had failed, but their threats were not forgotten:

Depuis le temps que partistes d'icy
Joue n'avons moralité n'histoire;
Si nous eussions tant seulement toussy,
L'on nous eust fait aller en l'auditoire.

Ll. 154–7: Since the time when you left here, We have not performed morality or story; If we had so much as coughed, We would have been brought before the judge.

As they judged the danger to be ever-present, the *sots* in the end abandoned their *jeu*, to try again the following year.

That was in Geneva, where the Enfants did not enjoy the favor of a king like Louis XII. But the French *sotties* also frequently express a similar fear of censorship, suppression, and reprisal, in particular during the last three decades of the fifteenth century. In *Les Premiers* Le Principal demands:

> Pour quoy t'es tu tant fait querir,
> Que ne vins tu des l'an passay?

Ll. 75–6: Why did you make us look so hard for you? Why didn't you come last year?

And, in an allusion to an *arrêt* of the Faculté de Paris that forbade performances (January 5, 1470), L'Ermite responds:

> Venir n'estoit pas tout aisay,
> Les festes estoient deffendus.

Ll. 77–8: It wasn't very easy to come, The festivals were forbidden.

In another play from this period, *Les Sots qui corrigent*, Roussignol is warned by the others not to attempt a play:

> Par Dieu, se vous en faictes guere,
> Ne doubtez qu'on vous pugnira.

Ll. 219–20: By God, if you do any [plays] at all, Have no doubt that they will punish you.

It was evidently a bad time for *sots* and *sottise*, a time when the players were haunted by the 'peur d'estre mys en prison' (*Deulx Gallans et Sancté*, l. 41).[83]

Although their attacks undoubtedly became more veiled, the *sots* were not deterred – they showed the same perseverance in the face of opposition as had the celebrants of the Fête des Fous. Both the revelries of the *festum fatuorum* and the satire of the *sotties* ran into frequent attempts by various hierarchies – ecclesiastical, feudal, or royal – to control or suppress them, and both continued to thrive. The plays themselves will show us how they were affected by censorship, or the threat of it, and by repression; they also show us how their satire succeeded in answering a popular need, despite the threat of official retaliation.

The traditional costume of the *sot* may have been in part an attempt to deceive the censor. Who, after all, pays attention to the babbling of a fool? Under the guise of *folie*, the *fou* could speak his mind, as long as the words sounded foolish. For this reason, the *sots* of *Les Béguins* refused to perform without the costume of the fool.

The *habit des fous* had certain traditional components, with some variations: something of an animal on the head, something variegated on the body, and something comical in the hand. On their heads, the *sots* usually wore a hood (*capuchon*) with long, pointed ears, a head-covering which became the symbol and badge of the *sociétés joyeuses*. As Chambers has pointed out, it is found on most of the seals and other devices of the Infanterie Dijonnaise, sometimes hung with bells on the ears and often scalloped at the bottom.[84] The *bonnet de folie* was used at Amiens, and at Rouen it was probably the origin of the term 'Cornards'. We have already seen that Marot ascribes it to a Parisian 'sot de la Bazoche'. This headgear, sometimes called a *sac à coquillons*, seems to have hidden a shaved head, another mark of the *sot*.[85] 'Teste pelée' is in effect an invective thrown at a rebellious *sot* in *Le Roy des Sotz* (l. 191; see also *Les Coquins*: 'Ou me tondre en guise de fol', l. 505). This baldness was probably a parodying imitation of the monk's tonsure.

In the many drawings, carvings, and woodcuts of fools that were produced in the later Middle Ages and the Renaissance, the fool is portrayed in variations of this hood.[86] Sometimes, as in the case of the fools in the ducal chapel of Dijon, the hood had a central peak or crest between the ears, similar to the crest of a rooster. Chambers believes that this eared and/or crested hood was originally 'a sophistication of a more primitive head-dress, namely the actual head of a sacrificial animal worn by the worshipper at the New Year festival'.[87] The ass's ears are undoubtedly a survival from the prominence of the animal in the Fête des Fous. In any case, the hood's association with religious custom can also be seen in its grotesque allusion to the religious cowl.

The fools also wore gay, eye-catching colors. Those of the Enfants-sans-souci were green and yellow: 'grande cape mi-partie jaune et verte, pourvu de sonnettes', in the words of Gustave Cohen.[88] The Infanterie Dijonnaise used three colors, adding red to the more traditional green and yellow, and other companies probably had their individual combination of colors.[89]

The third mark of the *sot* was the *marotte* that he carried in his hand. This was a kind of doll at the end of a short staff, usually representing in miniature the head and shoulders of the fool himself. Douce's figures sometimes carry a bladder on a stick, or some other type of bauble. The *marotte* as well as the rest of the costume was worn not only by the theatrical *sot* but also by the jester of royal courts or noble houses.[90]

The references to and dramatic uses of the *habit des fous* in the *sotties* are multiple. Most commonly a character is forced against his will to remove his outer costume in order to reveal that underneath it he is in effect wearing the fool's costume (e.g., *Les Sotz qui corrigent*). The entire second half of *Les Béguins* comprises the fools' efforts to put together the traditional costume, in order to play a new *sottie*. When they cannot find their hoods, one fool cuts new ones out of the ample gown of Mère Folie. Just as they are ready to perform, they notice that an ear is lacking, symbolizing that year's unfavorable atmosphere for *sotties*. Consequently, they refuse to play: as though in a religious ritual, the *sot* must have his entire *habit*. Gaultier, in *Les Sotz escornez*, makes sure that we understand this:

> Chascun viendra avec [ses] sotz et sotes,
> Ad ce dit jour chascun se trouvera
> Avec oreilles, testiere et marotes,
> Puis au surplus on y advisera.

Ll. 372–5: Each one will come with [his] fools, both male and female, On the agreed day each will present himself With ears, hood, and baubles; Then we will discuss the rest.

An unusual use of the fool's costume is found in *La Moralité de 1427*: Le Monde is required to don the costume before being permitted to hear the Master's lesson, which he would not otherwise understand (ll. 322ff.). This action illustrates the paradox of the wise fool (it is the four fools who later in the play reveal what is wrong with the world), for in medieval thought it is the foolish who have the gift of seeing beyond appearances.

This résumé of certain aspects of the literary history of the *sottie* and *sots* has necessarily been made up more of questions than of answers. Much research remains to be done on the origins of the genre; on the origins and type of person who wrote and performed the plays; on certain troupes, such as the Enfants-sans-souci, and their relation to other groups; on the attitudes of government and Church to the plays and the players. These questions are worth studying for their intrinsic interest. However, the main reason for discussing these problems in detail here is to see what light they might shed on the techniques, goals, and point of view of the plays themselves, and on their use of satire.

3

The *sottie* as drama

After a study of the literary history of the *sottie*, we can now turn to an examination of the plays themselves, of their structure and the popular attitudes that they express. But the values underlying satire in the *sotties* can be understood only when more is known about the dramatic characteristics of the plays, in particular the structure, types of comedy, and types of characters which are unique to the *sottie*. Therefore, after inspecting those characteristics, the rest of this study will consider attitudes and beliefs, hopes and fears expressed or implied by the *sottie* – ultimately, its conception of *folie*.

Questions exist today about the structure of the *sotties* that still – 450 years after the heyday of the genre – have not been answered. How are the plays structured in terms of number of divisions, for example? How many characters do they involve? Is there a dominant type of structure? Does the use of plot, characterization, and language differ in this theatrical genre from their use in other medieval genres? These fundamental questions have often been dismissed with generalizations and contradictions. Let us begin with a basic question, the number and types of roles in the *sottie*, which have been described both as 'numerous', and as 'few'.[1]

The existing plays contain a total of 283 roles, played by 157 different characters (some characters appear in more than one play). If exception is made of *Le Jeu du Prince des Sotz* of Gringore, which has an unusually large number of *personnages*, the average number of characters in a *sottie* is four or five. Furthermore, only eight plays have more than six characters. It is striking that more than half of the plays have three characters of the same kind:

three 'sots', 'fols', 'brus', 'compagnons', 'supposts', 'esbahys', 'gallans', or 'nouveaulx'. This is not fortuitous, for the *sots* themselves recognize the need to be three:

> Touteffoys se nous fussions troys,
> Nous serions ung peu mieulx sortis.

Trote Menu, ll. 88–9: However, if we were three, We would be a little better matched.

The number three was so rich in symbolic meaning to the medieval mind that all its nuances cannot be examined here. The theater public of the time was certainly aware of possible allusions to the Trinity, but perhaps the most appropriate Biblical reference is to the Three Wise Men, who are parodied by their counterparts, the Three Fools of the *sottie*. 'Three' is after all the 'odd' number *par excellence*. Because of the prevalence of three-of-a-kind characters, I would argue that a short satiric play with a trio of similar characters is almost certainly a *sottie*.

The names given to these characters are often indicative of the profound difference that exists between the farce and the *sottie*. In the farce, a character is usually called by a proper name: we find a community of ordinary people, made up of Guillerme, who ate the figs of the *curé*, Jean de Lagny, and Margot, who got in trouble when she confessed; people like Jenin Landore, who was resurrected; Martin de Cambray and Guillemette his wife; poor Jouhan and fickle Affricqué; Frère Guillebert, and, of course, the gentlemen of the Bar, best represented by Maistre Pathelin. These farce-characters, while representing recognizable types of human beings, are nonetheless individualized to a certain extent, as indicated by their personal proper names.

The characters of the *sottie*, on the other hand, rarely have a proper name, in the sense of a name that designates a person as an individual and not solely as a type or member of a group. Only eleven proper names are to be found among the more than 140 distinct characters of the plays, and seven of these are found in one play alone, *Les Béguins*. Several are questionable as proper names.[2] In the case of Maistre Pierre Doribus (*Les Sotz qui recueuvrent*), for example, we are dealing with an imaginative term for a charlatan, a *triacleur*.[3] This type (rather than individual)

appears also in the fourteenth-century Palatine Passion and in the
Farce d'un Pardonneur, and is related to the mountebank of the
Dit de l'erberie of Rutebeuf. Therefore, the *sotties* present a large
number of characters who are not individuals, who do not have
proper names, and who reappear many times from play to play.
Who are these 'inhabitants' of the *sottie*? Their names alone
reveal much about them.

Five categories of generic names are found in the *sotties*.[4] One
of these categories uses a title to designate a character. Eleven
sots are titled: there are five Seigneurs, two Abbés, two Generaux,
a Docteur, and a Prince (other than Prince des Sots). Most of the
titles suggest an imaginary place which summarizes the dominant
quality of the characters, as in the Abbé de Plate Bource (which
may be also an erotic *double entendre*), or the Seigneur de Joye.
Only two of these, the General d'Enfance and the Docteur,
occur outside *Le Jeu du Prince des Sotz*, but in spite of their
limited appearance in the *sotties*, Gringore did not invent them
for his play: they were the names that members of *confréries de
sots* frequently gave themselves.[5] This type of name served
several purposes, for in addition to parodying the clergy and the
nobility and indicating a particular quality of the character, at a
more general level many of them came to be synonymous with
the term *sot* itself.

The second category, and the most varied, consists of the use
of a compound word or of an adjective to indicate the dominant
personal quality of a character. In the manner of a synecdoche,
one characteristic is made to stand for the person as a whole.[6]
Sometimes a character's name implies that he is shrewd: L'Affineur
and Fine Mine are two names based on *fin*, indicating a person
who is capable of ruse or deception.[7] Deception is in effect one
of the favorite pastimes of the *sots*, who ask nothing more than to
'tromper le monde'. But if not *trompeur*, then *trompé*. A fool's
name more frequently suggests the opposite quality of *fin*, that is,
someone lacking in brains, as in the names Estourdi, Dando
Mareschal (from *dindo, dindin*), Nyvelet (from *niveler*, 'to waste
one's time with foolishness'), Guippellin, and especially as in a
group of names that include the word *teste*: Teste Ligiere, Teste
Creuse, Teste Verte. Evidently, the fool could appear to be, in

the words of Cotgrave, 'a foolish, humorous, hare-brain'd, giddie-headed fellow' (in the article 'Il y a de la lune'),[8] or he could be most *fin* and *rusé*. This opposition will recur again and again in the satirical view that the *sottie* offers of society, seen as an assembly of fools.

One name in this category deserves particular mention, that of the famous Triboulet. Meaning 'to torment', perhaps also 'to be excited or agitated', this name was one of the most popular terms for a fool in the period under discussion. A succession of court fools named Triboulet accompanied the French kings through history: Louis XI had his Triboulet, as did Louis XII and François I. Other noblemen, such as René d'Anjou, rivaled the kings with their own Triboulets.[9] In addition to the court fools, various *farceurs* adopted this stage name, in the manner of Turlupin, Gros Guillaume, or Gautier Gargouille of the seventeenth century. The Triboulet renowned as a *joueur de sotties* was the right-hand man of another famous actor, Maître Mouche,[10] and probably at one time directed his own troupe. His popularity on the stage induced his *suppôts* to pay him comic tribute in *Les Vigilles de Triboullet*, one of the most amusing of the *sotties*. Not only could he perform a large repertory (including, as we have seen, *La Belle Dame sans mercy*), but, like Shakespeare and Molière, he wrote as well as acted: 'Il a composé mainte farce', we are told, with panegyric hyperbole, and 'quattre cens moralitez', not to mention a great abundance of *sotties* (ll. 176 and 225–30). Thus, Triboulet was the name of various court fools, of actors, of a comic role, and a synonym for *sot*. In a series of metamorphoses, in and out of real life, in and out of the theater, Triboulet the *sot* and actor played 'Triboullet', the role in a *sottie*. Person and personification, reality and pretense are intertwined so thoroughly that the *sot* cannot be viewed as a purely theatrical invention, with an existence limited to the performing platform. Here again (if it were needed) is striking evidence, in the character of one *sot*, of the medieval fascination with the fool.

The next category of names is one step further removed from an individualized name. Instead of being called by a personal trait, some characters are simply labeled with the name of a social group to which they belong, such as occupation, sex, or condition in life. Most of the occupations are from two plays, *Le Monde* and *Les Povres Deables*. Aside from these two plays and a few assorted valets, tavern-keepers, messengers, prostitutes, and a shepherd, the traditional occupations are noticeably lacking in the *sotties*. (This is contrary to farce practice, where *savetiers*, for example, abound.) A few *métiers* are exploited or invented for comic effect, such as L'Escumeur de Latin of *Les Coppieurs*, and La Mère de Ville, who confronts three burlesque *gardes*, Le Garde Pot, Le Garde Nape, and Le Garde Cul. More often, however, a character is stripped even of occupation and called simply Femme, Amoureux, Pelerin, Hermite, or (referring to a life-style) Gorrier and Folle Bobance.

The most abstract category of all comprises the allegorical roles, which are almost as popular in the *sottie* as in the morality. The desires of the *sots* are made into abstractions, as are their enemies: they pursue Sancté, Joyeuseté, and, especially, Bon Temps, while struggling against Abuz, Malice, Grosse Despense, and, sometimes, Justice and Ordre. One-third of the allegorical roles in the *sottie* are personifications of a class or 'estat', or of society as a whole. No fewer than 11 plays put on stage Le Monde, or Tout, Peuple François, La Chose Publicque, Chascun, or Les Gens. Even Le Temps has a role. The *sots* are at grips not with an individual protagonist, as in the farces, but with society as a whole, or a large section of it, as they try to deceive Le Monde, or are in turn deceived by it. Thus, this category is the first to be made up almost entirely of characters distinguished in some way from the group of *sots* in a play. (The only exceptions are three Folies and La Bazoche in *Le Cry de la Bazoche*.)

In contrast to the allegorical names, the last category to be considered is made up entirely of *sots*.[11] About one-fourth of the total roles in the *sottie* are called simply *sot*, *sotte*, or derivatives of these terms. In addition to *sot* and *sotte*, writers of *sotties* gave their audiences (who evidently loved such characters) a variety of *sotins*, *sotouarts*, and *sottinets*; they gave them Mères and Grand'Mères Sottes; they included a Sot Corrompu, Sot Glorieux, and Sot Dissolu; a Sotte Mine, Sotte Commune, Sotte Fiance, Sotte Occasion; and even a double *sot*, so to speak: Sotte Folle (in *Le Monde, Abuz*). In an effort to control these 'giddie-headed' *sots*, the playwrights provided them with leaders: the *sots* know six Princes, a Principal, a Cappitaine, a Docteur, and a Roy des Sotz. This configuration of a group of followers around its leader was common theatrical practice as far back as the Roman Empire. According to Chambers, at that time an *archimimus* generally dominated the plays of the mimes, and he was provided with 'certain *stupidi* or *parasiti*': fools as foils.[12]

As a *sot* by any other name would be as foolish, the characters of a *sottie* are often called by terms more or less synonymous with *sot*. 'Compaignons', 'esbahys', 'nouveaulx', 'supposts', 'gallants', 'gorriers', 'sots' are all fools. Nine characters are indicated only by number (Premier, Second, etc.), as further description was unnecessary (what could they be but *sots?*). The largest category after *sot* is *galant*, which was evidently often interchangeable with *sot*.[13] In *Les Sobres Sots*, for example, the five Gallans of the cast are called Sotz in the rubrics. The relation of the terms *badin* and *sot* is less clear. Les Sobres Sots insist on distinguishing between *badin*, *sot*, and *sage* (ll. 92–5). Le Badin of *Le Bateleur* considers himself 'des gens de quoy on faict memoyre' (l. 163), 'qui ont le bruict' (l. 23), and he asserts that more glory accompanies the name of *badin* than of *sot*. These pretensions of a humble *bateleur* notwithstanding, the differences between the two types of role are in many plays unclear. It seems that the *badin*, whether he liked it or not, was *grosso modo* a variety of *sot*.[14] The term *fou* originally applied to the licentious character who had the right to say whatever he chose, as he is found in the Fête des Fous and the mysteries. The term slowly evolved to the point where it designated the 'wise fool', the omnipresent and omniscient fool situated outside the group, who comments in an ironic manner on the behavior of others (as in *Le Povre Jouhan*). At this point, when the *fou* has the characteristics of wisdom and frankness, without those of licentiousness and buffoonery, the character becomes the *sot* of the *sottie*.

Two other lexical groups that designated the fool should be mentioned: the constellations of words derived from the roots *coq* and *coquille*. The *sotties* have characters named Coquin, Coquibus (derived from *coq+ibus*, not from *quiproquo*, as Picot suggests[15]), Coquillart, and Coquillon (derived from *coquille*).

As in the case of *sot*, verbs, adjectives, and adverbs were formed based on the root word: 'coquarde, / Coquillarde, coquillonnée' (*La Folie des Gorriers*, ll. 567–8). These names based on *coq* and *coquille* combine a 'double message': they mean simultaneously *fol, niais, benêt* (stupid and foolish) and – what would seem contradictory – a shrewd fellow, scoundrel, dishonest or malicious person, in addition to just 'down-and-out'.[16] In other words, a Coquin could seem to be foolish while having the slyness of a rogue; Coquibus might be a *sot*, but he was just as likely to be a *trompeur*. This opposition has already been seen with regard to the descriptive simple and compound names; it will come up again in the course of this study, for it reflects the fundamental characteristic that made the *sot* the ideal spokesman for late medieval popular attitudes.

In summary, the characters in the *sotties* offer a variety of names, very few of which are traditional proper names. The great majority of the fools' names are to a large degree abstract, ranging from the least abstract, that is, a name fabricated from a personal characteristic, like a nickname; continuing, through invented titles, to a name derived from a social group (profession or sex, for example); and, finally, to the most abstract type of name, the allegorical ones (like Sancté, or Le Temps). In effect, all of these names, except for the allegorical, are but the varied, imaginative ways the *sottie* uses to say the same thing: *sot*. Is this just another illustration of that circular definition that critics sometimes fall back on when trying to define the *sottie*: 'a play performed by *sots*'? The *sottie* was not simply a play put on by a *confrérie des sots*, for if the actor were a *sot*, he was also playing a character who was a *sot*. Ultimately, then, the subject of the *sottie* is the *sottie*: its society of fools, their pleasures and vicissitudes, and their view of what is wrong with the world. Thus, the protagonist at the most general level becomes *sottise*. In fact, no fewer than six characters are called explicitly Sottie or Folie. This discovery must be a touchstone for any study of the *sottie*, for an understanding of the plays called *sotties* should lead to an understanding of the concept of *sottise* and the related idea, *folie*, in the plays, and consequently to an understanding of the medieval fascination with this idea. And, conversely, an understanding of the *sottie* depends on an understanding of its conception of what is *sottise*.

The names of the *sots* have revealed much of what the *sottie* will tell us about its characters. Almost never is there a mention in the plays of a family (except of course the great family of fools, for the fools love to trace their foolish genealogy); the *sots* sometimes have symbolic mothers or grandmothers, but rarely a spouse or offspring. In this way they differ markedly from the characters of the farce. Sometimes they reveal some individuality, in their courtings, for example (*Le Monde, Abuz*), or in their conspiracies (*Les Premiers*). Generally, however, neither family, nor work, nor personal characteristics are used to describe the *sots*: seemingly unemployed and orphaned, they are defined by what they do on stage, even more so by what they say. To understand how this theatrical conception of character fits into the *sottie*, we must now look at the structure of the plays.

As a *sottie* does not have 'characters' as we conceive them, neither does it have a 'plot' in the modern sense. There is rarely a simple answer to the question: What happens in a *sottie*? So little seems to happen that some modern critics, unamused by the 'facéties du roi des sots et de ses sujets', conclude that 'l'intérêt dramatique y est a peu près nul'.[17] A theatrical genre, however, does not flourish for a century and a half if the dramatic interest is *nul*. Therefore, we will try to avoid what one historian considered 'le péché des péchés – le péché entre tous irrémissible: l'anachronisme',[18] and instead try to see the *sottie* as a medieval audience might have seen it. At times structure may mean merely the particular order of subjects discussed, for the dramatic interest and humor of the *sottie* are largely verbal; more often however, structure in the *sottie* involves more than plot, for it incorporates dramatic elements such as musical interludes and poetic *formes fixes*, refrains, repetitions, exits and entrances. Let us see how these elements function in the *sotties*.

The *sotties* are generally very short: Gracien du Pont overestimated the length of a *sottie* when, in 1539, he said that they had about 500 lines.[19] To judge by the existing plays, the average number of lines is 375.[20] About half have between 300 and 400 lines, while only six plays are over 600 lines in length. Many have fewer than 300 lines. The lines of a *sottie* are usually octosyllabic verses rhyming *aabb* or *abab*. Some plays intersperse lines of other lengths, occasionally including stanzas of ten-syllable lines, more frequently mixing in short sections of four- or five-syllable lines (e.g., *Les Coppieurs*, ll. 32–81; *Les Rapporteurs*, ll. 318–44; and especially *Le Monde, Abuz*, which uses a variety of verse lengths: three-, four-, and five-syllable lines, as well as some of eight and ten syllables). The majority of the *sotties*, however, are written in the octosyllabic lines so common in the medieval theater (and in poetry in general).

With so few lines with which to work, the writer of a *sottie* usually chose to begin either with a very short prologue or *in medias res*. The opening of *Troys Galans et Monde* is typical: three *galants* are on stage, speaking one after the other, and in order (that is, 1er Sot, 2e Sot, etc.) about various projects, complaints, political observations, or fantasies; after a short time, another character enters. This formula is so frequent in the *sotties* that the medieval audience knew what to expect as soon as it saw three characters on the stage. The only possible source of suspense was the question: Who else might appear? Sometimes it was another *sot* or the group's leader; at times it was an exotic character such as L'Astrologue or Le Temps qui court. A limited number of traditional structures recur in the opening section of a *sottie*, so much so that the form of the typical *début* can be schematized thus:

X, Y, Z on stage / interaction / A enters / effect on interaction

X, Y, Z are *sots*, though variety is found in their differing names and guises; they form a group which is in the process of interacting in some way, generally verbally. A is a character from outside the group, usually either an antagonist, or a character representing a general concept (Le Monde, Le Temps, etc.); his appearance either contributes to the discussion already in progress, that is, he simply joins in (usually with 'news' of some sort), or it diverts the *sots* from their patter by opposing them in some way. There are a number of variations on this basic formula, of which two of the most common are:

X on stage / summons other *sots* / Y, Z, etc. appear / interaction
X, Y, Z on stage / seek non-*sots* / A, B, etc. found / interaction

If one fool is alone on stage, he soon (sometimes after a short prologue) summons others to join him and the play continues in the principal pattern. Or the beginning may vary, not in the number of *sots* on stage, but in the way that one or more additional, non-*sot*, characters are found or appear.

Thus, the attention of the audience is focused, from the beginning of the play and throughout it, on the question of the entrances of characters: Who will appear, and how many? Contrary to modern conceptions of dramatic structure, these entrances are non-motivated. Yet apparently they were of great interest to the medieval theater-goer, as suggested by the *sottie* that is today generally recognized as the best, *Le Jeu du Prince des Sotz*, in which no fewer than one-fourth of the total lines are taken up with the entrances of seven *sots* (ll. 66–192). The entire play, moreover, is a series of entrances: after these *sots*, there come Le Prince (l. 192), then Sotte Commune (l. 266), and, finally, Mère Sainte Eglise and her two counselors (l. 335). The medieval interest in the entrances of dramatic characters is revealed by the fact that these entrances, gratuitous as they seem, are in addition drawn out by introductions, presentations, and salutations that take up many more lines. This preoccupation with the appearance on stage of a character will prove to be symptomatic of a concern with appearance at another level, with what a character appears to be, and what he turns out to be in reality.

The drama of multiple entrances is sometimes increased by a modification of staging (the only significant modification to be found in the staging of the *sotties*). Whereas most of the plays were performed on a simple platform with few or no properties required, at least two of them use a second, raised level on which one or more *sots* make their first appearance. This double stage is clearly indicated in *Le Jeu du Prince des Sotz*: the followers of the Prince are first seen in compartments or loges from which they are invited to descend to the performing-stage. Similarly, Guippellin, in *Le Roy des Sotz*, is first spied at a *pertuys* from which he is forced to descend. By this method, the effect of the successive *entrées* was literally and figuratively heightened.

Variations on the use of entrances account for some of the most significant types of structure in the *sottie*. They are incorporated into the framework of a larger, tripartite structure, which will be called, for convenience, the 'triptych' form. The great majority of the *sotties* begin with a short prologue and conclude with an epilogue, between which is sandwiched the *matière* of the play. The prologue was an opportunity for the playwright to show some poetic skill in strophic arrangements, such as ballades and other *formes fixes* more complex than the ubiquitous rondeau. Sometimes the opposite practice was followed: that is, instead of beginning with long stanzas recited by one character, the playwright wrote a fast, lively prologue, in which a line is divided among two, three, or even four *sots* (in *Les Sobres Sots*). The prologue itself, which is usually about 30 lines, is in most cases a brief discussion of the situation to be developed in the play. *Les Coquins* is typical: Maulevault delivers a brief monologue followed by the separate entrances of the other *sots*, who introduce and praise themselves to the public. Then the play begins.

Although the large central portion of a *sottie* does not fall into acts and scenes as in later theatrical practice, the plays do show a distinct, if rudimentary, concern for scenic structure. Many *sotties* are clearly divided into two sections. *L'Astrologue*, for example, after a prologue on the state of society, presents first the problem and then its remedy, followed by the conclusion. Similarly, in *Les Coppieurs*, Teste Creuse and Sotin are *lardés* (ridiculed) in the first section and take their revenge in the second. (For other examples of this type of construction, see *Le Cry de la Bazoche*, *Les Esbahis*, and *Troys Galans et Monde*.) Entrances play an important part in the 'triptych' structure, for the appearance of a new character usually serves to mark the beginning of a new section, or a turn of events in the development of the play.

The epilogue may be an extended one, as in the 80-line 'Eloge de la Folie' at the end of *La Folie des Gorriers*. More commonly, the conclusion is another example of traditional forms in the *sottie*, for certain set phrases occur over and over:

Prenez en gre tous esbatz.

En prenant congé de ce lieu,
Une chanson pour dire adieu.

A Dieu toute la compaignie.

Frequently a *sottie* simply stops, without coming to a logical resolution.

Although this dramatic construction was simple, it allowed for significant variations. At times, the opening and conclusion, or even the two parts of the central action, were structured to envelop or hide a theme which the *sots* did not want to state clearly because of some risk involved, from which they wanted to divert attention. We have seen how they often feared the effects of speaking their minds. In *Le Cry de la Bazoche*, for example, there are tucked away, between the accepted moral sentiments that open and close the play, attitudes that were less acceptable (on war, in particular). This *noyau–écorce* structure is also found in *Le Roy des Sotz* (see the remarks on Protestantism, ll. 137ff.), and in *Les Brus*, whose 'kernel', a bitter condemnation of monks for their hypocrisy and lechery, is enclosed in the shell of the prostitutes' story. In *Les Esbahis*, the structure of insertions is more diffuse – acerbic comments on God and politics are interspersed among remarks on mythological persons, such as Jason and Medea, in an effort, perhaps, to make the dangerous remarks less noticeable. (The mythological names may also be veiled references to powerful individuals.) Finally, there is one case in which this structure is used in a way that seems harmless. In *Les Coquins*, a comic bet takes place in a tavern: several *coquins* want to see which one can refrain the longest from scratching or from blowing his nose – a scene inserted between two long passages made up of *propos divers* and tall tales. In this way these *sotties* express divergent messages: there is the 'official' subject matter, stated in the opening section and on which the dénouement moralizes, and a second subject, inserted somewhere in the middle, where it will be less conspicuous. At the most general structural level of the *sotties* a theme appears that will be dominant at all levels: the concern with that which is seen and with that which is hidden; with what appears to be and what is.

The second set of variations of the basic 'triptych' structure makes use of the characters' entrances in several imaginative ways. First of all, the entrances sometimes develop from simple stage business to the point of constituting much of the play. This development has already been pointed out in *Le Jeu du Prince des Sotz*. Similarly, in *Les Povres Deables*, each character introduces himself with a short speech, so that the entrances in effect punctuate the play. Other plays based on a similar structure are *La Reformeresse* and *La Mère de Ville* in particular. In these plays, and almost every time a character makes an appearance in a *sottie*, his *entrée* is used to introduce him immediately to the audience. We are led to think that there is to be no surprise or discovery for the audience. Thus, in *Le Pelerin et La Pelerine*, Le Pelerin states openly in the very beginning what he is and has done. And as soon as Mère Sotte appears in *Le Jeu du Prince des Sotz* (ll. 335–55), she delivers a long monologue (long, that is, for the *sotties*), in the manner of a Shakespearian soliloquy, in which she meditates on her evil schemes and explains her plans. That is, she explains them to herself and to the audience, but not to the other *sots*. The playwright evidently wanted to tell the audience immediately who a character was and why he had appeared there before them. The three fools of *Folle Bobance* could be expressing the anxiety felt by the public when they exclaim to the lady who has just entered:

> Dea, dame, pas ne nous celez
> Vostre nom; dictes en presence.

Ll. 29–30: Indeed, lady, do not hide from us Your name; say it in everyone's presence.

'Pou d'Acquest?' 'Pou d'Acquest?', repeat the *sots* of the *sottie* by that name, when Pou d'Acquest first introduces himself. 'Is that really your name? Did we hear you right?' The character thus had to 'fix' his identity, or he might turn out to be someone other than he seemed. And, in spite of these precautions, he often did.

Disguises, revelations, changes of costume, concealments – all these variations on the 'appearance', in both senses, of a character are among the principal dramatic techniques of the *sotties*. In *Troys Galans et Monde*, for instance, the three *sots* try to deceive Le Monde by playing hide-and-seek with him. The costume furthermore is often the key to these *péripéties*, as the characters may hide behind a misleading costume. A character may appear in one costume, one that symbolizes his nature or estate, only to change to another one later (to no fewer than four others in *Mestier et Marchandise*). More frequently, the first costume is an intended disguise: Le Prince in *Le Prince des Sots* enters dressed in a long robe, but the stage directions tell us that 'desoubs est habillé en sot' ('underneath he is dressed like a fool').

Is a character's costume a disguise? What is under the disguise? How can a character be made to reveal his true identity? These are questions that recur in the minds of the *sots*. This difficulty of knowing who a character really is leads to various developments, all variations of the theme of appearance and concealment. In the scene in *Le Prince des Sots* mentioned above (p. 45), the two *suppôts* beg their leader to remove his robe, to assume his true nature of *sot* by revealing his fool's costume: otherwise, he cannot 'folloyer en folloyant' (l. 91: 'have a good time by playing the fool'). If a character will not reveal himself voluntarily, however, the *sots* will compel him to do so. In *Les Premiers, Les Sotz triumphans, Le Prince des Sots, Le Roy des Sotz,* and *Le Jeu du Prince des Sotz*, characters have their outer costume forcibly removed to reveal the *sot* underneath. Mère Sotte makes two 'entrances' in this way: one intentional (as Mère Sainte Eglise), one forced (as Mère Sotte). These concealments, disguises, *déshabillements forcés*, revelations, and disclosures of various kinds are motivated by the same concern as that which lies behind the *noyau–écorce* type of dramatic construction. A *sot*, as well as a *sottie*, may have two levels: the 'official' character, indicated by the false costume that he wears on entering, and the real one hidden beneath the other. Furthermore, the *sottie* suggests that a character is hiding behind the role itself:

> Sy tu joue ton personnage
> Si le dy: t'ose tu monstrer?

Troys Galans et Monde, ll. 123–4: If you are playing your part, Say so: do you dare show yourself?

This theme of different realities will reappear in many ways and on many levels in the course of this study.[21]

There are still other types of dramatic structure in the *sottie*. A series of affirmations and denials, of claims and counter-claims, or of similar opposing speeches, constitutes a binary structure in some *sotties*. This type of alternating construction makes use of the wise fool as commentator on the words or actions of another character, in the tradition of medieval 'debate' literature. *Le Gaudisseur et le Sot* and *Les Cris de Paris* are the clearest examples of the affirmation–denial construction.[22] In these plays the dramatic interest lies in the conflict between two points of view, or two mutually exclusive activities. In *Le Gaudisseur et le Sot*, Le Gaudisseur has his self-laudatory, exaggerated claims corrected by a *sot* whom he pretends to ignore. In the same way, Le Badin, in the *Fragment for three characters*, denies everything the beggars assert; and Le Second Suppôt, in *Le Cry de la Bazoche*, opposes his pessimistic view of the state of society to the more optimistic one of Le Premier Suppôt. The binary rhythm is further emphasized by the symmetrical construction of their speeches: each two- or three-line assertion is countered by a two- or three-line counter-assertion, both often beginning with the same word: 'Tel'. *Les Cris de Paris* is a more complicated case, for the street-vendor interrupts the discussion of two *galants* in a seemingly haphazard way. Nonetheless, the same mechanism is at work in this play as in *Le Gaudisseur et le Sot*: his *cris* for cakes and herrings are not irrelevant; they comment on what the other two are trying to say, but with a crudeness that shocks them.

The *sot* as truth-speaker appears in several other plays, as a part of the dramatic structures discussed above. In *Le Jeu du Prince des Sotz*, for example, the three *sots* comment on the action at a critical moment, that of the battle; it is they who ultimately reveal the truth about Mère Sotte to the Prince, who has turned to them for counsel. Once again the *sottie* indicates a concern with the conflict of truth and appearance: the *sot* as commentator reveals what the hypocritical words and actions of others attempt to hide. One type of *sot* makes clear the *sottise* of another. This dichotomy in the ranks of the *sots* will prove essential to understanding the *sottie*.

Some *sotties*, like *Les Menus Propos*, seem to have no discernible dramatic structure. In this play, one of the better known of the *sotties*, three *sots* are on stage, exchanging small talk. And all that happens is talk. Critics have considered this type of *sottie* as the most rudimentary and least dramatic. Yet *Les Menus Propos* presents a complex interweaving of fantasies, political allusions, and comments on the problems of daily life in the Middle Ages. That the choice between talk and action was one of the major options of the medieval playwright is shown by the fact that two plays deal with the same subject in these opposing ways: *Folle Bobance* represents in words alone what *La Folie des Gorriers* puts into action on the stage. When language becomes action, the arrangement of the topics, what has been called the 'textual syntax' of a work,[23] becomes a dramatic structure of greater subtlety than the more obvious stage actions discussed above.

Therefore, if we look for structure in the *sottie* based on division into scenes and acts, with motivated entrances and exits, as some scholars of the *sottie* seem to have done (Picot and Petit de Julleville in particular), then we will have to conclude with them that the plays are simple and unstructured. But other kinds of formal 'markers' can be discerned that are intrinsic to the texts. The question of music – *chansons*, *danses*, and *pauses*, in particular – as a structuring device in this theater, is beginning to be explored in works such as H. M. Brown's excellent *Music in the French Secular Theater*.[24] There is now little doubt that music and, in particular, *chansons*, made up part of the structure of the *sotties*.

Chansons sometimes seem to be inserted for the sheer love of music, with little relation to plot, characters, or structure of the play. *Deulx Gallans et Sancté* includes the largest number of such *chansons:* nine songs, which existed previously to the play, are interpolated into the text. The *sots* simply interrupt the play by saying something like: 'Chanton(s) de courage / Une chanson à la plaisance' (ll. 162–3). Frequently, however, a song reinforces an idea that has just been expressed (see ll. 200ff.). In addition, a variety of pretexts served for the inclusion of a song: the three *badins* sing while L'Astrologue star-gazes (*L'Astrologue*); in *Les Croniqueurs*, all five *chansons* reiterate a satiric point that one of the *sots* has just made. Brown feels that the *sots* themselves had to be musicians in order to sing, accompany themselves on instruments, and dance, as most acting societies were not rich enough to hire their own singers or instrumentalists.[25] Songs therefore could serve, for the medieval playwright, as a pleasing way to mark the major ideas or divisions of a play.[26]

Instrumental passages are, after songs, the most common way of indicating changes in scene or action. Flourishes at important exits and entrances usher in the leading fools, the princes, generals, and other *grands personnages* of the *sotties*, in a manner worthy of their 'dignity'. The term *pauses* (or 'poses'), which probably indicates musical interludes, occurs in a number of *sotties*. Sometimes music separates one scene from another – the single musical reference in *Les Béguins* occurs when Printemps leaves the stage to fetch Bon Temps. Similarly, *Le Monde* is clearly divided into little scenes, marked by 'poses', and 'silètes'. Instrumental music was probably interpolated into the action more frequently than the rubrics indicate;[27] here, though, we are still forced to conjecture.

Other means may have been used to indicate divisions in a *sottie*; repetitions and refrains, and poetic forms such as the rondeau, often occur at a moment that intensifies a preceding speech (in the manner of the 'poetic' passages in a T. S. Eliot play), or at a moment that marks a change in the direction of the plot. In *Les Brus*, five refrains (including two rondeaux) clearly mark the stages of the play, in a kind of internal résumé. As music may celebrate the entrance of a character, rondeaux are frequently used to introduce him to the other *sots* and to the audience (see *Mestier et Marchandise*, ll. 70–7 and 115–22). Refrains are used in some plays to emphasize uncompromising attitudes and obsessions (as do the refrains in *Les Gens nouveaulx*).[28]

Thus a variety of formal means were available to the medieval playwright, a range of theatrical procedures that were to a large extent traditional. The author's 'freedom of choice' lay not so much in a freedom to structure his play as he wished as in the ways that he could vary and combine already established procedures and techniques.[29] The *sottie* therefore is to be recognized as more structured than has been previously thought. The plays must be interpreted in the light of the dramatic traditions on which they draw, for on the threshold of the innovations of the Renaissance, the *sottie* looks backward – in its dramatic form and, as we shall see, in the attitudes which that form expresses.

The superficial structure of the *sottie* – the narrative sequence of events, or *récit* – is provided by the realization, in individual plays, of the three fundamental roles of the *sottie*. These roles determine the significance of what characters do and say on stage, the relative positions they occupy in the structure of the play. The primary roles of the *sotties* are: evil-doer, victim, and accuser. Some person or group is accused of wrong behavior by another, who may or may not be the victim of the harmful behavior. The role of victim, whether represented by a character on stage or conveyed verbally, is the necessary counterpart of the evil-doer. The accuser voices the denunciations of wrong-doing. This basic configuration of evil-doer / victim / accuser underlies and structures all the satiric *sotties*, whether or not all three roles are incorporated in specific characters; they also affect the narrative structure of the non-satiric *sotties*, although in a less well-defined way. The term 'role' is used here in the way that Vladimir Propp used it in *The Morphology of the Folktale*, to indicate a category that is more general than a specific character.[30] As we shall see, several characters may play the same role, in the same or different plays, and one character may play more than one role. The inter-relationship of the three basic roles of the *sottie* exists at a deeper, more abstract, level of analysis than that of either character or *récit*, for it is these roles that determine the specific manifestations of character and plot which constitute the various types of *sotties*.[31]

The variety and complexity with which these roles are realized in individual plays are the result of three factors. First, a character may embody more than one role at a time. The combination, in a character or group of characters, of the accusatory and victimized roles is the most common (as in *Mestier et Marchandise* and *Les Gens nouveaulx*). As we shall see, the merging of these two roles is largely the result of the identification of the *sots* with the troubled lower classes. The combination of evil-doer and victim can be seen in those plays in which the role of victim manifests itself at two levels: the immediate victim of harmful actions, and the indirect victim of those actions, the evil-doer himself. As in *Le Monde, Abuz*, the evil-doers are sometimes made to suffer as the result of their own actions.

Second, one or more roles may not be represented on stage at all – they may be incorporated in individuals who remain off stage, so to speak, and who live dramatically only in the words of the on-stage characters. The role most often left off stage is that of evil-doer, a situation which at first seems surprising – the maleficent role is fundamental to the *sottie*, as to all satiric literature, for without pillaging knights, ambitious prelates, and dishonest merchants, for example, there would be no object of satiric attack. But the fact that the author of a *sottie* chooses verbal rather than physical representation of this particular role is largely a reflection of the danger involved in putting on stage evil-doers who were powerful enough to retaliate. The *sots* evidently thought it less dangerous to refer verbally to certain powerful people whom they wished to accuse than to represent them on stage. Some *sotties* could put the evil-doers on stage because the playwright had official support (as did Gringore in *Le Jeu du Prince des Sotz*). More frequently the *sots* chose to disguise the identity of the evil-doers by incorporating them in characters called by obscure names, like 'Les Gens Nouveaulx' or 'L'Un et l'Autre'. Other ways were sometimes used to avoid trouble – the seemingly maleficent characters could be shown to be relatively innocent: the evil-doers represented on stage are not the real culprits (*La Reformeresse*). This role is consequently sometimes divided between two groups, a group of lesser evil (represented on stage) and a group responsible for more serious wrong-doing (usually represented only verbally).

Unlike the other two roles that of accuser is at once stable and universal in the *sottie*. Although the roles of evil-doer and victim are at times not embodied in particular characters, that of accuser is always present in the *sottie*, as it seems to be intrinsic to satire. It is also the role which, in an economy of means, is most often combined with another.

The third factor influencing the configuration of these roles is the possibility of shifting a character from one role to another during the play. In an illustration of that popular medieval notion of the *trompeur trompé*, the victim and the evil-doer sometimes change places. In rare cases, the accusers take on the role of evil-doer in a cynical expression of the all-pervasive nature of injustice (*Chascun, Plusieurs*). It should be pointed out, however, that the dénouement which destroys the evil-doers, either through physical defeat or through their repentance, does not simply shift characters from one role to another, but neutralizes all the roles and removes the possibility of further satire.

These three roles have a relationship similar to three of the *actants* proposed by A. J. Greimas in *Sémantique structurale*, for the analysis of narrative.[32] The victim can be seen as the *Sujet*, the accuser as the *Adjuvant*, and the evil-doer as the *Opposant*. An additional *Adjuvant* sometimes appears under the name 'Ordre', or something similar; an *Objet* is represented or alluded to by terms such as 'Bon Temps'. But the roles that I have described are better adapted than are the *actants* to delineating the peculiar structure of the *sotties*, because they are predicated on the fundamental purpose of the plays – the denunciation of wrong-doing: the *sottie* finds the vicious more fascinating than the virtuous. For this reason, it seems more appropriate to reverse the distribution of *actants* in those plays in which the evil-doers occupy the center of attention, as in *Le Monde, Abuz*. In such plays, the evil-doers are in effect the *Sujet*, or rather *Anti-Sujet*; their *Opposant* is represented by a character like Le Monde; and their *Objet* is domination, their *Adjuvant*, deceit (and money). Such a play is primarily about these evil-doers, their machiavellian principles, goals, and methods. In addition, it should be pointed out that both the accuser and the victim are *Opposants*, one aggressive, the other passive, of the evil-doer. Thus, although the relationship of the primary roles to Greimas's *actants* varies from play to play and within a play, the relationship among the three roles remains stable. After we have looked at specific manifestations of these three roles, we shall be able to suggest the reason for the development of this unique configuration of roles in the *sottie* (see p. 163, below).

Scholars of the *sottie* have frequently raised the question of the evolution of the genre.[33] Since the *sotties* comprise a number of different kinds of comedy, the question arises as to whether one kind evolved from another. Which is *la sottie primitive*? Is lack of dramatic action a sign of primitiveness? Or are simple *jeux de scène* or *grossièretés* the criteria? These questions are difficult for us to answer – in an attempt to measure 'primitiveness' in a form of theater that is quite alien to modern conceptions we must try to avoid definitions of complexity or primitiveness based on present-day theatrical practice. The dates of the plays cannot help us, for the question of evolutionary types is further complicated by the synchronic existence of all the types of *sottie*, as indicated by the extant texts. The dates give no clear evidence of the evolution of one from another – some of the more 'primitive' (i.e., simpler) *sotties* were written later than some of the more complicated ones. The evolution of the genre may one day be established, but it cannot now be presupposed. Therefore, the following consideration of the comic types of *sottie* will necessarily be synchronic, not diachronic.

The four classic types of comedy are generally suggested to be comedy of situation; words, or language; character; and *comique de geste*, or slapstick.[34] To this list, Felix Gaiffe would add 'le comique d'idées', a type of comedy that is based on language, but whose humor lies not in word-play but in an attempt to say something amusing about an individual, event, or idea. The humor is therefore not in the way in which words are used, but in what they say about something or someone. It is already clear from the preceding study of characterization and structure that these types of comedy are not equally represented in the *sottie*: slapstick and the comedy of situation are rudimentary, while the comedy of characters is limited to one kind; the comedy of words and of ideas is on the other hand highly developed.

A preliminary division of the *sotties* separates them into two large categories: satiric (including parodic) and non-satiric. Each of these main categories can in turn be subdivided into three more specific types, giving six in all.[35] The types of non-satiric *sotties* are made up of plays based on the comedies of situation, character, and words. The satiric *sotties* are in turn divided according to the level of generality, or specificity, of their satire. The most general type is the satire of society as a whole; the satire of a type of person, class, *métier*, or institution is less general; the satire of real events and individuals is the most specific. These categories are not purely hypothetical, for each does exist in 'pure' form in one or more plays, which will serve as models, or prototypes, for the study of the types of comedy in the *sottie*. In addition these models will help us understand the various combinations of the six types found in the other *sotties*.

How do the non-satiric *sotties* differ from the satiric? Briefly, they are generally shorter, less complex, and emphasize language, character, or physical humor rather than 'ideas'. The physical comedy (which in the *sottie* underlies and is almost synonymous with the comedy of situation) takes the form of *jeux de scène*, games, scuffles, processions, and other stage business. It is the type of comedy most closely tied to plot, for these *jeux de scène* answer the question: What happens? Common to many of the plays are certain *jeux de scène*, such as *entrées* and *sorties*, blows, and acrobatics. In some plays, however, a more extended stage action forms the nucleus of the play.[36] *Trote Menu* is one such play: the two fools decide to play a game, one that involves attaching a coin to the forehead of one *sot*, while the other, blindfold, tries to take it in his teeth. The second time round, Trote Menu fixes the money not on his forehead but above his other cheeks, that is, on 'le plus parfaict / Cul qui soit d'icy a Romme' (ll. 160–1). Mirre Loret discovers that he has been tricked, and a fist-fight ends the play. Some critics have tended to take this type of play as representative of the genre and have consequently dismissed the *sottie* as unimportant, although plays of this type are by far the rarest. (Most plays like *Trote Menu* must have been lost, as they are slightly more than improvised buffooneries.) Such *sotties* evidently served to entertain the spectators while they waited for the performance of a serious play (see ll. 192–3: 'Tu vois cy les gens attendant / A veoir jouer ce mestere [*mystère*]?'). Thus, it is their purpose that determines the nature of these plays, their simplicity, liveliness, and use of obscenity.[37]

The other major type of *jeu de scène* consists of parodic actions such as ceremonies, processions, liturgies, all of which the *sots* seem to have enjoyed immensely. The ceremonial side of life, the 'actes sociaux à forme arrêtée', as Bergson calls them[38] – from a simple distribution of prizes (*Les Premiers*) to an elaborate funeral service (*Les Vigilles de Triboullet*) – were a favorite pastime of the fools. The burlesque processions, which in *Les Sotz nouveaulx* include macaronic Latin and wine-drinking, could have been simple or elaborate, depending on the troupe and the performance, since the *pauses* could allow for the inclusion of musical interludes. In either case, with or without music, these ceremonies, although amusing in themselves, usually take on an aspect of religious parody.

Games, fights, 'gabs' (boasts), processions: the elements of the typical *jeu de scène* are accessible to all publics, of any age, national or cultural background, because this type of theater – like the silent comedies of Chaplin – can be easily understood without translation; it is conveyed directly by visible gestures. But the word, rather than pantomime or slapstick, is usually the basis of a *sottie*. Those *sotties* that are made up of a particular form of verbal humor called *propos sans suite* are the least accessible today. This form of word-play is a kind of *fantaisie verbale*, which Robert Garapon has defined as 'un jeu libéré du souci de la signification et placé sous le signe de la gratuité. Pratiquement, il y a fantaisie verbale dès que le plaisir d'assembler les mots et de jouer avec eux prend le pas sur la volonté de signifier.'[39] This definition will be discussed at length in Chapter 5; at this point it is useful to see how such a definition of verbal gratuitousness applies to the *sotties*. The model of this type of comedy, *Les Menus Propos*, suggests an answer.

Three *sots*, called simply Le Premier, Le Second, and Le Tiers, recite consecutively, in strict numerical order, a series of two- and four-line speeches (more than 570 lines of such *répliques*). The form of the play is as rigid and monotonous as the content is capricious and free of the constraints of logic. (In fact, the form seems to be most rigid where the content is most free.) The gratuitousness of *Les Menus Propos* lies not so much in the words themselves as in the way one subject follows another in a seemingly incoherent manner.[40] Yet, attention to what the *sots* are saying shows their words to be anything but *fatrasiques* (devoid of intelligible meaning): only six of the many speeches in *Les Menus Propos* express images that are nonsensical, impossible. The *sots* speak mostly about the details of daily life, about political and

religious subjects, intermixing with their comments proverbs
and diverse – but mostly useless – information:

> Mais que la paix si soit criée,
> Je troteray bien les pays.

Ll. 101-2: But if peace were proclaimed, I would go running around the
country.

> Qui vouldroit avoir bons cousteaulx,
> Il fault droit aller a Saint Lo.

Ll. 185-6: Whoever wants to have good knives, He should go straight to
St Lô.

> Ma mere dit que, se Dieu meurt,
> Que Saint Benoist si sera Dieu;
> Mais je ne sçais pas à quel jeu
> S'il ne le gaignoit aux festus.

Ll. 391-4: My mother says that, if God dies, St Benoît will be God. But I
don't know at what game [he would win the post] If he didn't win it at
drawing straws.

Because there is no plot, a spectator could arrive at any time
and would not be at a loss to know what was happening. Yet
despite this advantage, it is difficult to conceive how this long,
disconnected speech could hold the attention of a crowd of
spectators just entering the play-area. This is another example of
the ability of audiences of former centuries to sit for long periods
of time and listen to a sermon, speech, or drama: the Puritans in
America are known to have listened attentively to their minister
for three or four hours. While *Les Menus Propos* is not nearly so
long as a sermon, it also requires solely auditory attention in
order to appreciate the remarks of the *sots*. After the decline of
the *sottie*, theater-goers will not be expected to listen to a play that
is almost entirely verbal, a play in which virtually nothing
happens, until *En attendant Godot*.

Robert Garapon, in an attempt to explain the phenomenon of
Les Menus Propos, has offered the ingenious theory that the play
was never given as the text reads, that in effect it is not a play at
all, but a 'florilège de menus propos', 'un recueil de "sottes
nouvelles", où les acteurs d'autres sotties pouvaient puiser
librement pour meubler tel ou tel endroit de leur jeu'.[41] Plausible
as his theory is, some of his arguments do not really support it.

Garapon points out, for example, that the *sots* are called only by numbers, an anonymity which he qualifies as 'rarissime'.[42] In reality, however, no fewer than one-fifth of the *sotties* include characters called only by number. In particular, in all the plays in which three *sots* appear, if they are not given another name ('Gens Nouveaulx', for example), they are called simply Le Premier, Le Second, etc., in the rubrics. Furthermore, the play begins and ends with a rondeau, so giving a definite opening and closing to the composition. On the other hand, it is true that large sections of *Les Menus Propos* were written into another *sottie*, *Estourdi*. (The *Sermon joyeux d'ung fiancé qui emprunte ung pain sur la journée* also borrows from *Les Menus Propos*.) Such borrowing is a tribute to the popularity of the play, a popularity attested also by the number of editions that remain from the sixteenth century. *Les Menus Propos*, and its borrower, *Estourdi*, are the only *sotties* made up entirely of this type of verbal fantasy. But other plays do include this kind of comic 'small talk': *Les Coquins* is two-thirds *menus propos*. (Other plays that include large sections are *Le Prince des Sots*, *Les Rapporteurs*, *Les Sotz ecclesiasticques*, and *Les Sotz escornez*.) So we are still faced with the problem of trying to understand the comic effect of these disconnected remarks on the audiences of the *sottie*.

Striking is the fools' preoccupation with – and joy in – words. Even when a play is not simply *propos sans suite*, it is still largely words: in *Les Troy Galans et un Badin*, Le Badin talks, for most of the play, about what would happen if he were God: the new paradise is talked about, not dramatized. Similarly, in *Le Pelerinage* and *Les Cris de Paris*, the subject of marriage – which is acted out in malicious detail in farces like *Le Cuvier* and *Le Povre Jouhan* – is in the *sotties* only talked about. Finally, one *sottie* sometimes takes the same subject as another, divests it of what little dramatic action it did have, and turns it into pure talk (we have seen how *Folle Bobance* describes what happens in *La Folie des Gorriers*). The meaning of this choice of words over action, for the *sots* and for their conception of *folie*, will become clear as we look more closely at the plays.

The sole type of character comedy to be found in the *sotties* is illustrated by *Les Vigilles de Triboullet*. Maître Triboullet, the

'Vray sot sotouart', whose exploits and pretended decease are described humorously and in great detail, was a master of words. He could speak 'ung tres-divers langaige' (l. 220) composed of Latin, Picard, Flemish, French, and jargon; and 'Il faisoit rage d'exposer' (l. 315) in language either crude ('lourdoys') or academic ('rethorique'). He talked as well as he drank (and the two are clearly connected, as he talked better the more he drank). *Les Vigilles de Triboullet* offers a portrait of a foolish character ('character' in the two senses that it has in English), a parody of a real actor (whose stage name was Triboullet), a song of *sottise* which the *sots* pretend to sing in all seriousness (thereby increasing the humor). Triboullet and the *sottie* that celebrates his gifts are an example of a *comique de caractère* to be found in a few *sotties*, which we shall call *sotties de bande*.

The term *sottie de bande* is not a modern one: the *sots* themselves suggest it in *Les Coppieurs* (see l. 177, where a play is called 'farce de bande'). This term describes those *sotties* that are based on the idea of the *sot* as a fascinating person, whose life and activities – particularly his life in the troupe of *sots* – are dramatic subjects of great amusement (cf. the praise of *badins* in *Le Bateleur*). *Les Vigilles de Triboullet* is the model and masterpiece of this type of comedy. In addition to the portraits of particular fools, their relations to their prince are often the topic of a *sottie*: *Les Premiers*, *Le Prince des Sots*, *Le Roy des Sotz*, and *Les Sotz escornez* are plays about the attempts of *sots* to revolt against their leader. Rather than parodying specific political events (as far as can be determined), these plays laugh at the life of the *sot* and his foolish problems; they are a mockery of the *sot* by the *sot*.[43]

After the comedy of slapstick, language, and character, we come to the comedy of ideas in the form of the satiric *sotties*. These constitute the majority of the plays. Because of their 'tendance moralisatrice, politique, sociale, ou littéraire', the satiric plays are generally considered more important than the 'simples parades'.[44] They may be more important according to our criteria of 'important theater', but are frequently, for us, less comic. For it is difficult today to appreciate the full meaning of the satiric *sotties* without knowing the political and social circumstances to which the plays refer. Unfortunately, our understanding of satire in the *sotties* has grown slowly and haltingly and will probably remain incomplete. Nevertheless, we shall see that on certain levels the *sotties* are still intelligible. In the satiric *sotties*, action, language, plot, character – all become means to a satiric end. Satire in the *sottie* may be verbal, usually in the form of allegory or allusion; or it may derive from gesture or action. In other words, the *sots* may talk about those who try to 'mener paistre le roy par simulation' (*Le Monde, Abuz*, ll. 676–7: 'put the king out to graze [i.e., to dupe him], through deception'), or they may hand another character, named Le Monde, a bunch of grass (*Troys Galans et Monde*). But whether verbalized or acted out, the satire is expressed at one of three levels of generality.

The first of the satiric types are the *sotties* that remain on the most general level, those that attempt to satirize the state of society as a whole. This broad satire usually takes the form of a 'proverb in action'. A number of plays – *Deulx Gallans et Sancté, Les Gens nouveaulx, Les Sotz triumphans, Troys Galans et Monde –* could serve as the model for this type. In *Les Gens nouveaulx*, three *sots* decide to house Le Monde 'de Mal en Pire'. And so the poor Monde finds himself moved from one ramshackle home, named appropriately Mal, to another, called, of course, Pire.[45] By acting out a proverb, familiar expression, or similar verbal formula, the *sots* make concrete their view of a general state of affairs, while leaving in shadow the individuals to whom they may be referring.

Some *sotties*, clearly involving a more specific kind of satire, constitute the second level of generality; this is the satire of a particular institution, class, *métier*, or type of individual. Most of the satiric *sotties* belong to this group, for the *sots* ridicule a great variety of people (from hawkers of patent medicine to the king's favorites) and institutions (the Church in particular). The usual professions – lawyer, *sergent*, innkeeper – are satirized, and so, it has been claimed, are all classes of society. (The validity of this claim will be examined in the following chapters; for the moment let us just note that these plays constitute one type of satire.) The model of this type could be *Les Povres Deables*, in which a priest, a monk, a lawyer, a prostitute, and a roué are the objects of satire, or any of a number of plays which deal with a specific type: *Le Gaudisseur et le Sot, La Folie des Gorriers,* or *Les Sotz ecclesiasticques.*[46] It was undoubtedly *sotties* of this type that led Petit de Julleville to view the medieval comic theater as 'un acte d'accusation contre tous les vices du siècle; un réquisitoire à la fois railleur et passionné'.[47]

The accusations of the *sotties* at the third level of specificity are aimed not at society as a whole or at particular classes or institutions, but, in the tradition of *Le Jeu de la feuillée,* at specific events and individuals. While rarely 'naming names', the plays of this type do make clear to whom or to what they are referring; they speak out for or against a certain cause, government, or head of state. *Le Jeu du Prince des Sotz* is an excellent model for this class. Since this is the only *sottie* commonly read, it is unnecessary to summarize it here; suffice it to say that the object of the satire – Pope Jules II – is both precise and clearly designated. Both language and action are used to unmask (literally and figuratively) this head of the Church, to show that he is, in the eyes of Gringore and of his patron, Louis XII, just another *sot.* Gringore uses all the satiric means at his disposal in such a masterful way that it is difficult to believe that this is a work of his youth – his first comic play (as far as we know). Thus, while the quality of the satire may vary enormously from play to play,[48] the *sotties* of this type are all characterized by their attacks on specific objects of satire.[49]

Most *sotties* are not pure types, but a combination, frequently complex, of several kinds of satire. One of the most common syntheses is that of the satire of society as a whole and of certain institutions, *métiers,* etc. (see *Les Sotz fourrez*). *La Reformeresse* presents the combination of all three satiric kinds of comedy, and, in addition, a *sottie de bande,* as the company that performed the play (the printers of Rouen?) satirizes itself in several passages. Other types of comedy can be combined with the three levels of satire, as in *Les Sotz ecclesiasticques,* where 30 lines of *menus propos* (ll. 44–76) are interjected in the midst of a biting satire of the clergy. Consequently, since the text of a *sottie* frequently contains diverse elements, it is necessary to avoid a static principle of classification, despite the use of certain plays to illustrate one principal type. Instead, I have tried 'to have recourse to criteria related to the very dynamism' of the plays, as Zumthor has expressed it.[50] This procedure has permitted us to isolate the various kinds of comedy in the *sotties*, but the isolation must be short-lived, and now the plays can be seen again in their comic complexity.

To sum up, the approach to the *sottie* through the names of the *sots* has brought out a significant quality of many characters, their dual nature of *trompeur* and its mirror image, *trompé*. It has been seen that their antagonists often take the form of society as a whole, thereby revealing the concern of the *sots* with the general state of society. Finally, the names of the *personnages* made clear that the major character was the *sottie* itself, and, consequently, the larger concepts of *sottise* and *folie*.

The structure of the *sotties* has shown a preoccupation with the theme of appearances, in the form of entrances, costumes, disguises, revelations, and concealments. The costume symbolizes the two levels of perception, appearance and reality, for the *sots* often wear an official (false) costume over the hidden (real) one. In addition, the theme of appearance and reality is suggested by some of the basic types of structure in the *sottie*, in the *noyau–écorce* play, in the play of extended entrances, and in the plays involving a fool–commentator.

Last of all, and most important, we have discovered the primary roles – evil-doer, victim, and accuser – that underlie the structure of the *sottie*, and the general types of comedy in the plays. The most important forms of comedy were found to be language and ideas – the use of words instead of action was striking. The various forms of satire, which are crucial for an understanding of the attitudes expressed in the plays, were analyzed briefly in this chapter. In the next, I will examine in more detail the nature and use of satire in the *sotties*. In particular, the following chapter considers the general view of society – Le Monde – in the plays; the classes, institutions, and types satirized; and how and why certain individuals are satirized.

4

Satire in the *sottie*

A! mes amys,
Les abus au monde sont mys.
La Mère de Ville, ll. 109–10

The *sottie* is a satiric genre – about this there is little disagreement. But what do the plays satirize, from what point of view, and for what purpose? In the preceding chapter a preliminary analysis was conducted by grouping the *sotties* according to the generality of their satiric object: society as a whole; certain classes, *métiers*, institutions, or types of individuals; and, lastly, specific events and individuals. This division of the plays will help to answer the question just raised about the object, point of view, and purpose of satire in the *sottie*. Help in an analysis of satire in the *sottie* is also provided by the only thorough study, to my knowledge, of the problems involved in analyzing medieval French satire, the study of anti-bourgeois satire by Jean V. Alter,[1] the precision and consistency of which stands out against previous studies. From Lenient's *La Satire en France au Moyen Age* of 1859 and Petit de Julleville's *La Comédie et les mœurs* of 1885 to a recent doctoral dissertation,[2] the discussion of satire in the *sottie* has alternated between the poles of extreme specificity (a paraphrase of the texts) and over-generalization (sweeping statements not always visibly rooted in the texts). But as Alter's work does not study the *sottie* specifically, there is still a need for a close look at satire in the *sottie*.

The term 'satire' has been succinctly defined by Northrop Frye as a tone or attitude comprising two essential ingredients: 'one is wit or humor, the other an object of attack'.[3] Attack without humor is not satire but denunciation or invective; humor without attack is gaiety or exuberance. Therefore, humor is not always satire, for, in the words of Charles Mauron, 'La satire suppose une agressivité de l'auteur contre son objet.'[4] As we have seen, the object of this aggressiveness may be a class, profession, individual, or institution.[5] 'Satire' in this sense is to be distinguished both from broader terms like 'ridicule', and also from 'parody', a term that will be used here in its extended sense, that of an intended imitation, for comic effect, of the language, mannerisms, or other characteristics of a type of person or of a member of an institution. Criticism is often implied by such an imitation, but the primary purpose of parody may be humor, not abuse.

The most fundamental problem relating to satire in the *sottie* is that of the object of satire: who and what is criticized, and to what extent? But it is not sufficient to determine the satiric objects, for every criticism, being a negative view of something, is also the reflection of an ideal, a standard that the object of satire fails to live up to. The satiric object is always satirized in view of a value or set of values, whether or not made explicit. Priests, for example, are satirized in the medieval theater for their lasciviousness, the ideal being a life of celibacy. Therefore, we must ask a further question, concerning the positive values that underlie satire in the *sottie*. A third set of questions centers on the problem of the satiric function of the *sottie* (and, ultimately, of the medieval comic theater). What was the social effect of satire in the Middle Ages? What were the *sots* hoping to accomplish by their satire? These last questions are difficult to answer, but this study will at least suggest some new perspectives.

If scholars have found it difficult to determine either the point of view implied by satire in the *sottie*, or its social function, or even its object, the fault has not been entirely theirs. For the *sots* do make it difficult to answer such questions. The barrier between the fools' thought and our understanding of it has frequently been called the 'mask of folly'. The costume of the *sot* was itself a kind of mask, in the sense of a standardized and schematic representation of a state of being, a sign of an assumed and artificial *folie*. (It is perhaps significant that the word 'mask'

is derived from the Arabic word 'maskharah', meaning 'buffoon'.)
Moreover, this state of being, *folie*, is itself a 'mask', for the *sot* is
allowed to speak the truth if he covers it with the mask of his
madness. In the classical theater of Antiquity the mask was an
ambivalent code, for it was intended both to disguise and to
identify. Similarly, in the late Middle Ages, the mask of folly was
two-sided: it granted an unusual freedom to reveal the truth to
the 'wise', while at the same time it covered up with foolish words
what the *sots* meant to say. The mask is an essential part of the
fool's role, and he never completely removes it. Therefore,
satire by a *sot* is continuously ironic.[6]

Since one can never accuse a fool of 'meaning' anything, this
irony allows him a liberty of criticism whose chief literary
evidence is the *sottie*. Without the *sottie*, in the opinion of Barbara
Swain, the liberty of the fool to criticize 'might otherwise have
remained a legend connected with the vanished domestic fool'.[7]
This liberty depended on preventing the listener from taking the
fool seriously:

> Ce n'est que pour passer le temps
> Et resjouyr la compaignie

Ll. 442–3: It's only in order to pass the time And amuse the company

the *sots* themselves remind us, at the end of *Les Cris de Paris*. The
sots of *Le Prince des sots* also point to the mask of folly:

> Fol ne demande qu'à galler.
> C'est un fol; laisse-le aller,
> Il ne sçait qu'il demande.

Ll. 27–30: A fool asks only to have fun. He's a fool; let him go. He doesn't
know what he asks.

The public evidently accepted in a *sottie*, *Le Jeu du Prince des Sotz*,
an insulting view of the Pope that, according to Picot, it would not
have accepted in a morality: 'mais le masque de la folie permettait
toutes les audaces; aussi la sottie a-t-elle plus d'importance que la
moralité et que la farce'.[8] As Stultitia remarks, in Erasmus's
Eloge de la Folie: 'on leur permet [aux fous] de tout dire et de tout
faire'.[9] Thus, the artificial fool of the *sottie* was at liberty to
criticize in a way that would have been unacceptable elsewhere,

at the price of imitating the seemingly senseless chatter of the natural fool.

Although the audience knew that the *sots* were not real fools, nevertheless they were permitted to satirize the Pope, the king, and almost anyone else. Some scholars have found this attitude incomprehensible: 'La raison d'une telle liberté, nous la comprenons fort mal aujourd'hui.'[10] However, as we have seen, the threat of censorship, fines, or worse limited the freedom of the *sots*. The characters of *Les Sobres Sots* were probably alluding to individuals and events known to their audience, but they disguise their remarks to the point where their meaning is now lost. Censorship itself is one of the principal themes of this play:

> On ne saroyt pas trop farder
> Le penser qu'on a sur le cœur.

Ll. 282–3: One cannot go too far in disguising The thought one has in one's heart.

While in some plays the *sots* express themselves with greater openness, in other *sotties*, such as this one, the mask increases the difficulty of understanding the satire, with the result that interpretations of such satire will frequently remain tentative. The pilgrims of *Troys Pelerins et Malice* invent the expression 'mangeurs de lune' (ll. 241–7) in order to indicate, while hiding it, the object of their satire: are these 'lunatics' real or imaginary? Did the audience understand who was referred to? The need for such a mask to hide one's thought varied from one period to another, from one parliament or king to another. In times of repression (under François I, for example), the mask of folly became a useful means of avoiding censorship or punishment. Yet as it is only the *sot*, among social critics, who was permitted that mask, it must be viewed not as simply a way to avoid repression, but as essential to the satire in the *sottie* and to its conception of folly.

Because of this mask it is understandable that there is enormous discrepancy in critical views of the satiric object in the *sottie*, while there is general agreement about what the farce laughs at – the town mayor, the village priest, especially all kinds of women and rogues.[11] In contrast to the farce, the *sottie* is most frequently seen as a general satire of society. The *sots* themselves tell us how broad the topics of their discussions are:

> Nous devisions du temps, des gens,
> Du commung foulle, des sergentz,
> De paix, des amours, de la guerre,
> Qu'on veoyt preparer sur la terre.
> ...
> Bref, de tout qu'on peult adviser
> Nous pretendons en deviser.

Le Cry de la Bazoche, ll. 87–90 and 103–4: We are chatting about the times, the people, The common man, the *sergents* About peace, loves, the war, That we see being readied on the earth... In brief, about everything that one could consider, We intend to talk.

A contemporary discussion of the *sottie* also expresses this view: Jehan Bouchet, in 1545, wrote that the *sots* satirize 'les grands follies... des gens de grand renom / Et des petits... / Sur eschaffaux en parolles polies'.[12] Modern critics would enlarge the scope of the *sottie* to comprise not just medieval society, but 'la nature des hommes de tous les temps', 'toute l'humanité ridicule et grotesque'.[13] Charles Lenient believed that this satire was indiscriminate, attacking everything and everyone – abuses and reforms, the people as well as the king, 'laissant à chacun le droit de rire aux dépens de son voisin'.[14] Other scholars would limit the satire of the *sottie* to that of social classes. In the words of the editor of the largest collection of *sotties*, Emile Picot, 'la sottie transporta sur la scène la satire dirigée contre les diverses classes de la société'.[15] Petit de Julleville describes this satire as more specifically political, for he asserts that from 1450 to 1550 'tous les grands événements publics' were satirized on the comic stage.[16] Droz could not be in greater disagreement with this position, for she believes that 'les événements politiques du xve siècle finissant, la régence, les guerres d'Italie aient passé au dessus des amuseurs et de leurs auditeurs'.[17] In her opinion, the price of bread and wine concerns them more than the Italian campaigns.

If the question of the satiric object of the *sottie* has caused difficulties, the next question – 'Who is doing the satirizing?' – is even more difficult to answer, particularly if satire is seen, as it usually is, not as an individual and isolated opinion, but as the point of view of a group of individuals, of a social or economic class. The problem can be dismissed by seeing the *sottie* as an expression of the opinions of the *foule*,[18] but positing the relationship *fou–foule* does not tell us very much – we still need to know the composition of the crowd. It must still be asked whether the *sottie* reflects the ideas of its public, or only of its author or troupe. What is known today about the make-up of the public at the time of each play and about the relationship of a play to this public? Can the satiric treatment of the object in the *sottie* tell us anything about the milieu in which that satire arose?

In comparison with other forms of literary expression, the theater has a unique rapport with its public. A text becomes a play only when performed, when it is embodied in actors in the presence of spectators – with all that means in terms of oral delivery, gesture, costume, and *mise en scène*. The comic playwright depends on the judgment of his public, for he writes or adapts plays in the hope of winning the favorable reaction of an audience and usually also a financial reward. Therefore, in the words of Alter, 'Leur opinion personnelle compte peu, seul importe l'opinion publique.'[19] For this reason the theater is, of all the arts, the most receptive to changes in the social structure, and the most revealing of such changes.[20] Particularly is this true of the late medieval period, for at few other times has the theater been more intimately connected to the society in which it developed.[21] Plays were evidently put on by a social group (town, guild, or other association) for that social group; rarely by professional actors performing for an élite. The medieval theater, including the *sottie*, is essentially a collective work, like the cathedrals of the same period.

Unfortunately our knowledge of the authors of the *sotties* is slight. Most of the plays are anonymous: it is not known even whether they were the work of an individual or of a company. The name of an author, even conjectural, can be associated with no more than 8 of the 61 plays, and of these, three are attributed to Gringore. It is believed that Gringore came from the bourgeoisie and represented its ideas; Alter argues that not only Gringore but most of the writers came from the bourgeoisie.[22] More specifically, the authors of many *sotties* show signs of having been Basochiens, *clercs*, or civil servants.[23] An exception is the author of *Le Bateleur*, who most likely came from the milieu

that he dramatized, the world of the penniless, struggling mountebank. On the other hand there is almost no evidence to suggest
that the aristocracy wrote or was particularly interested in the
sotties.

As the *sotties* are a satiric form, their connection with an
audience must have been particularly close, closer perhaps than
that which existed for non-satiric types of theater. Northrop
Frye argues that 'in order to attack anything, satirist and audience
must agree on its undesirability'.[24] The *sotties* still in existence
must have won some approval from an audience, for they were
not only produced but also copied or printed for sale. Though
it cannot be known to what extent the satiric opinions expressed
in a *sottie* are those of either its author(s) or its public, it can be
assumed that those opinions were shared to a large degree by the
audience. Therefore, the plays will be treated in this study as the
attitudes and opinions of a group, and not solely of an individual
playwright.

For this reason we need to learn more about the public of the
sotties. The *sots* were clearly aware of the audience to which they
were playing, for they frequently address themselves to the
spectators, they bid them adieu and ask their indulgence (and
their *sous*). One *sottie* even mentions the public that saw the play
performed: *Le Monde* records that 'Monsieur de Morienne [a
bishop] et plusieurs courtisans y furent et tout plein de marchands, car la foyre estoit alors.'[25]

Three conflicting answers have been given to this question of
the nature of the audience at medieval comic plays. Most scholars
believe that 'there can be little doubt that these plays are primarily
directed at the lower and middle classes and may be aptly described as "popular" entertainments'.[26] If, as Petit de Julleville
claims, the comic theater was 'l'écho fidèle des opinions popu-
laires', that is, the spokesman for 'le peuple et la petite bourgeoisie',[27] then Bakhtine is correct in concluding that this theater
was characterized by a 'lien essentiel avec la *vérité populaire non
officielle*'.[28] Alter has modified this point of view with respect to a
particular form of satire, that directed against the bourgeoisie:
'Pas plus qu'au moyen âge, la satire anti-bourgeoise au XVIe
siècle ne peut être ramenée à une authentique inspiration

populaire.'[29] He goes so far as to maintain that satiric literature was 'l'apanage de la bourgeoisie et des classes supérieures' throughout the *ancien régime*.[30] Although popular troubles are frequently lamented in satiric writing of this period, the dominant voice, according to Alter, belonged to the nobility and the bourgeoisie. Harvey has offered yet a third possibility. If the milieu of the *sottie* is, as he has argued, predominantly that of the Basoche, then the point of view of the plays is that of a particular association, the law clerks of Paris and Rouen: 'It should never be forgotten that the *sots* of the Basoche represented a clan, and were primarily concerned with themselves, with the fortune of their clan, with the complaints of their clan.'[31] Finally, the *sottie* could also be at times the expression of an official (usually royal) point of view, as in the case of *Le Jeu du Prince des Sotz* and other plays of the reign of Louis XII.

The relationship of satire to its source is not a simple one, for it is incorrect to see the public in which a satiric point of view originates as different from, exterior to, the object of the satire. Satire of the bourgeoisie, for example, does not necessarily indicate a source outside that class and hostile to it: the bourgeoisie was known to satirize itself.[32] In principle, there are three possible 'directions' of satire: it can be directed at a higher class (ascending direction), at a lower class (descending), or within the same class or group. Whether the audience of the *sottie*, and consequently the source of its satire, is seen as the 'common people' (however defined), as a certain social class, or as a clan, will depend on the adoption of one of these three possible views of satiric direction.

The concept of the ascending direction of satire posits the lower (and weaker) strata of society as the source of satire directed at those higher and more powerful. In this view we would expect to see 'the people' satirized relatively less in the *sottie* than, for example, the nobility. Most scholars have adopted the ascending view of satire, to the point where this direction has come to be considered the 'démarche générale de l'esprit satirique'.[33] Lenient, among others, sees satire as the product of the lower classes criticizing the more powerful, 'le faible contre le fort'.[34] Brown argues that the strongest attacks in many *sotties* are reserved for abuses which directly affect *le menu peuple*, and that, therefore, the source of the *sotties* is the lower classes.[35]

The second view of satire argues that the dominant levels of society satirize those beneath them because they feel threatened by them. The Church and the nobility, therefore, are seen as the source of much satire of the bourgeoisie. Alter, principally, argues that anti-bourgeois satire 'est dirigée de haut en bas',[36] thus contradicting the general direction of most satire.

Third, satire can originate in a particular group or class and can be directed at that same class. Lenient points out that the most damning accusations against the clergy came from the clergy itself.[37] Moreover, the bourgeoisie was probably the source of much anti-bourgeois satire. Gringore, for example, was a bourgeois who turned his satiric barbs against the élite of his class in *Le Jeu du Prince des Sotz*.[38] As Alter has expressed it (p. 138): 'tout indique que les bourgeois ont toujours été de friands amateurs de la satire anti-bourgeoise'. Harvey's view of the *sottie* as satire by a clan also sees a group satirizing its own members.[39] The medieval audience thus laughed at itself.

These three types of satiric direction are useful concepts for several reasons. First, by keeping them in mind, simplistic judgments can be avoided – judgments that assume that anti-bourgeois satire, for example, must originate in non-bourgeois classes of society. Instances of all three types of satire can be found in the *sotties*, in varying degrees. Second, this concept of three different directions of satire helps to clarify the third and last question that was raised at the beginning of this chapter: What was the purpose, or at least the social effect, of satiric theater in the Middle Ages? The answers that have been offered to this question are in still greater disagreement than the answers given to those preceding. Droz, for example, denies the social import of the *sotties* and argues that the principal interest of the plays for us is their vocabulary.[40] Harvey, on the contrary, sees the plays as an expression of the royal struggle against the feudal powers of the nobility and the church, whereas Swain believes that the function of the *sotties* was to protest abuses of the Valois kings.[41]

If the basic direction of satire is seen as 'ascending', then the effect of satire is thought to be more or less progressive. The lower classes, from this point of view, turn to satire as a consolation for their miseries and as a vengeance against the abuses from which they suffer.[42] Many scholars hold this view of the purpose of satire: Petit de Julleville for one believes that satiric theater 'est un instrument très actif et très puissant de progrès, ou (pour ne rien préjuger) de changement dans les Etats'.[43] As an instrument of progress, satire is viewed as a plea to those in authority for governmental reform.[44] Ultimately, this view conceives of the purpose of satire as one of liberation: according to Lenient, satire 'a combattu toutes les tyrannies, féodale, clericale, monarchique et populaire'.[45] In general, this positive view of the social function of satire involves a range of theories, from the vaguely progressive, through the consoling and reforming, to the liberating.[46]

Understandably some critics are sceptical. The idea of progress, besides implying a theory of history, implies also that all satire is revolutionary, or at least reforming, which is, in Northrop Frye's opinion, nonsense.[47] This supposed impetus to change has been viewed as disruptive, by Petit de Julleville, for example, who points out that Henri IV, when he re-established law and order generally, had to bring order to the stage as well. At times Petit de Julleville sees satire as the 'subtil poison de la raillerie universelle', which contributed to undermining the political and religious structure of the Middle Ages.[48]

Finally, there is the theory that satire, at least the satiric theater of the late Middle Ages, did not promote change at all – neither positive social change nor undesirable social unrest. The satiric theater was rather a conservative force, attempting to laugh away all *nouveauté*, or change, whether political, religious, or simply sartorial. Although the *sottie* was frequently aimed at particular abuses, and although the plays did express the discontent and suffering of the lower classes, I hope to show that this theater was not fundamentally progressive (in the sense of advocating new forms of social organisation). The *sots* judge the abuses of the present from a retrospective vantage point: things are not what they should be, the fools believe; but long ago, they were as they should have been. Thus, the view of satire as a conservative force is the conception that best describes the *sottie*.

The term 'class' has been used when discussing satire and will continue to be used throughout this study. What social and economic structures does this term refer to in the late medieval period? What were the medieval conceptions of the divisions of society, and what were the economic realities? Most economic historians today believe that the relative homogeneity of earlier centuries was profoundly changing in the late Middle Ages.[49] Henri Pirenne has written that a working class began forming in the first half of the fifteenth century which was 'très différente de celle des artisans privilégiés du moyen âge'.[50] *Compagnons* and *apprentis* no longer had the same possibility of moving up to become masters,[51] and already in this period journeymen began to be degraded to the condition of proletariat. Although it is difficult to determine the extent and nature of this urban proletariat, it is clear that French society at this time comprised two large classes: in the words of Gaston Zeller, 'celle des privilégiés et celle des non-privilégiés'.[52] The historian of the Renaissance, Emil Lucki, has divided the non-privileged into the poorer craftsmen and apprentices that Pirenne refers to, adding to their number the 'day laborers, street-hawkers, boatmen, servants, and vagabonds that constituted the great majority' of the urban population. He estimates that the peasants and the town masses combined probably made up more than 75 percent of the entire population of France at this time.[53]

This division into privileged (both financially and socially) and non-privileged groups, which was found in society as a whole, was mirrored in the merchant class. The bourgeoisie[54] was in the process of dividing into the wealthy, influential members at the higher levels, and the poor, economically insecure craftsmen and merchants at the lower levels.[55] This concept of two bourgeoisies will prove crucial to an understanding of satire in the *sottie*.

What was the medieval conception of class in this period? The idea of class – usually expressed by the terms 'estat' (estate) or 'ordre' – was a fundamental and tenaciously held notion in

medieval thought. So important was this concept that it permeated a wide range of literary works grouped under the generic
name of 'estats du monde'.[56] Sometimes the term 'estat' meant
simply a style of living: the *sots* of *L'Astrologue* speak of the
'estas des gorriers' (ll. 526–7). More frequently, it meant one of
the major divisions of society, classes based on the idea of service
to society. Each order or estate was generally believed to have
been given by God a certain duty to perform for society, a
contribution to make for the good of all. The knight (Noblesse)
defended the weak; the priest (Clergé) prayed for all Christian
souls; the peasant (Labour) provided the necessary daily bread
for himself and the other classes.[57] In this view of society there
was little or no awareness of the economic function of a class.
Mohl has summarized certain well-defined theories or beliefs
relating to the idea of estate, which include:

The divine origin of the three classes of society, the importance to the state of
every class, the obligation resting upon each class to do its duty, the desirability
of every man's being content with his degree and the folly of trying to change
his estate, the superiority of the good old times when estates did their duties
and men were content with their station in life.[58]

These beliefs underlie the view of the estates in the *sottie* and
orient its satire.

The number of estates seen as constituting society varied, as
did the names given to them. Although Mohl claims that 'there
were clearly defined classes or "estates" to be catalogued',[59] the
works she cites give rather a fluctuating delineation. Three
estates, usually Noblesse, Clergé, and Laboureurs,[60] are the
earliest and most commonly mentioned number. Three orders
are found in *Le Debat du laboureur, du prestre et du gendarme*, for
example, and in *Le Débat de Félicité*. It is most likely that at the
end of the eleventh century the bourgeois, by his intrusion into
the traditional scheme of medieval society, began to break up
this conception of three estates. The medieval writer had difficulty
knowing in which order to classify the bourgeois.[61] Sometimes
he created for the new estate a separate, fourth category: Clergé,
Noblesse, Marchandise, and Labour.[62] Toward the end of the
Middle Ages the bourgeois began to replace the ecclesiastic in
the listing of the estates. In *Folle Bobance*, for example, the charac-

ter by that name summons her 'Troys Estas', represented by
Noblesse, Bourgeoisie, and Laboureur (l. 36). A third approach
to the difficulty is sometimes attempted, a kind of compromise
exemplified by the solution of *Tout le Monde:* the character Tout
le Monde is said to represent three estates, but they turn out to
be four: Noblesse, Marchant, Labeur, and Eglise (ll. 81–2). In
Le Jeu du Prince des Sotz, it is unclear whether the phrase 'Bourgeois, laboureurs et marchans' (l. 544) refers to three distinct
estates, or whether the first includes the following two. In *Le
Jeu du Capifol*, we first see Commun and Labeur opposed, then
united. Finally, in the play *Mestier et Marchandise*, the working
class itself is seen as divided in three: Mestier, Marchandise, and
Le Berger. This brief survey of the concept of estate in medieval
thought, in the *sottie* especially, gives some idea of its fluctuations.
The idea of estate or order will recur in the discussion of satire
in the *sottie* that follows, for this question is one of the major
preoccupations of the *sots*. They are concerned not only with
the number and composition of the estates, but particularly with
the relation between them and with their fluidity or fixity.

If the medieval concept of *état* differed from the modern
notion of 'class', similarly the idea of 'the people' did not connote
what it does today. The idea of lower classes, beneath the bourgeoisie or overlapping its lower economic limits, only slowly
evolved in the Middle Ages from the idea of the 'bas estats' as
including all those who were neither noble nor clergy. In the
early centuries of the growth of the bourgeoisie, the term 'bourgeois' frequently meant everyone (as Alter points out[63]) in an
urban area. Gradually the idea developed of a *menu peuple* that
was distinct from the bourgeoisie (in particular, from the higher
bourgeoisie). Sotte Commune, in *Le Jeu du Prince des Sotz*, probably represents both the bourgeois and the non-bourgeois
classes. Yet less than a hundred years later the jurisconsult Loyseau
insisted on the distinction between them: 'Les viles personnes du
menu peuple n'ont pas droit de se qualifier bourgeois. Aussi
n'ont-ils part aux honneurs de la cité, ni voix aux assemblées, en
quoi consiste la bourgeoisie.'[64] The *sotties* reflect the confusion
of their times with regard to the terms 'bourgeois' and 'peuple',
that is, with regard to the bourgeois and non-bourgeois groups

of the working classes. The plays use terms with shades of meaning ranging from the lower (non-bourgeois) class to the entire nation. This confusion in thinking about class in the late Middle Ages must be kept in mind if modern confusion is to be avoided, that is, if we wish to understand terms like 'Le Commun' in the sense in which they were used in the *sotties*.

Six characters in the *sotties* represent the people in the sense of either the lower classes or the population as a whole: Le Commun, Sotte Commune, Chascun, Sot Ignorant, La Chose Publicque, and Peuple François.[65] The last term clearly refers to the French nation, a meaning close to the present-day sense. The other terms, especially Chascun and La Chose Publicque, would seem to refer to the nation as a whole, but when attention is given to the specific complaints of the characters by those names, it is seen that they are speaking for the lower classes. The *sots* leave their meaning somewhat vague:

> Chacun, déa!
> C'est un grant commun.
> Chacun, se sont beaucoup de gens.[66]

On the other hand, Sot Ignorant clearly represents only the lower classes. Sotte Commune and Le Commun speak now for *le menu peuple*, now for the lower classes plus the bourgeoisie, at times even for the nation as a whole.

As the meaning of these terms fluctuates, so do the attitudes of the playwrights toward the social groups they refer to. Nineteenth-century critics tended to see a favorable glow around the terms 'commun' or 'chascun' when encountered in the plays. Lenient, for example, remarks that the theater was 'animé d'un esprit bourgeois et libéral, il prit la défense du pauvre Commun'.[67] The *sots* were not always so enthusiastic about 'le pauvre Commun'. Those of *Les Sotz triumphans* not only have little sympathy for Chascun – they are positively insulting toward him although they admit that he is 'ung peu de nostre parenté' (l. 100). The *sots* of *L'Astrologue*, on the other hand, show real sympathy for Chascun, and this character is treated much better by them than by their foolish colleagues. The fools of *Les Sotz qui remetent* praise 'la cour de Parlement' for showing itself 'la nourisse du commun', that is (probably), for having brought order to the troubled estate of the lower classes. Despite the seeming antipathy of some *sots* for the 'bas estats', a deep-felt sympathy with the troubles of the lower classes is shown in many *sotties*. Very few characters representing the lower classes are satiric, that is, held up for criticism; and what satiric treatment there is of Le Commun in the *sotties* is much milder than that of the other classes and of certain professions. Furthermore, the authors of the plays side with these characters against their enemies, the characters called by such names as 'Gens Nouveaulx'. The following study of social satire in the plays will discuss in more detail the reason for and ramifications of this point of view.

After listing three or four principal 'estats', much of the literature of estates adds a supplementary one: women. For example, Etienne de Fougères, after discussing the three estates in the *Livre des Manières*, continues with a discussion of women, as though they constituted a class apart, as though the wife of a merchant, the lady of a manor, and a 'prestresse' were not divided by differences as great as those which separated their men. Evidently, this view of the distinctiveness of women as a class was widely accepted, for the *sottie* adopts it also. I will follow its example: the satire of women in the *sottie* will be discussed separately from the social or economic class to which they belong. I will diverge in one way from medieval practice, however – I will consider the satire of women not after the other estates, but before.

There are very few women in the *sotties* – women as women that is. There are many seemingly female characters (though fewer than male ones) since allegorical names in the feminine gender appear on stage as females.[68] Thus, although Folle Bobance, Sancté, Sotte Fiance, and Sotte Occasion are all nominally women, these roles, like those of Folie and Sottie, are not individualized, as are female characters in the farce: Folie is not a woman, but an allegorical portrayal of a moral state. Even La Mère de Ville and La Reformeresse, characters who would appear to be more clearly women, are simply means to a satiric end (they examine the abuses of others). In *Le Jeu du Prince des*

Sotz, Mère Sotte is so little a woman that she is used to portray and thereby to satirize a man, the Pope. Only La Chose Publicque is an exception, for this incarnation of the common weal is treated by the *sots*, for erotic–humorous effect, as a whore.

Almost every farce has its women (principally mothers, wives, mistresses, servants, and fishwives), but only a dozen *sotties* put women on stage or even refer to them at any length. This state of affairs is a little puzzling, since women are clearly associated in the minds of the *sots* with *folie* itself. In *Le Monde, Abuz*, for example, Woman (in the guise of Sotte Folle) makes her appearance after five estates or occupations have been satirized by five *sots*; each *sot* is named by an adjective that designates his principal quality (the priest is called Sot Dissolu; the knight, Sot Glorieux, etc.). What is the qualifying adjective given to the Sotte who represents women? She is Sotte Folle. And the first 'pillar' of Sotte Folle will be Folye, the 'droit fundement' of women (ll. 1221–2). The author of *La Folie des Gorriers* is just as explicit: when Folie tells her life story (ll. 135–57), she ascribes to herself all the world's follies and all its crimes of passion, but especially those inspired by women. (When Erasmus put the *Moriae encomium* in the mouth of a woman, he was following a traditional association of women with Folie.)

Except for the allegorical roles of Folie, Sottie, etc., which have just been described, there are 13 characters in the *sotties* that portray individualized women. Four of these are *pèlerines* and four are prostitutes (a remarkable numerical representation of the Ave–Eva conception of women).[69] The pilgrims are again simply the means to discuss a particular subject, that of marriage. On the other hand, the three *brus* and La Fille Esgarée are necessarily less abstract mouthpieces for a point of view; they are (given their *métier*) more flesh and blood. The five remaining characters appear in *Le Bateleur* (Bynète and two unnamed women), and *Le Jeu par Jehan Destrées* (two unnamed women). (*Le Bateleur* has been considered a farce, in part because the presence of individualized women tends to create the mood and situation of the farce.) The only activity of women that is observed to any extent in the *sotties* is that of prostitution: women belonging to 'la religion publique / Observantine de Cuissy' (*Les Povres Deables*, ll.

199–200) are those who interest most the public of the *sottie*. There is even the suggestion that La Chose Publicque is one of them, thus making the not unlikely association between politics and prostitution (see *Les Sotz fourrez*, ll. 186ff.).

Satire of women in the *sottie* is not limited to the use of dramatic characters, however. Many satiric remarks are made about women when they are not present, remarks made behind their backs, as it were. Five types of complaints are made against them: they talk too much; their sexual appetites are wrong (too great or not great enough, or too promiscuous); they are bad-tempered; they are too changeable; and they spend too much of their husbands' money.[70] These accusations are not unique to the *sottie* – they are found not only in the farce (where they constitute the stock characteristics of women),[71] but also in nearly all criticism of women in the Middle Ages. It should be pointed out, however, that the last two complaints mentioned above are particularly significant in the *sottie*, for the accusations of instability and of excessive financial desires are linked to two of the principal preoccupations of the *sots*, deception and money.

It is difficult to know why the idea of the loquaciousness of women was held to tenaciously in the Middle Ages. Whether or not women really did talk too much, the *sots* certainly thought they did. The fools themselves hold forth at great length on the subject of the *caquet* of women:

> Quant une femme se taira
> Pour son mary, menés la pendre.

Ll. 231–2: When a wife will shut up For her husband, take her to be hanged,

say the *sots* of *Les Menus Propos* (cf. ll. 261–2.)
Le Badin in *Troys Galans et un Badin* would hesitate to let women into heaven if he were God, for fear that their chatter might break his head, 'Et engendrer grand maladye' (l. 237). He would let them in on one condition:

> Si tost qu'en paradis iroyent,
> A jamais il ne parleroyent
> Jusque a ce que leur fise signe.

Ll. 243–5: As soon as they would go to Paradise, Never would they speak Until I should give them the sign.

The second type of complaint is more equivocal. The *sots* (and medieval man in general, I suspect) held conflicting opinions about the sexual drives of women. In the farces, and to some extent in the *sotties*, women are seen as suffering from unbounded desires: the *sots* of *Le Pelerinage* ask to be free from 'femme qui a doys menus, / Courtes mamelles et nés camus', for she does it 'sans lict encourtiné' (ll. 414–16: 'a woman who has small fingers, / Short (high) breasts and a snub nose / Does it without a curtained bed'). The image of women also sees them 'faisant la beste à deulx dos' ('making the two-backed beast'; see ll. 453–5) whenever their husbands are away. The infidelity of women is a complaint based in part on their supposed sexual appetites. Not content with husband and household, the woman permits that 'aultres...leur batent les cus / Et facent leurs maris coqus' (*Le Pelerinage*, ll. 452–3: '...others pound their arse / And make cuckolds of their husbands'). This unfaithfulness of wives is seen as one of the greatest evils of marriage: 'Gardez vous d'y estre trompé' ('Watch out that you are not deceived') is the seven-times repeated refrain of *Le Pelerin et La Pelerine*. Yet, since women are variable, they are sometimes seen not as licentious but as cold:

> Cul de femme et museau de chien
> Si sont tousjours froiz comme glace.

Les Menus Propos, ll. 509–10: Woman's arse and dog's muzzle Are always cold as ice.

In general, however, the satiric view of women in the *sottie* – their sexual appetites and their unfaithfulness – corresponds with the view of women in the farce.

If the *sotties* disagree at times about a woman's sexual desires, they are in complete accord about her bad temper. After Folye, the second trait that characterizes Sotte Folle is Despit (insolence, anger) according to *Le Monde, Abuz* (ll. 1229ff.). In their burlesque procession, the *sots* and *sottes* of *Le Pelerinage* offer this prayer:

> Deffens nous de leur malle teste,
> Mulerye, tenson et tempeste,
> De leur bec, gryz [*griffes?*], ongles, ergos;
>   *Te rogamus, audi nos.*

Ll. 460–2: Protect us from their bad temper, Stubbornness, disputes and rage, From their beak, claws, nails, spurs; We pray you, hear us.

The Sobres Sots, in the play by that name, are concerned with how they should react to a wife who scolds and beats them: should they flee like cowards, or should they stand their ground and give two blows for one (ll. 445–62)?[72] The *sotties* agree, then, with the farces, that 'c'est une furye / Que de femmes' (*Les Sobres Sots*, ll. 415–16: 'women are a fury').

As though this image of women weren't bad enough, the satire of them in the *sotties* continues with two more complaints. The charges that women are *variables* and that they live beyond their means are both viewed as forms of *folie*. If, as the plays suggest, deception permeates every level of society, women are particularly suffused with it. Especially are they guilty of the worst form of falseness, the attempt to change one's class or, at least, to appear to have changed it. Two of the 'pillars' given to Sotte Folle, in *Le Monde, Abuz*, refer to the unreliability and deceptiveness of women, the 'pillars' Variation and Foiblesse. Variation (the instability of a woman's opinions, desires, and actions) is the fault 'que a commandé / Les fammes et leur nation' (ll. 1244–5: 'that has ruled / Women and their kind'). They are so changeable in fact that not one but two pillars will be given to this failing: to Variation is added Foiblesse, signifying the little faith that can be placed in a woman's word: 'Est ce / Moy que l'ay dit?' a woman will ask innocently ('Was it / I who said that?').

Underlying this satire of women as unfaithful, changeable, and socially pretentious is the theme of deception. That women are profoundly two-faced is suggested by a tall tale told in *Les Sotz nouveaulx* (ll. 50–4). Le Tiers Sot claims to have brought back from 'La Fontaine de Jouvence' an animal 'de grant essence': this beast reveals, every Sunday, all that women have secretly done during the week. This marvelous animal makes known the truth by destroying secrets and is therefore an arm against the deceptions of women. Moreover, women are sexually unfaithful only partly because of their sexual appetites – they are also motivated, according to the *sotties*, by the desire to deceive their husbands. The second half of *Le Cry de la Bazoche* is a series of anecdotes recounting various illicit love affairs in which the wife and lover deceive the husband. These stories, concerned with dissimulation and deception in love, or rather, in marriage, are part of the more general idea, dear to the *sottie*, that falseness and dissimulation have become the means to all ends.

Finally, squandering money is one symptom of *folie* from which women suffer acutely. It is the wife who wastes the household's resources:

> Si le mary a tout vendu
> Et la femme l'a despendu,
> Que avront ilz après la grant messe
> A desjeuner?

Les Cris de Paris, ll. 195–8: If the husband has sold everything, And the wife has spent it all, What will they have after High Mass For lunch?

Stylish and expensive clothes symbolize for the *sot* this foolish squandering, and again it is the woman who is particularly liable to this folly:

> De femme tranchant du grobis,
> Qui depend tant en ses habits
> Que son mary est mal disné,
> Gardez vous d'y estre trompé.[73]

Le Pelerin et La Pelerine, ll. 237–40: By a woman putting on airs, Who spends so much for her clothes That her husband has a poor supper, Watch out that you are not deceived.

'Trancher du grobis' is an indication of women's efforts to rise above their social class, for women appear as 'instigatrices de la prétention bourgeoise de dépasser sa condition', according to Alter.[74]

Satire of women in the *sottie* is congruent with the image of them in the farces (and elsewhere in medieval literature): they are above all verbose, unfaithful, and bad-tempered. In addition, this satire suggests three of the principal themes of the *sottie*, the themes of money, clothes, and deception, for women are above all seen as squandering, deceitful, and preoccupied with appearances. Why these three elements play an essential part in the *thématique de la folie* will be seen more clearly upon analyzing the satire of individuals and especially that of social classes.

On a scale of frankness, of explicit satiric comment, the subject of women in the *sottie* would constitute one pole, for on that topic the *sots* speak their minds. The opposite pole may well be satiric treatment of high-placed individuals. When referring to members of the ecclesiastical or political Establishment, the *sots* carefully cover themselves with the mask of folly, for the reason that allusions to powerful individuals undoubtedly provoked greater and more immediate repression than did references to more general objects of satire, such as women (see discussion of censorship above, pp. 29–32). Yet the *sots* and their public evidently reveled in such attacks. *Le Journal d'un bourgeois de Paris* speaks at length of the amusement provoked by a play that satirized 'un monsieur Dishomme' by means of ingenious allusions.[75] Thus, it is not improbable that certain *sotties*, such as *Les Croniqueurs*, *Le Cry de la Bazoche*, *Les Sobres Sots*, *L'Astrologue*, and possibly other plays, are entirely or in large part allusions to prominent people. This pleasure in alluding to individuals was particularly noticeable among the members of the Basoche. According to Harvey, the Basochiens spiced their dramas 'by revealing, or pretending to reveal, private scandals involving the names of clerks or lawyers known to the audience'.[76]

Two methods were used by the *sots* to refer obliquely to individuals without revealing the identity of their victim. The most dramatic way was to put on stage a character who represented, more or less explicitly, the individual to be satirized. This is the approach that Gringore used in *Le Jeu du Prince des Sotz*, in which Pope Jules II is symbolized by Mère Sotte. Other characters in the same play may have represented well-known clergy and nobility, just as it is possible that the character La Reformeresse in *Les Povres Deables* was a veiled representation of Louise de Savoie, who from 1515 to her death in 1531 wielded enormous power. Maxwell points out that her 'rapacity was notorious, and, as early as 1516 she had been satirized under the cloak of Mère-Sotte'.[77] The satire of Louise de Savoie and of other notables is based on the widespread belief that individuals in high places are the primary cause of the miseries that plague the country. Over and over again, wars, taxes, the high cost of living, even natural catastrophes are attributed not just to the vices of prominent people, but specifically to their avarice and desire for power.[78] The *sots* of *L'Astrologue*, for example, blame the accident of July 2,

1498, in which the collapse of platforms at a tournament killed
and injured many people, on the noxious influence of Anne de
Bretagne (ll. 91–9; see also l. 147: evil-doing causes epidemics).
God punishes public sin by public catastrophe.

Individuals could also be discreetly satirized by references using
allegorical and mythological names. *Les Croniqueurs*, for example,
is made up of allusions which use animal names emblematically
to indicate individuals and countries: Holland is 'le Lion em-
parqué', Marie d'Angleterre is described as having ended the
war between 'le Porc apic et des liepars passans' (l. 191). Similarly,
in *Le Cry de la Bazoche* allegorical animals represent powerful
people and countries: the play is a menagerie of Aigles, Phenix,
Léopards, and Lyons *rampants*. *L'Astrologue* prefers mythological
names – Gemini, 'le haust dieu Mars', Virgo, Venus, and Cancro
allude to various members of the court of Louis XII. The Amboise
brothers, Georges, first minister of Louis XII, and Louis, Bishop
of Albi, are bitterly satirized, under the 'code name' Gemini (see
l. 60: 'Par ta faulte vileine'), for conducting military operations,
an illegitimate activity for men of the Church:

> Mars, qui est prince de feureur,
> Par prebstres conduit ces bataillez
> Et les commet en sa chaleur
> A lever suscites et taillez.

Ll. 116–19: Mars, who is Prince of Furor, Conducts these battles by means
of priests And commits them, in his heat, To levying taxes and assessments.

Until the traitorous Gemini are banished, the world will know
no peace.

In the satire of the Amboise brothers, the *sots* indicate another
of the fundamental attitudes that underlie their satire of all the
estates. Each individual, they believe, should remain in the place
for which he was destined, should do the work which is proper
for him as a member of a particular estate; any change of estate
produces terrible consequences. These themes – the public
consequences of individual sin, especially of the desire for money
and power, and the ambition to change one's station in life – are
at the heart of the satire of individuals in the *sottie*. Furthermore,
they reappear again and again in the satire of social classes,
constituting one of the fools' primary preoccupations.

PART II. SATIRE OF THE NOBILITY AND THE CLERGY

The *sotties* rarely omit the nobility when discussing the world's follies or vices. Everyone is 'fourrée de malice', the *sots* tell us, 'En l'ostel de ces grans seigneurs' (*Les Sotz fourrez*, ll. 123–33: 'furred [covered] with malice / In the home of these great lords'). *Le Monde, Abuz* is more specific about the nature of this 'malice' (ll. 823–934): the 'pillars' accepted by Sot Glorieux (i.e., the *gendarmes* and the nobility) include: Lascheté, Bobance, Avarice, Pilherie, Mespris, Menasses et Courroux, Trayson, and l'Art de Domination (replacing the 'pillar' of Aid to Others).

Only two *sotties* offer favorable views of the nobility: the *Satyre* of Roger de Collerye, and, in part, *Les Croniqueurs*. The admiration of Roger de Collerye for the king and the nobility is clear in his description of the court and the magnificent procession of the royal family, and in his praise for the princes and the queen. *Les Croniqueurs* attributes the country's woes to the fact that Louis XI allowed non-nobles to run the government, men who were 'pretz et dilligens / De despriser seigneurs et princes' (ll. 45–6: 'ready and diligent / To look down on lords and princes'). In particular, he permitted priests to conduct wars, which is the proper domain of the nobility (ll. 29–30). However, in the good times that will come again, the *sots* envisage the return to power of the nobility; then they expect to have 'Planté de biens', they will see again

> jouxtes [*sic*] et tournoys,
> Et que on rompra encor gros boys
> Pour l'amour des dames de brief.

Ll. 300–3: jousts and tourneys, And that thick wood [lances] will be broken again For the love of the ladies, in brief.

Such nostalgia for a return of the true nobility is rare in the *sotties*. Nonetheless, it does reveal what all the plays hold in common in their view of the nobility: that *l'état de noblesse* has degenerated and become corrupt. Sot Corrompu, in *Le Monde, Abuz*, laments that once

> Noblesse avoit provision
> De Vertu et prou vision
> De hardiesse, au passe temps.

Ll. 830–2: Nobility had a great supply Of Virtu and an ideal Of Courage, in former times.

Now it has come to ridicule ('irrision'). A close look at satire of the nobility in the *sottie* reveals the nature and cause of the aristocratic decline, as the *sots* see it.

The satiric view of the nobility in the *sottie* can be understood only in relation to the nature of war and peace at the time of the plays. By the end of the fifteenth century (the peak of the popularity of the *sottie*), war in Europe was nearly continuous: major campaigns were mounted by the important European powers in three out of every four years between the beginning of the Italian wars in 1494 and the end of the sixteenth century. Entire generations lived under its shadow, knew nothing but its miseries.[79] The complaints of the *sots* express the suffering caused by war and their intense desire for peace. The *sotties* repeatedly sympathize with the victims of this incessant strife; for example, with

> Les povres laboureurs des champs
> Qui a maulx sont tousjours marchans
> Et par la guerre desolés.

Troys Galans et un Badin, ll. 155–7: The poor laborers in the fields Who are forever walking with misfortune And desolated by war.

If Le Badin of the same play were God, 'la guerre / Jamais ne seroyt sur la terre' (ll. 259–60: 'there would nevermore be war on the earth'), and all armaments would be made of 'sucre candis' (l. 263: 'sugar candy'). Several plays assert that Bon Temps is now imprisoned by war and will return only when war ends (e.g., *Faulte d'Argent*, ll. 182–91; *Les Sotz qui remetent*, ll. 288–91). The *sots* rightly see the non-noble classes as those who suffer most:

> Le grant dieu Mars se lassera-il point
> De tant nous battre et d'estoc et de taille?[80]

Pou d'Acquest, ll. 20–1: The great god Mars, will he never tire Of beating us, both cutting and thrusting?

Each estate, it has been pointed out, had a specific service to perform for the good of society; the duty of the nobility was to conduct war, so defending the defenseless. Imbued from earliest feudal times with the ideal of protecting the weak and helpless, and moreover prohibited from engaging in commerce,[81] the nobility saw its *raison d'être* in the practice of arms. The *guerriers* exerted continual pressure on their king to give them the opportunity to show their valor; this pressure was a major force behind the aggressive attacks on Italy that began in 1494.[82]

The *sots* recognize this social function of the nobility (see *Tout le Monde*, ll. 130–8), but they believe – and this is the basis of their criticism – that the knightly ideal of the defense of the weak is no longer being lived up to. War in the fifteenth and sixteenth centuries is no longer a praiseworthy struggle against a military adversary: it has become characterized more and more by violence against those whom the nobility was in principle established to protect. A grim state of affairs existed at the end of the Middle Ages, for when the French army was left unpaid (during times of nominal peace), the soldiers turned into 'pillaging mobs, mercilessly sacking cities and ravishing the countryside'.[83] According to one historian,

Des grandes Compagnies, dont Froissart relate la naissance et les exploits, aux Ecorcheurs du temps de Charles VII, il existe une effroyable continuité dans la destruction, le pillage, la dévastation. Compagnons, routiers, brigands, écorcheurs: autant de termes différents que la réalité a rendus synonymes…le brigandage devient le but exclusif de l'activité guerrière, aux périodes de trève et de paix.[84]

Cities as well as the open country were ravaged, villages disappeared, formerly prosperous areas were left fallow, important towns were emptied of inhabitants. As it was during peace-time that the brigands were most active, peace came to be more dreaded than war. Ultimately, this pillaging by 'gens d'armes' showed how false was the belief that the knights protected the innocent and the weak. No longer are the soldiers 'Servans au royaulme de France'; they are nothing but 'ung tas de paillars, / Meschans, coquins, larrons, pillars' (*Les Gens nouveaulx*, ll. 183–5: 'a pile of good-for-nothing, / Evil people, scoundrels, thieves, looters'), and Le Mond prays God to confound them (see also ll. 154–5 and 199).[85]

The view of the nobility in the *sottie* corresponds to that presented by Raymond Lincoln Kilgour, who has studied the pillaging bands of the fifteenth century and the resultant decay of the knightly ideal as it is revealed in the literature of the period.[86] He cites, for example, the following passage from the *Chroniques* of Monstrelet: 'Les gens de guerre qui avoient été évoqués à venir autour de Paris, tant par le duc de Bourgogne comme par les autres seigneurs, furent licenciés et retournoient chacun ès lieux dont ils estoient venus, *en mangeant le pauvre peuple*, selon la coutume d'adonc.'[87] The *sotties* echo these words, for in *L'Astrologue* Chascun laments:

> Car, par mon Dieu, je suis lassé
> D'avoir eu tant, le temps passé,
> De pertes et de mengeries.

Ll. 153–5: For, by God, I am weary Of having had, these past days, so many Losses and devourings.

Sottie after *sottie* picks up and reiterates the complaint: discussions of 'la grande pilerie qui ne cesse de courir' are to be found in *L'Astrologue* (ll. 248–50), *La Folie des Gorriers* (l. 181), *Deulx Gallans et Sancté* (ll. 12–21), among other plays (cf. *Pou d'Acquest*, ll. 190–2 and *Les Rapporteurs*, ll. 214–16). The *sots* see the marauding bands everywhere:

> Y ne court plus que pillerie
> Au monde et tout traison.

Deulx Gallans et Sancté, ll. 14–15: The world is overrun with pillaging And every treasonous act.

In *Le Monde, Abuz*, Sot Glorieux ('Habillé en gendarme') admits openly his intentions:

> Je feray plourer mainctes lermes
> A ses gros villains de village.

Ll. 152–3: I will make many a tear fall From the eyes of those fat village peasants.

The same *sottie* makes Pilherie one of the foundation stones of Noblesse: the 'pillar' of Pillage 'joinct si bien que c'est raige' (l. 890: 'fits so well that it's astounding').[88]

Most of the complaints of the *sots* are directed specifically at the 'gens d'armes'.[89] As far as I have been able to determine, this term did not refer to all men of arms, but instead, in the great majority of cases, to mounted armored soldiers of noble origin.[90]

Thus it was the knight who was largely responsible for the wide-spread pillaging. The greatest lords of France, the most famous knights of the day, were the leaders of these bands, torturing and robbing their own countrymen.[91] The captain of the *écorcheurs* (active after the Peace of Arras, in 1435), for example, was known to have been a nobleman, one Jacques de Pouilly.[92] Ferdinand Lot has written that the soldiers who composed the bands

semblent bien, du moins pour les compagnies françaises, être d'authentiques 'gentilhommes', en majorité; mais ils sont le déchet de la classe noble, cadets de familles pauvres, bâtards sans espoir d'avenir – et ils pullulent en ce siècle. Rebut de la société de leur temps, ils sont pour elle sans pitié.[93]

The noble origin of the *gendarme* is also indicated by the literature of the period, in such titles as *Le Débat du laboureur, du prestre et du gendarme*, for the latter represents the nobility. Finally, in *Folle Bobance*, 'gens d'armes' are referred to as 'grans seigneurs' (ll. 129–30).

The crucial fact remains that the nobility was seen as primarily responsible for the misconduct of war. For this reason, Louis XII ordered in 1505 that the infantry captains (noblemen) were to turn in those who pillage or 'fait des maux au peuple'.[94] Thus it was pillaging and the role of the nobility in it that revealed most strikingly the conflict between the knightly ideal and the brutal reality, between the illusion that the nobility still tried to main-tain (in the extravagant banquets of the Burgundian court, for example) and the everyday atrocities, pillaging, and treachery which the people saw as the real practice of knighthood. This conflict between illusion and reality went beyond a nostalgic regret for a past order of things and became disillusionment, clearly expressed in the *sotties*, which at times mounted to despair or to rage.[95] It should be pointed out that this criticism of the nobility in the *sottie* is clearly from a non-noble point of view (except for the two favorable plays mentioned above); the com-plaints against war and pillaging express the sufferings of the lower classes. 'Que toute guerre soyt finée', exclaims Sancté,

Marchans seront en joye remys,
De quoy je seray consolée.

Deulx Gallans et Sancté, ll. 59–61: If all war were ended, Merchants would be joyful again, By which I would be consoled.

But as well as being the victims of the violent aristocracy, these classes suffered in another way from the military actions of the nobility. The *sots* also complain about the heavy taxes that the people must pay to support these wars that they abhor. By the fifteenth century, war had become, in the words of Duby and Mandrou, 'terriblement coûteuse, dévoreuse de monnaie',[96] and it was in order to raise funds for their wars that kings in this period instituted regular taxation.[97] If an army were mobilized during only two or three months, even a small army (2,000 or 3,000 *chevaliers*), expenses multiplied and the royal treasury was emptied. When La Commune complains, 'Enfin je paye tousjours l'escot' (*Le Jeu du Prince des Sotz*, l. 568: 'In the end I always pick up the tab'), she does not exaggerate.[98] Therefore, the *sots* doubt whether the time will ever come

> ...que plus il ne viendra,
> A mon huis, un tas de merdailles
> Pour demander l'argent des tailles.

Les Esbahis, ll. 181–3: that no longer will there come To my door, a bunch of scoundrels To ask for the tax money.

To sum up, the *sots* condemn war and lament its miseries, so indirectly questioning the validity of the very role of the nobility in the structure of medieval society. But they go further: they also openly satirize the nobility for not waging their wars properly, that is, for pillaging their own people. Finally, the *sots* complain of the heavy taxes that they must pay to support these wars. This satiric view of the nobility suggests one of the recurring themes of the *sotties*: the conflict of reality and illusion, as revealed in this case by an estate's pretense of fidelity to a purpose which it had long ago abandoned in practice.

Most often these criticisms of the nobility are expressed with a minimum of humor, so that there is much malice but little wit. On the other hand, humor *is* the object when the fools choose to parody the nobility, and they do so frequently. Of the principal estates, only the nobility and the clergy are parodied in the *sotties*. For parody to flourish, I propose that two conditions must exist.

First, the object of parody (in the sense defined above, pp. 65–6) must be an institution, class, or social group (or a member of one) that has distinctive characteristics: language, rites, mannerisms, or clothing, for example. Second, this institution or group must be in decline from a peak of power, so that it begins to appear ludicrous. The bourgeoisie was neither in decline at the time of the *sotties* (on the contrary, it was rapidly growing in power), nor was it characterized by traits that were both visible (to the fools) and distinctive. The nobility, on the other hand, fulfilled both requirements, and it is the estate most frequently parodied.

The humor of the *sotties*, as we have seen, is largely verbal. Not surprisingly, this also holds for their parody of the nobility. Two aspects of noble life and manners are the principal objects of the fools' parody: feudal relations and customs, and the language of courtly love. In two plays a foolish *dame* is courted by *sots* competing in the language of courtly love to win her favors. In both cases this game is drawn out for the comic effect it would have on the audience. In *Le Monde, Abuz*, the *sots* parody poetic and amorous competitions for the love of Sotte Folle, who has told them:

> Qui mieux me sera [saura] exhorter,
> Mon amour en appourtera.

Ll. 1316–17: Whoever will be able to woo me best, He will carry off my love.

There follow some 30 lines of comical love poetry, of which this is a sample:

> Tes plaisans jouettes,
> Doulces et dehettes,
> Ton penetrant viz
> Et les babinettes
> Qu'as tant popinettes
> M'ont faict tout raviz.

Ll. 1330–5: Your pleasing little cheeks, Sweet and desirable, Your penetrating glance And the lips That are so delectable Have made me completely lose my head.

The *sots* of *La Folie des Gorriers* enact a similar parody of courtly love poetry in their wooing of Folie: 'vous estes celle / Qui a mis mon cueur en ses las' (ll. 64–5: 'you are the one / who has ensnared my heart'). The rondeaux (ll. 176–87 and 199–210) recited in her honor parody rhetorical styles of the period as well as the language of *courtoisie*.

The parody of this aspect of noble language is accompanied by a parody of feudal terms. The *sots* of *La Folie des Gorriers* shift easily from courting the Lady to treating her as a great Lord:

> [Nous] vous octroyons par accords
> Foy, loyauté, mambres et corps;
> A vous servir sommes entiers.[99]

Ll. 216–18: We grant you as sign of peace between us Faith, loyalty, body, and limbs; To serve you we are whole-hearted.

Phrases such as 'soublz votre seigneurye', 'porteron le guydon', 'tres-redoubté prince', 'tenir table ronde', and 'voz vassaulx', occur frequently in the plays.[100]

If Folie could speak of herself in courtly terms ('Car je suis liberalle et franche': *La Folie des Gorriers*, l. 87), it was because she ruled a court that paralleled and parodied the courts of the nobility, for the *sots* imitated not only the language of the court, but the social structure as well. The satiric element in this imitation is that the prince 'par sus tous estimé' was a Prince des Sots, that the 'tresgracieuse Dame' was Dame Folie, and their 'vassaulx', a bunch of *sots*. Not only the structure of the troupe of *sots* but also their plays parodied the feudal aristocracy. In *Les Premiers*, for example, parody is no longer limited to language: a scene of court intrigue, of revolt by vassals, and their final appeasement parodies court activities that were undoubtedly familiar to the audience (see also *Les Sotz escornez*). The most extended parody of the structure and activities of a feudal court is to be found in *Le Roy des Sotz*: Guippellin is appointed 'gros veneur', 'grand maître des sots', 'connestable du roy', and his relations to the other *sots* and to his king constitute a detailed and amusing imitation of a real court.

Thus, the *sots* parody the nobility by means of both language and action. A third form of parody in the *sotties* combines both of these types. In the stories of 'hauts faits chevaleresques' that the *sots* frequently and enthusiastically reel off, the parody is still essentially in verbal form. Yet in these tales language is used to reconstruct certain specific actions (which are thereby experienced vicariously by the audience), or perhaps to imitate certain literary accounts of this type of action. Such parody is found in the funeral service for the great fool, Triboullet, a rite which serves as the pretext for a celebration of the heroic deeds of 'le vray champion', of 'le chevalier' (*Les Vigilles de Triboullet*, ll. 120, 126, and 201). The three *coquins* in the *sottie* of that name tell at length of desperate combats against a flea, against the English, and of the events at the tournament of a certain King Jude. The ruffians of *Les Maraux* boast of their exploits in chivalric terms, which do not hide the true nature of their acts: pillage.[101]

So three types of parody of the nobility are found in the *sotties*: parody of noble language, both courtly and feudal; parody of the feudal social structure and court activities; and, finally, narrative parody of supposed acts of knightly heroism. This last type brings us back to the satire of the military role of the nobility, based on a vision of that class's betrayal of its consecrated duty. Here is perhaps an indication of the function of parody, and ultimately of satire, in the context of the *sottie*. Parody is satiric insofar as it transposes 'en familier le solennel'.[102] This transposition constitutes a lowering of the knight from his lofty social status, a reversal of the high and the low (in the spirit of the Fête des Fous), for the noble becomes ridiculous and even blameworthy, while the foolish pretends to assume a noble air. This satiric overturning is a kind of revenge of the victim against the oppressor, represented by the *sot* and the *noblesse* respectively, a revenge aimed at the empty pretense of noble service to society. There is no evidence that the *sots* hoped for or expected real and prompt reform of the military system. Instead, they chose to laugh at the gap between reality and appearance, thereby acting out – as Mauron would express it – a symbolic solution, a symbolic revenge that was psychically satisfying, though sterile in terms of practical social effect.

When we turn to satire of the clergy, we find that the theme of pretense arising from a class's betrayal of its duty is again the basis of satire, and that the symbolic revenge of the *sots* over their enemies is more clearly acted out. From its beginnings, the Church condemned mortal life as wicked and corrupt. One might say

that, in return, the *sots*, representing a mortal life of frivolity and
pleasure, condemned the Church as wicked and corrupt. The
corruption which they saw in the Church, from Pope to parish
priest, drew from the *sots* their most violent tirades, as in this
eloquent condemnation pronounced by Le Medecin in *Le Monde*:

> Monde? Tu ne te troubles pas
> De voyr ces larrons attrapars
> Vendre et achepter benefices,
> Les enfants ez bras des nourrices
> Estre abbez, evesques, prieurs,
>
> . . .
> Tuer les gens pour leur plaisir,
>
> . . .
> Faire la guerre a tout outrance,
> Pour un rien, entre les chrestiens?

Ll. 246–56: World, are you not upset To see these deceiving thieves Sell and
buy benefices, Children in the arms of their nurses Become abbots, bishops,
priors... Kill men for their pleasure... Wage war without limit, For
nothing – among Christians?

Ecclesiastical satire goes back beyond the beginnings of the
sottie to the Fête des Fous, which laughed at churchmen from
within the Church itself. This satire of the Church which began
in the twelfth century was still continuing with such force four
centuries later that a parliamentary *arrêt* of April 1556 attempted
to stop all 'bateleurs, enfants sans souci, et autres joueurs de
farces, de jouer aucune pièce concernant la foi chrétienne, la
vénération des saints et les saintes institutions de l'Eglise'.[103]
Maxwell has pointed out that in the late Middle Ages the clergy
'were favorite game of the Connards [of Rouen], and charges of
pluralism, simony, immorality and the like might belong to any
time in the early sixteenth century'.[104] Anti-ecclesiastical satire
extended not only over a considerable period of time, but also to
all levels of the ecclesiastical hierarchy. For if the *sottie*, like the
farce, condemns the lasciviousness and soft life of the priest, it
attacks in addition the corruption of the highest, the Pope, who
is after all represented as no more than Mère Sotte.

Critical discussions of ecclesiastical satire in the *sottie* have not
always distinguished between the treatment that different kinds
of clergy receive. Yet, in the *sotties*, the four basic types of

churchmen – priests, monks and other members of religious orders, hermits, and prelates – are satirized to different degrees and for different reasons. Another problem suggested by anti-ecclesiastical satire in the *sottie* arises from the unique nature of the *état de clergé*. Part of the function of this estate was the preservation and dissemination of a body of doctrine. Consequently, the question has often been raised as to whether the object of satire is simply the abuse of the clergy or the teachings of the Church itself: Was the *sottie* attacking dogma as well as individual vice? Petit de Julleville has argued that the Church tolerated the acerbic satire of the comic theater for the very reason that its doctrines were not questioned: 'A condition qu'on ne touchât pas aux dogmes, elle abandonnait les personnes.'[105] In general, the *sotties* attack overtly only clergy, not doctrine, as can be seen from this opening tirade of Sot Dissolu, representing the clergy in *Le Monde, Abuz*:

> Ribleurs, chasseurs, joueurs, gormens,
> Paillars, ruffiens, plains de tormentz,
> Reigneurs dissolutz, appostates,
> Yvrongnes napleuz, a grant hastes
> Venez, car vostre prince est né.

Ll. 126–31: Debauched people, hunters, gamers, and gluttons,   Lechers, ruffians full of frenzy,   Dissolute renegades, apostates,   Syphilitic drunkards, in great haste   Come – for your Prince is born.

This outrageous list of sinning churchmen evidently does not attack any particular doctrine (unless the allusion to the Nativity is such an attack). Yet the problem is not so easily resolved, for the attitudes of the *sots* must be viewed in the context of the troubled times in which they developed. A clearer view of these attitudes can be gained by a study of the basic satire of the Church in the *sottie*.

Ecclesiastical roles in the *sottie* are more common than aristocratic ones, for 11 characters (appearing in 16 roles) make up the ecclesiastical class of the *sottie*. These include Sot Dissolu, in *Le Monde, Abuz*; three *sots ecclésiastiques*, in the *sottie* by that name; the Ministre d'Eglise, in *Le Jeu du Capifol*; two priests, in *Les Povres Deables* and *Le Monde*; three hermits, in *Les Brus* and *Les Premiers*; a monk, in *Les Povres Deables*; the two characters probably representative of lower churchmen, in *La Mère de Ville*: Le Garde Nape and Le Garde Pot; and, finally, the roles with ecclesiastical titles, in *Le Jeu du Prince des Sotz*: L'Abbé de Frevaulx, L'Abbé de Plate Bource, Mère Sainte Eglise.[106] A category of quasi-religious characters are the eight *pèlerins* and four *pèlerines* that appear in a number of *sotties*.[107] However, these characters do not represent satire of pilgrims so much as a convenient way to discuss certain topics, such as marriage and the state of the world.

The two vehicles of the satire of ecclesiastics in the *sottie* are these characters, who are embodiments of the clergy (that is, direct satire), and the remarks made about members of the Church (indirect satire). (Plays which contain much indirect ecclesiastical satire are: *Les Rapporteurs*; *Le Monde, Abuz*; *L'Astrologue*; *Les Gens nouveaulx*; and *Le Jeu du Prince des Sotz*.) The charges made against the clergy are similar in both the direct and the indirect satire. The 'pillars' offered to Sot Dissolu summarize all the accusations, for his vices are: Hypocrisie, Ribaudise, Apostazie, Lubricité, Simonie, and Irrégularité. As the vices attributed to the clergy are studied in more detail, they are seen to fall along a continuum, beginning with the vices of a more physical nature (soft living, drunkenness and gluttony, and debauchery), continuing through vices that are more spiritual although still physical in their desire for material goods (avarice and simony); next come satirical charges of irregularity in the practice of Church functions (multiple benefices), and last of all, the most spiritual of vices, the desire for temporal power and the concomitants of that desire (in the eyes of the *sots*), falsehood and hypocrisy. The satire of the *sottie* does not attribute these vices equally to all levels of the Church hierarchy. Instead, the more physical sins are generally ascribed to the lower echelons, while spiritual corruption is seen as the peculiar characteristic of the higher clergy. Priests are most often charged with gluttony and other forms of sinful living; monks are seen as suffering mainly from the vice of *lasciveté*; prelates are given to abuse of their functions, to the buying and selling of benefices, and to simony; the Pope seems to be guilty only of the desire for temporal power and of hypocrisy.[108] It can be seen, from this analysis, that in the *sottie* the view of the lower ranks of the clergy corresponds generally with the view in the farces. But it also becomes clear that the *sottie* differs significantly from the farce in the amount of attention it gives to the corruption of the higher clergy, which the farce generally ignores. Let us now look at these vices in more detail.

The *sots* are forever searching for Bon Temps, but war and its miseries prevent Bon Temps from returning. Where is he living while away? With the men of the Church, for Sot Dissolu has

> Putains et cartes a foyson,
> Vin cleret et tout gormandise.

Le Monde, Abuz, ll. 134–5: Whores and playing-cards a-plenty, Claret wine and good things to eat.

The *sots ébahis* only appear to be surprised at this state of affairs, in particular at the gluttony of priests:

> Assez ne me puis esbahir
> De la tromperie et finesse
> D'aucuns prestres qui chantent messe
> Après qu'ils ont mengé et beu.

Ll. 175–8: I cannot be too surprised At the deceit and cunning Of some priests who sing the Mass After they have eaten and drunk. (Cf. *Le Pelerinage*, ll. 4–5.)

The Gens Nouveaulx propose to include all the lower clergy in their reforms: they would no longer have 'garces ne chevaulx' (l. 62: 'whores or horses'); furthermore, they 'ne mangeussent plus gras morceaulx' (l. 66: 'they would no longer eat juicy morsels'). If the *sots* could accomplish this, they would indeed be 'gens nouveaulx'. It should be noted that this condemnation of the good life of the clergy is not a condemnation of such a life *per se* – only as inappropriate, or sinful, for ecclesiastics. The *sots*, as we shall see, sometimes ask nothing more for themselves than to lead just such a life.

The accusation of lack of chastity is made principally against the lower clergy in both the *sottie* and the farce.[109]

> Que Chasteté et gens d'Eglise
> Ne se congnoissent nullement

Le Monde, Abuz, ll. 697–8: That Chastity and churchmen Know one another not at all

exclaims a *sot*. But whereas the farce includes priests, monks, and nuns among the debauched, the *sottie* concentrates to a remarkable degree on monks and the religious orders. In the earlier period of the *sottie*, monastic satire may have been related to the struggle between the University of Paris and the mendicant orders.[110] By the late fifteenth and sixteenth centuries, an anti-monastic feeling expressed itself both in the *sottie* and in evangelical and Reform writings. According to Lucien Febvre, monastic life was judged 'sans indulgence dans son principe et dans ses effets'.[111] A striking example of the growth of anti-monastic satire can be seen by comparing two *sotties* from different periods which are similar in images and ideas, but which reveal a significant difference: *Les Rapporteurs*, a generation after *Les Gens nouveaulx*, has added 44 lines of obscene invective against monks in general and mendicant orders in particular. The *sots* rage:

> Moynes, que le mal feu les arde
> Tant portent ilz la cuille verd.

Ll. 189–90: Monks! May the fires of hell burn them So green [lively] are their balls.

'Carmes, cordeliers et chanoynes, / Jacobins, augustins et moynes' – the *sots* pray 'le grand dyable' to take them all. Then they add a remark that reveals a popular point of view:

> Si m'ont dit les dyables d'enfer
> Qu'ilz les y feront bien chauffer
> A quelque pris que soit le boys.

Ll. 200–2: The devils of hell themselves have told me That they will roast them well No matter what the price of firewood.

Given the inflated price of firewood through much of the later Middle Ages, the devils are indeed relentless.[112] Thus the *sottie* clearly reflects the growing anti-monastic sentiments of the times.

The *sottie* begins to move away from the type of ecclesiastical satire found in the farces when it attacks the corruption, irregularity, and hypocrisy of the higher clergy. The *sots* claim that the corruption of the Church arises in part from love of money. Where is the money of La Commune going?

Les marchans et gens de mestier
N'ont plus rien: tout va à l'Eglise.

Le Jeu du Prince des Sotz, ll. 548–9: Merchants and workers Have nothing left: everything goes to the Church.

Tout le Monde claims that the clergy takes not only the wealth of the people, but also of the Church, 'l'espouse saincte' (l. 174), and they do so by committing 'maincte chose faincte'. Once again the themes of avarice and deception are seen to be connected in the minds of the *sots*. The principal way of acquiring wealth, for the clergy, was of course the buying and selling of benefices.[113] The large number of satiric protestations against simony reflect the importance of this particular sin in the minds of the *sots*. The sale of offices is rampant; it has become one of the 'pillars' of the clergy:

> Simonie a tant de complices
> D'auctorité superlative
> Qu'il n'est dignité elective,
> Ne benefice collatif,
> Qui ne soit au jour d'uy natif
> D'elle, selon le temps qui court.

Le Monde, Abuz, ll. 788–93: Simony has so many accomplices With superlative authority That there is no elective office Nor collative benefice, That isn't today born From her, according to the times.

Furthermore, clerical avarice is part of a general social phenomenon: the churchmen are simply acting 'selon le temps qui court'. If Justice would only make Chascun keep to his proper estate, the reign of Simonye would end.[114]

Related to the practice of simony is that of pluralism or the accumulation of the revenues of a number of benefices. Primus in *L'Astrologue* rails against the 'docteur preschier' who wants 'cinc ou .vi. prebendes' (ll. 380–3). The fiercest satire of the corruption and irregularity of the clergy is to be found in *Les Sotz ecclesiasticques*. Three *sots* have risen from lowly estates (one was a 'fringuereau de court', another the son of a shoemaker, the third a keeper of hounds) by means of simony. They have accumulated enough benefices to satisfy the average clergyman: one *sot* has three *cures*, as many abbeys, seven 'prieurez', and fourteen 'chanoyneries'. Still they are discontented, and under the instigation of Haulte Follie they play 'au content', a game of swapping their *prébendes, évechés,* and their revenues from other benefices. Never satisfied, they demand either the papacy, apotheosis, or at least the highest place in paradise.

The wealth gained through these various irregular procedures is used principally, according to the *sots,* to gain power – not just ecclesiastical but also temporal.[115] Gringore states clearly the means by which Mère Sotte has mounted to the papal chair:

> Car elle fut posée de fait
> En sa chaire par symonie.

Le Jeu du Prince des Sotz, ll. 632–4: For in fact she was placed   On her chair by simony.

In particular, it is the growing temporal power of the clergy that scandalizes the *sots. L'Astrologue* protests against those churchmen who involve themselves in the conduct of war:

> Chasses moy ung tas de prebstrailles
> Qui s'entremettent des assaulx.

Ll. 122–3: Get rid of a gang of low-down priests   Who get mixed up in military assaults.

By their actions they are abandoning their true estate: 'Chascun doit faire son mestier' (l. 379: 'Everyone should do his job'. Cf. ll. 116–19, 538–41; and *Les Croniqueurs,* ll. 29–30 and 319–21). Although Petit de Julleville has claimed that in the medieval comic theater, 'Les prélats, qui étaient puissants, ne sont attaqués que d'une façon vague et générale',[116] several *sotties* indicate clearly to which prelate they are referring: *Les Croniqueurs* protests against the evils caused by the famous Cardinal Balue (ll. 21–32), *L'Astrologue* and *Le Monde, Abuz* satirize the powerful Amboise brothers. These men became favorite objects of satire in the *sottie* because of their attempts to hold in their hands, illegitimately, both 'la temporalité' and 'l'église'.

The *sots* evidently differentiated between one kind of evil – the failure to fulfill the legitimate functions with which one was entrusted, as the nobleman did when he pillaged or the priest when he lead a soft life – and another, greater evil, that consisted of the attempt by one estate to usurp the functions of another.

This is an abuse which the *sots* see as the supreme hypocrisy or deception:

> O damnation
> Que avoir des coronnes tondues
> Pres des royalles!

Le Monde, Abuz, ll. 678–9: Oh damnation! To have tonsured crowns Near royal ones!

exclaim the *sots*. For this is Ypocrisie (l. 683), the new foundation of the clergy, replacing the former cornerstone, Dévotion.[117] In the same way, *Le Jeu du Prince des Sotz* is fundamentally a condemnation of the falsehood of members of the higher clergy, who have risen in the hierarchy by means of money, and who attempt to annex 'la temporalité', again by means of money, to their other powers.[118] Thus the *sots* define hypocrisy in a particular way: it is the falsehood of a prelate attempting to wield temporal (and therefore unalterably illegitimate) power.

Decadent living, debauchery, avarice and simony, pluralism, the illegitimate use of temporal power, and finally, hypocrisy: these constitute the major abuses of which the *sottie* accuses the clergy. This portrayal of a thoroughly corrupt clergy is not limited to the plays and lines that have just been examined. Like the nobility, the clergy is not only satirized in the *sottie*, but also parodied, for, like the nobility, the clergy meets two of the requirements for parody: as a group it was distinguished by clearly recognizable forms of behavior and language, and it was 'decadent' in the sense that it had supposedly fallen from a former state of purity to its present state of corruption. Consequently, parody of the Church, its rites, and its clergy, is a recurring form of comedy in the *sottie*.

Like the parody of the nobility, that of the clergy is two-edged, for the *sotties* imitate both language and behavior. The use of Latin abounds in the plays, from one or two words inserted at random to extended passages that parody the liturgy. Le Sot of *Le Gaudisseur et le Sot* mocks the braggart by means of ecclesiastical Latin (ll. 201ff.). *L'Astrologue* includes both Latin words (*mirabilia, cantabunt, minor bursa*) and latinisms such as 'orbiculaire' and 'pecune'.[119] However, the use of Latin and latinisms is not necessarily a parody of the language of the Church, for in some

sotties such language is instead a mockery of law clerks or pretentious schoolmen (as in *Les Menus Propos* and *Les Sotz qui
corrigent*).

More clearly a parody of the Church is the comic liturgy
found in several *sotties*, particularly in *Le Pelerinage* and *Les
Vigilles de Triboullet*.[120] Divine service is parodied by a technique
that recurs throughout the comic theater – the singing of an
irreverent text in the vernacular to a Gregorian chant. Another
technique is the joining together of liturgical fragments in a
macaronic jumble to create a pseudo-religious effect, as in *Les
Premiers* (ll. 173ff.). In some cases, the *sots* may intend the parody
of a sermon, as perhaps Estourdi does in his long disquisition on
the *Croniques* of the theologian Dorie (*Estourdi*, ll. 99–132). This
type of parody is by no means unique to the *sotties*, for parodies
both of sermons and of the liturgy, and the use of Latin, constitute
the basis of a related theatrical form, the *sermon joyeux*.[121] Furthermore, jesting about religious subjects was widespread in the
literature of Rabelais's time, as Febvre has shown.[122]

Therefore, satire of the Church in the *sottie* must be seen in the
context of a satiric tradition, as part of what Febvre has called
'cette monnaie courante des bons raillards daubant sur les moines,
les pardons et les chambrières des curés'.[123] The profoundly
religious nature of medieval society contrasted with an equally
deep-seated anti-clericalism,[124] and this contrast, as reflected in
the comic theater, is 'une des questions de psychologie collective
les plus embarrassantes que pose l'histoire de notre théâtre', in
the words of Felix Gaiffe.[125] Satire of the clergy similar to that in
the *sottie* was to be found 250 years earlier, in the *Bible au Seigneur
de Berzé* (1215–20). This satire continued throughout the Middle
Ages, constituting a tradition that provoked from Michelet this
remark: 'Trois cents ans de plaisanteries sur le pape, les mœurs
des moines, la gouvernante du curé: c'est de quoi lasser à la
fin?'[126] In the sixteenth century, attacks on the abuses of monks,
prelates, and theologians are to be found not only in the works of
Rabelais, but also 'dans les écrits et dans la pensée des Evangéliques;
et des Réformés de ce temps'.[127] On this topic Erasmus and
Gringore, the learned humanist and the popular *farceur*, worked
together to proclaim that the Church was badly run.[128]

Placed in this context, religious satire in the *sottie*, especially of the lower clergy, seems less outrageous than when it is seen in isolation. The conventional nature of parody and of much (but not all) of the satire in the *sottie* suggests a partial answer to the question raised at the beginning of this discussion about the purpose of satire: evidently neither the parody of the Church in the *sottie* nor its satire was expected to reform the abuses they protest, for the same accusations are repeated not just year after year, but century after century, although they had no effect on the abuses themselves.

Though this non-reforming nature of satire is generally true of the *sotties*, it is not entirely so. There are several plays that are to a lesser or greater degree advocates of the Reformation, although the *sottie* was not actually adopted as a weapon by the new cult.[129] Nonetheless, *La Mère de Ville*, written in Rouen at a time of significant Protestant sympathy on the part of the population, shows reformist tendencies in its satire of a priest (Le Garde Pot), a character whose 'pratique' is to make the faithful believe the contrary of the truth, namely, 'espargner la vérité / Et faire du faulx le certain' (ll. 181–2; see also ll. 186–7). Discreet references to reformist doctrine can be gleaned from several other plays: Le Monde is criticized, in *Le Monde*, for not savoring the 'texte de la Bible, / Qui est chose irrépréhensible' (ll. 210–11; see also *Les Troys Galans et un Badin*, ll. 312–13; and *Faulte d'Argent*, ll. 221–5). The pro-Catholic side is represented mainly by *Troys Pelerins et Malice*, 'écrite par quelque plume catholique dans les premiers temps de la Réforme', according to Fournier.[130] And, in *Les Sobres Sots*, the *réformés* are called 'fols mutins et obstinés', '[qui] se font bruller a credit' (ll. 335 and 338: 'obstinate, rebellious fools', 'who get themselves burned [at the stake] gratuitously').

These are nearly all the pro-Reformation or evangelical allusions in the *sotties*. The charges of corruption and irregularity, which were discussed above (pp. 98–103), have not been cited as evidence of reformist tendencies, since the mere existence of abuses, and the protests against them, are inadequate to explain the birth or development of the Reformation.[131] It is likely, however, that indirect, perhaps unconscious, support was given to the Reformation by a certain view of the Church that is expressed in the *sotties*. Like many other people of the time, the *sots* seem to long for a simple, clear, and efficacious religion – the religion they suspect was once given to the world and has since been lost. The Church was formerly founded on Dévotion and Bonne Foy. Now the 'pillar' of the Church is ruined from capital to base. Bonne Foy, once 'vraye sotte principalle' of Mère Sainte Eglise, has become 'le viel jeu' (*Le Jeu du Prince des Sotz*, l. 406). To restore the Church to its original purity, to bring back Bonne Foy, was the aim of many reformed clergy-men.[132] This particular attitude in the *sottie* helped to prepare the ground for the Reformation in France.

In some of the *sotties*, there is great pessimism about the Church, a pessimism which expresses itself most clearly in a certain view of the higher clergy. Unlike the satire of priests and monks in the *sottie*, that of the prelates is both less traditional and more filled with anxiety. The higher clergy is, in the eyes of the *sots*, intent on gaining illegitimate temporal power, power that means more war and higher taxes for the people. Several lines in *L'Astrologue* suggest that the attitude of the lower classes is being expressed. Chascun protests, for instance, that

> Pour poier le chapeau d'ung moyne
> Ma bource est toute évacuée.

Ll. 162–3: To buy a [cardinal's] hat for a monk My purse is completely emptied.

To gain its ends, the higher clergy uses not only the corrupting influence of money, but also all the devious stratagems that a profound hypocrisy can devise.

This important difference in the view of the two levels of clergy is indicated first by the greater intensity of the attacks on the prelates. But it is also important to recognize that the ways in which the two types of ecclesiastics are treated in the *sotties* indicate a major element of the plays' attitude toward them. Until now, the significance of the dénouement has not been recognized in analysis of satire in the *sottie*. In the two plays in which members of the lower clergy appear as major characters, they either escape unpunished or are actually rewarded (*Les Brus* and *Les Povres Deables*). Yet in the three principal *sotties* which deal with the problem of the hypocrisy of the higher clergy (*Le Monde, Abuz*; *Le Jeu du Prince des Sotz*; and *Les Sotz ecclesiasticques*), the characters representing this level of the clergy are not simply defeated, but unmasked, exiled, and in one case eternally damned. The wily prelates are first shown acting out their evil ways – buying and selling benefices; trying to build a new world in which Ypocrisie, Simonie, and Irrégularité dominate; corrupting the king's ministers in order to gain temporal power. When the anxiety created by their machinations reaches its peak, the prelates are suddenly denounced, dethroned, and condemned to the fires of hell. In this way the *sottie* expresses first a profound anxiety and then a symbolic triumph over it.[133] The anxiety provoked by what the *sots* see as hidden evil is allayed by the symbolic, ritualistic defeat of the evil ministers. Thus, anti-ecclesiastical satire in the *sottie* suggests one of the primary functions of satire in the late Middle Ages: symbolic triumph over the anxiety provoked by dangerous people. This function of satire will become clearer as the final parts of the picture are studied – the satire of the lower classes, and in particular the satire of the bourgeoisie.

PART III. SATIRE OF THE THIRD ESTATE

> Feste bieu, que de gens nouveaulx!
>
> *Les Rapporteurs,* l. 41
>
> Il n'est rien pire soubz la nue
> Que gens nouveaulx de maintenant.
>
> *Les Gens nouveaulx,* ll. 227–8

Satire of the Third Estate in the *sotties* differs significantly from that of the previous two groups. For one thing, the most populous medieval estate is the object of the smallest amount of satire. And yet the lower classes do pervade the *sotties*; a representative of them appears in one form or another in most of the plays. Why, then, is there so little satire of this part of society? Is satire of the Third Estate veiled, and if so, why? If Le Commun is not an object of satire, what is its function in the dramatic world of the *sots*? These are the principal questions to be taken up now.

The Third Estate differs from the noble and ecclesiastical estates in the vagueness of its conceptualization. The *sotties* are almost always clear about the object of their satire when they deal with the nobility or the clergy. The concept of the *roturier*, on the other hand, is an imprecise one: sometimes it indicates the laboring classes, sometimes these classes plus the bourgeoisie (as it has been defined above, p. 75), sometimes 'the people' becomes the French people, the nation as a whole. In effect, the 'tiers estat' in the Middle Ages was defined negatively, by what it was not – all who were neither noble nor ecclesiastical.

The Third Estate appears only twice in a purely satiric role; its other appearances have a non-satiric function. These two satiric representations are Sot Ignorant, in *Le Monde, Abuz*, and Sotte Commune, in *Le Jeu du Prince des Sotz*. The satiric accusations made against the Third Estate in these *sotties* are as precise as they are limited, for one central accusation is made: the people are charged with being rebellious. Three of the six 'pillars' of Sot Ignorant, for example, are a form of disobedience to one's superiors. Murmurement, Rebellion, and Fureur par Desperance (ll. 1137, 1146, and 1155). Similarly, the virtues that Sot Ignorant rejects are those that the governing classes would have liked to see instilled in the people: Recongnoissance ('Pour recongnoistre un dieu, ung roy, / Ung seigneur', ll. 1099–1100), Obéissance ('Pour obeyr a ton seigneur, / A chacum comme a ton greigneur', ll. 1141–2), Patience ('Comme plus bas tousjours se offrant', l. 1134), with Ignoscence, Simplesse, and Puzillanimité included to complete the desired image of the 'innocuous lamb' (l. 1117). The author of *Le Monde, Abuz* seems to reflect the rulers' view of the supposedly rebellious masses, a view which is also expressed in *La Croix Faubin*, at the end of which the character Patience advises Le Pain and Le Vin to bear their difficulties without complaint. Gringore, in *Le Jeu du Prince des Sotz*, also counsels obedience for the common people. Although he himself was a member of the bourgeoisie, Gringore did not hesitate to satirize his class when it served the policies of the king. Therefore, his satire of Sotte Commune must be seen in the context of political propaganda. In particular, Sotte Commune is accused of complaining too much:

> La Commune grumelera
> Sans cesser et se meslera
> De parler a tort a travers.

Ll. 321–3: The Commonfolk will grumble Without stopping, and will get mixed up in Talking about everything at random.

Above all, she complains about war:

> Et! que ay je a faire de la guerre,
> Ne que a la chaire de saint Pierre
> Soit assis ung fol ou ung saige?
> Que m'en chault il se l'Eglise erre,
> Mais que paix soit en ceste terre?

Ll. 271–5: Ah, what do I have to do with war, Or that on the chair of St Peter There may be a fool or a wise man? What do I care if the Church errs, So long as there be peace on the earth?

It is this attitude of 'peace in our time' that Gringore must combat in order to mobilize the people behind his king. When Sotte Commune threatens to become too persuasive, the other *sots* brusquely silence her; and she is finally pushed into the background by the arrival of Mère Sotte herself.

Two other satiric barbs are thrown at the Third Estate. In addition to being rebellious and complaining, the *vilain* wants to become ennobled:

> Chascun se dict estre gentil,
> Fust il plus vilain c'un rat mort.

Tout le Monde, ll. 122–3: Everyman claims to be of gentle birth Were he more common than a dead rat.

Once again we see that any attempt to change one's estate is severely criticized by the *sots*. Furthermore, one play sees the lower classes as hungry for power. In *Mestier et Marchandise*, Le Temps rages against the lower classes:

> Cuydes vous gouverner le Temps,
> Et en faire a vostre devise?

Ll. 246–7: Do you think to govern Time And do with it as you wish?

It will be a long time before the lower classes have such power. In the meantime, they do, in the *sottie*, exactly what Gringore said they do: they protest against the state of the world in general, and they lament certain more specific troubles, such as war and taxation. But in few plays are these various complaints spoken by the lower classes in their own name. In *Mestier et Marchandise* and *Pou d'Acquest*, three *sots* assume the roles of Mestier, Marchandise, and Le Berger in order to lament the wretched state of these classes. In other plays it turns out that certain allegorical characters are in effect speaking for the lower classes: characters such as Chascun, Le Monde, Tout, and Tout le Monde.[134] Although Chascun is sometimes scornfully treated by the *sots* (see above, pp. 78–9), he generally voices their own lamentations on the state of the world, that is, the lamentations of the lower classes. These complaints reveal a popular point of view on the part of the authors, for the abuses and miseries that most affected the lower classes are those that provoke the protests of Le Monde, Chascun, and their counterparts.

As numerous as the complaints about specific troubles are the expressions of despair over the state of the world in general. A few examples will give an idea of the tone of these lamentations. For example, the ballade that opens *Le Monde, Abuz* reiterates the woeful refrain, 'Cest grand pitié de ce povre Monde.' Le Monde itself laments in *Les Gens nouveaulx*:

> Fortune, tu m'es bien contraire,
> Contraire dès que je fuz né.

Ll. 249–50: Fortune, you are quite contrary to me, Contrary since I was born.

Frequently the complaints of the *sots* were particularly intense at the beginning of a reign (provoked either by preceding troubles or from fears of what might be coming) – *Les Gens nouveaulx* and *L'Astrologue* draw sad pictures of the situation in France at the beginning of the reigns of Louis XI and Louis XII respectively. When the lower class speaks in its own voice, the same plaintive words recur. Marchandise, Mestier, and Le Berger, representing the three principal parts of the Third Estate, describe at length their problems in *Mestier et Marchandise* and *Pou d'Acquest*. Le Temps agrees with them: 'Vous déclinés en piteux termes' (*Mestier et Marchandise*, l. 205: 'You are deteriorating pitifully'), but they are not to blame:

Combien que soyons innocens
Si n'avons nous de chanter cause.

Ll. 214-15: However innocent we may be,   Still we have no cause to sing.
(Cf. the beginning of *Le Jeu du Capifol.*)

Although these complaints had become largely conventional
by the end of the Middle Ages, like the accusation of ecclesiastical
debauchery, yet the conventionality of the form does not negate
the validity of the complaints themselves. It was painfully true in
the late Middle Ages that 'Si chacun se deult, / Croyez que ce
n'est point sans cause' (*Le Cry de la Bazoche*, ll. 64-5: 'If everyone
complains / Believe me that it's not without cause'). The mass of
the peasants of Europe led a life which was barely above sub-
sistence level, and the life of the urban poor was frequently as
bad. The ravages of the Hundred Years' War aggravated this
poverty in France, where the picture is truly pitiful. For those
with meager resources, a crop failure, an increase in taxes or rent,
or the outbreak of war would reduce them to destitution. It is no
wonder, then, that Renaissance Europe had more beggars than
any other age, and that states began to enact poor laws.[135] One
sottie, Les Povres Deables, takes as its principal theme the poverty
of the citizens of Normandy (suffering from drought, plague,
and famine), and the taxes with which they were burdened in
about 1520. Tout le Monde, in the play by that name, recognizes
the severity of the situation and decides to get rid of the costume
representing the laborer: 'J'arroys trop de peine et labit'. (L. 252:
'I would have too much pain and affliction.')

The miseries caused by war and taxation were aggravated, in
the minds of the *sots*, by the fact that even in times of trouble
some people still prospered. The fools protest the unjust disparity
of social conditions that existed at the end of the Middle Ages,
a period described by Edouard Fournier as 'ces temps de luxe et
de misère, de luxe sans pitié, de misère sans consolation'.[136] The
sots are equally eloquent:

> Tel menge trop.
>   Tel meurt de faim.
> Tel se tue de labourer
> Sa vigne, mais il n'ose grain
> Sa gorge du vin arrouser.

Folle Bobance, ll. 141–44: So-and-so eats too much. So-and-so dies of hunger. So-and-so kills himself in working His vineyard, but he dare not Wet his throat with wine.

> On veoyt qui a grand paine peult
> Se nourir qui aultre nourist.
> On veoyt mainct pauvre qui s'en deult.
> On veoyt mainct riche qui s'en rit.

Troys Pelerins et Malice, ll. 80–3: We see people feeding others Who can hardly feed themselves. We see many a poor man lamenting, We see many a rich man laughing.

The authors of the *sotties* seem to have been economically sophisticated enough to realize that their difficulties resulted in part from the cycles of deflation and inflation that afflicted the economy. *Mestier et Marchandise*, for example, contains a discussion of a deflationary period, in which money is worth more than formerly, but is more scarce (ll. 298–319), and the *sots* find they cannot earn enough. This is disastrous, since everyone knows 'Que l'argent faict partout la voye' (l. 306). A century later the *sots* complain that 'on a crié l'argent', that is, devalued it (*Le Jeu du Prince des Sotz*, l. 268). At the end of the period under consideration, about 1560, rising prices were a serious economic problem. Wages lagged behind prices, so that real wages in Spain, France, England, and Germany had fallen 20–40 percent below their average levels between 1450 and 1500.[137] The effect of this situation on the lower classes varied, depending on income. For wage workers the price rise meant economic regression and a serious fall in living standards. For the higher bourgeoisie, however, higher prices meant larger profits. Here again is evidence of a growing split in the Third Estate, a division which will prove to be significant for understanding the *sottie*, for it will help to explain the attitude of the *sots* toward the higher bourgeoisie.

In short, the lamentations of the *sots* express, to an overwhelming degree, the difficulties of the lower classes in the period 1440–1560. Very rare are the instances which reflect the complaints of the nobility, the clergy, or the higher bourgeoisie. From this observation, it is reasonable to conclude that both the public of the *sottie*, and more generally the social and economic framework in which the plays were conceived and to which they refer, were popular. It is striking that authors of works that sympathize with the injustice and troubles which the people suffered were frequently members of the educated élite: Jean Juvénal des Ursins, Jean Meschinot (in *Les Lunettes des princes*), Roger de Collerye, and Pierre Gringore – all were writers who had moved up in the social scale. Yet they remained spokesmen, to a large extent, of popular grievances.[138]

If there were any doubts about the popular origin of the *sotties*, the numerous details concerning the daily life of the lower classes would dispel them. Although critics have rarely considered these remarks as worthy of attention,[139] they are significant for what they indicate about the public of the *sottie*. Many remarks allude to the economic difficulties of the lower classes, as we have seen, while some details are purely descriptive of lower-class life. *Deulx Gallans et Sancté* sketches an image of lower-class life in two lines:

> Quant je suys en ma maison
> A faire mon petit menage.

Ll. 16–17: When I am in my home, Doing my little housework.

Les Menus Propos offers many examples of this kind of detail:

> On ot les nouvelles au four,
> Au moulin et chiez les barbiers.[140]

Ll. 25–6: We hear the news at the oven, The mill, and at the barber shop.

> Il fait bon aller a la cache
> Aux lievres quant il a negé.

Ll. 137–8: It feels good to go hunting Hares when it has snowed.

The Rapporteurs look forward to the day when 'Tous pietons iront a cheval', and 'Cloches ne feront plus de bruit' (ll. 257–8: 'All pedestrians will go on horseback', and 'Bells will no longer make noise'). We no longer hear the incessant bell-ringing that evidently annoyed the *menu peuple* of the Middle Ages. But five centuries ago, the bells of numerous churches, cathedrals, chapels, monasteries, and nunneries seemed to ring almost continuously.[141] The subject of bells is frequently mentioned by the *sots*: they believe, for example, that

Quant ung povre meurt, l'en ne sonne
Sinon les cloches d'un costé –

Les Menus Propos, ll. 343–4: When a poor man dies, they don't ring The bells
except maybe on one side.

– an amusing way of saying that the poor do not receive the
same attentions from the Church (and society) as do the rich.

Therefore, the source of the plays can now be argued to be
the lower classes, that is, the peasants, the urban poor and wage
laborers, and the *petite bourgeoisie*. New questions can now be
put to the *sots*: what are popular reactions to the difficult life
that they describe in the *sotties*, and, in particular, whom do
they blame for their troubles? A variety of reactions to their
lamentable life are expressed by the *sots*, from patience, to good-
humored acceptance, to pessimism. Le Prince counsels his
suppôts not to despair:

Enfans, nous airons patience
Tant que la revolucion
Du cours du temps a l'influence
Aist austre disposicion.

L'Astrologue, ll. 591–4: Children, we will be patient Until the revolution Of
the course of time May have a different disposition. (See *Chascun, Plusieurs*,
ll. 55–7.)

The Wheel of Fortune is continuously turning: and so, 'après
grant mal vient grant bien' (*Satyre*, ll. 1 and 11). Most of the time
the *sots* are content to wait until the Wheel spins back to Bon
Temps. When will that be? When 'la voix du Commun a course'
(see *Les Béguins*, ll. 103–13). The state of poverty is frequently
accepted as a joyful one. If in 'la bourse commune, / Il n'y a plus
rien, grant piessa' (*L'Astrologue*, ll. 300–1: 'in the wallet of the
common people, / There has not been anything for a long time'),
the *sots* find reason to rejoice in this very poverty:

Fy de thresor! Je ne desire
En se monde qu'avoir Sancté
Et demener joyeuseté
Pour vivre en plaisir et léesse.

Deulx Gallans et Sancté, ll. 118–21: A fig for wealth! I want but To have
Health, in this world, And to carry on joyously, In order to live in pleasure
and gaiety.

The *sots* value more highly 'Gallans justes et loyaux' than 'ceulx qui ont or a plains boysseaux' (*Faulte d'Argent*, ll. 29–30: 'those who have bushels full of gold'). The qualities of high spirits, loyalty to the *confrérie*, the ability to sing when there is little about which to be happy, the ability to 'raconter nouvelles' that amuse the 'povres engelés' of the *sottie*: all these qualities matter more than wealth. Conversely, 'Souci d'argent n'est que labit.' (*Le Bateleur*, l. 296: 'Concern about money is nothing but distress.') Therefore, if the *sots* have 'Autant en la ville que aux champs' (*Les Menus Propos*, l. 375: 'As much in town as in the fields') – that is, nothing – they are proud of their ability to laugh at their own poverty.

A final attitude of the *sots* is expressed in pessimistic prophecies of a terrible end to the world. This view is not the official Apocalypse envisioned by the Church, in which the Resurrection will bring a purified Christian people into the Kingdom of God. On the contrary, the *sots* predict that 'chascun declinera / A meschanseté et misere!' (*Les Menus Propos*, ll. 105–6: 'Everyman is falling into / Misfortune and misery!') The world is changing, yes, but 'de mal en pire':

> Le monde devient tousjours pire;
> Je ne sçay que sa fin sera.

Le Monde, ll. 110–11: The world is forever getting worse; I don't know what its end will be.

> Je m'esbahis, à bref parler,
> Où en fin l'en pourra aller
> Et que le monde deviendra.

Les Esbahis, ll. 29–31: I am astonished, to put it briefly, Where in the end we will be able to go, And what will become of the world.

The world seems very old, very decrepit – Sot Dissolu exclaims to Le Monde: 'Jesus, mon Dieu, que tu es vieulx' (*Le Monde, Abuz*, l. 357).[142] Yet any attempt to create a new world is not only doomed to failure but is condemned vigorously. The *sots* are decidedly not imbued with the Renaissance spirit of hope and faith in man's ability to build a better world.

Thus, on the one hand, the *sots* express quite clearly their feelings about the state of their world. On the other hand, they feel less free to state openly what they see as the causes of the problem. When the *sotties* satirize those who are seen as the trouble-makers, they do so with a vagueness that makes this object of satire the most difficult of all to delineate. The vagueness results from the kind of allegory found in some *sotties*, for if the *sottie* is satirical, like the farce, it is also allegorical, like the morality. The kingdom of *sots* is an allegorical parallel to the kingdom of France, and a *sot* becomes a vehicle for a range of allegorical representations: we have seen that varieties of *sots* symbolize social types, estates, occupations, institutions, and abstract ideas, such as Le Temps. The transparency of this allegorical cloak varies greatly from one type of play to another, depending on the kind of allegorical characters. The referent of one type of character, incarnating the nobility and the clergy, is fairly clear. But another type of allegorical character is also found in the *sottie*, one whose meaning is not clear, who demands an effort of interpretation on the part of the audience or reader – these are the characters called variously 'Gens Nouveaulx', 'Les Gens', 'gorriers', and sometimes 'gallans'.[143] At times the plays allude to those blamed for the world's miseries by means of such terms as 'privez loups', 'broulleurs', and 'mangeurs de lune'. It is clear that the *sots* blame these 'gens nouveaulx', for 'On doit bien mauldire celluy / Par qui le commun se doulloit.' (*Les Sotz qui remetent*, ll. 25–6: 'One should curse him / By whom the common people are afflicted.') But who might be represented by these vague names is on first reading obscure.

At this point in our study of satire it is easier to say who the 'gens nouveaulx' are not than who they are. They are not any of the categories of characters analyzed so far: they are not the clergy *per se*, nor the nobility, for these two estates are the objects of explicit satire in the *sottie*. There is no reason to suppose that the *sots* would satirize them openly at one moment and then veil their satiric attacks on them at another moment in the same play. Neither do the lower classes blame themselves for their own difficulties. There is a distinct division in the *sotties* between the *sots* who lament (the victims, representing the lower classes) and those who cause the lamentations (the evil-doers). Therefore, the group of characters given the vague names or alluded to in veiled terms may be found in the only satiric object that remains, the bourgeoisie.

It was not generally characteristic of medieval social thought to distinguish between the working class and the bourgeoisie. Especially in the twelfth and thirteenth centuries the merchant was classified with other members of Labour, that is, with all *roturiers* who earned a living by working. Jean V. Alter has argued that abuses of the class were satirized, while the nature of the merchant's activity itself was not questioned. Merchants were consistently attacked as '*menteurs, deceptifz, fins et subtiles, à tromper inventifz*'.[144] Several centuries later, it was becoming clearer that the bourgeoisie was somehow fundamentally different from, even antagonistic to, the working classes. This evolving view of the bourgeoisie is evident in the writings called 'estats du monde' and in satiric writings like the *sottie*. By the sixteenth century, the comic theater is the genre in which anti-bourgeois satire conserves the greatest vitality.[145] This is especially true of the *sottie*, which therefore makes a rich and varied field for the study of anti-bourgeois satire.

From the viewpoint of the Middle Ages, imbued with the ideal of service, individual profit implied generally some kind of deception or fraud, either in regard to merchandise or to the law. In Alter's words, 'sans mentir, comment les marchands et les légistes pourraient-ils s'enrichir?'[146] Therefore, the themes of *mensonge* and *tromperie*, of the conflict of pretense and reality, are concentrated to a remarkable degree in satire of the merchant, from the earliest appearance of the bourgeois type. When speaking of Marchandise, *Troys Pelerins et Malice* sums up this fundamental aspect of anti-bourgeois satire:

> Les faulx sermens, les tricheryes,
> Les regnymens, les tromperyes,
> Les moqueryes et faulx marchés
> Qui se font sont tant cachés
> Entour Desordre.

Ll. 104–8: The false oaths, the trickery, The betrayals, the deceptions, The mockery and false deals Which are done are so hidden Around Disorder.

Because of its connection with *tromperie* (the *sot* representing the

merchant in *Le Monde, Abuz* is called Sot Trompeur), the bourgeoisie becomes one of the principal objects of the fools' satire.
For *tromperie,* or the theme of illusion and reality, is the theme
par excellence of the *sottie.*

When studying anti-bourgeois satire in the *sottie,* it is useful to
distinguish between this traditional image of the merchant and
other satiric conceptions that were a later development. At the
end of the Middle Ages, a displacement can be observed in the
satire of the bourgeois; greater emphasis was placed on his
social comportment and on his social and political ambitions.[147]
As the focus of satire shifted from one aspect of bourgeois
activity to another, from economic activity to social and political
behavior, the theme of *mensonge* and *duperie* was carried over into
the new sphere and intensified. Whereas earlier satire protests
duperie concerning quantity or quality of products, later satire
concentrates, for instance, on the *tromperie* of the bourgeois as a
public official. Moreover, a complementary displacement occurred within the bourgeoisie itself. The higher bourgeoisie came
more and more to occupy the attention of the *sots,* as small
merchants remained the object of more limited satire, for the
higher bourgeoisie was seen as the primary group engaging in
moral and political deception, while the trickery of the lower
bourgeoisie stayed focused on quantity or quality of products.

When the *sotties* see the merchant as simply one part of the
working classes, he is the object of some sympathy. In two plays,
Mestier et Marchandise and *Pou d'Acquest,* both from the period of
Charles VII, the difficulties of the merchants are expressed in full.
In the latter play, the character called Marchandise complains of
having 'Pou d'Acquest et Grosse Despense' at the same time
(ll. 239–42), that is, he must pay heavy taxes to support Grosse
Despense (those making fortunes in government posts, or perhaps
even Agnès Sorel), although he is not earning very much: 'Qu'a
grant peine puis avoir mes despens' (l. 5). In *Mestier et Marchandise*
this character is even given some encouragement:

> Coures, faictes a vostre guise,
> Le Temps vous sert presentement,
> Et se vous aves longuement
> Esté petits, il vous fault croistre.

Ll. 429-32: Go about, do as you like, Time serves you now, And if you have for a long time Been small, you must begin to grow.

Concern for the difficulties of the merchant is relatively rare in the rest of the *sotties*. Occasional sympathy for the merchant, who also suffered from war, taxes, deflation, and inflation, did not deter the *sots* from denouncing the many abuses which were commonly attributed to him. Within the framework of *tromperie*, the *sotties* make a variety of criticisms of the merchant and of the lawyer and other *légistes*. Although satiric references to merchants are to be found in many of the *sotties*, the only fully developed role in which the bourgeoisie is the object of satire is that of Sot Trompeur, in *Le Monde, Abuz*.[148] The faults attributed to Sot Trompeur are Tromperie (of course), Usures,[149] Faulces Mesures, Parjuremens, Faintise, Avarice, and Larrecin. Several of these abuses relate to the exercise of his occupation (constituting what Alter calls 'la satire professionelle'): Usures and Faulces Mesures (perhaps also Larrecin) refer to the belief that the merchant betrayed the 'service' that he was to provide for society by taking interest on loans and by cheating on the amount or quality of the merchandise.

The rest of the abuses listed constitute the moral, rather than professional, satire of the bourgeoisie. In Alter's opinion, six major faults make up the moral satire of the bourgeoisie in medieval literature: 'avarice, crédulité, grossièreté, lacheté, mensonge et impiété'.[150] Given the widespread distribution of these vices in satiric writings on the bourgeoisie, it is remarkable that the *sottie* concentrates on only two, avarice and *mensonge*. Avarice in particular is among the most condemned of the faults of the bourgeois (appearing in medieval satiric literature as the fundamental vice to which are attached the secondary ones). This sin appears 'comme la caractéristique la plus évidente de la mentalité bourgeoise; et, par suite de cette préséance, elle est dénoncée avec une violence et une fréquence toutes spéciales'.[151] Avarice is viewed in the *sottie* too as a vice to which the bourgeoisie was particularly prone. In *Les Gens nouveaulx*, for instance, the misconduct of jurists is attributed to avarice. The *sots* are particularly alarmed by the corrupting power of money and its connection with the falseness of the bourgeoisie. Money corrupts doubly, according to the *sottie* – it corrupts him who has it, and it is used by him to corrupt others.

In addition to general satiric treatments of the merchant, as found in the role of Sot Trompeur, the *sottie* offers the satire of more limited types of bourgeois, that is, of certain tradesmen, and the satire of the legal profession. These two satiric treatments correspond to two of the sub-groups that make up the middle class, thus revealing again the lack of a unified conception of the bourgeoisie as a homogeneous class.[152] Three *métiers* are the objects of the greatest satire in the *sottie:* bakers, tavern-keepers, and *sergents*. (The *sergent* was technically part of the legal establishment, but the *sots* treat him as a separate enemy.) The frequency with which these particular occupations are satirized is explained not simply by their commercial character, but also by their importance to and unpopularity in the daily economic relations which existed between them and the lower class (another indication of the popular background of the plays). For the people, these groups often represented the category of *marchandise* as a whole.

Given the daily contact between the tavern-keeper or baker and his clients, it is not remarkable that the *boulanger* and the *tavernier* were the objects of intense satire.[153] The longest tirade against the 'paillards boulengiers' (*Les Premiers*, l. 145) is found in the *Satyre* of Collerye: thirty-five lines denounce their ruses and frauds, their underhanded activities:

> Croy qu'ilz ressemblent l'escrevice
> Qui va tousjours a reculons.

Ll. 123–4: Believe that they resemble the crayfish,   Which always walks backwards.

They cheat on both quantity and quality (ll. 117–18), but one day 'payez de leurs gages / Seront, pour vray' (ll. 131–2: 'paid they will be / With their own wages, for sure'; cf. *Les Sotz qui remetent*, ll. 161–7 and 242–3). Bakers are again threatened in *Les Troys Galans et un Badin*, threatened this time with damnation, should Le Badin ever become God. The unpopular *tavernier* is also accused of engaging in fraudulent activities, principally of mixing wine with water, or old wine with new:

Taverniers qui brouillent le vin
Meslant le viel o les nouveaulx.[154]

Thus, the two principal trades are accused of the same type of wrong-doing as was the nobility: they do not honorably fulfill the social function entrusted to them. As the nobility had cloaked itself in the ideal of national defense in order to pillage, as the lower clergy had betrayed its 'estat' by gluttony and debauchery, so the lower bourgeoisie, petty merchants like the bakers and tavern-keepers, are accused in the *sottie* of exploiting their position as purveyors of food and drink in order to cheat and, the *sots* suspect, to grow rich at the expense of their clients. Therefore, the attitude of the *sottie* toward the vices of the lower bourgeoisie is not exceptional, it is not predicated on the special function of the merchant in society. The satiric view of the lower bourgeoisie is consistent with that of other estates, also seen as failing to fulfill their duties.

Like the satire of the baker and the tavern-keeper, the satire of the *sergent* reflects a fundamentally popular point of view. The *sergent* was a law officer attached to a court, whose duty it was to 'signifier les sentences, les faire exécuter, et au besoin arrêter les malfaiteurs'.[155] As such he seems to have been feared and hated by his most frequent victims, the lower classes. The *sots* believed that his main function was to torment them:

Les sergens, qui sont dangereulx,
De tourmenter ne sont peureulx.
Tout cela iroyt en enfer
Plaider aveques Lucifer,
Pour accomplir tous leurs travaulx.

Les Troys Galans et un Badin, ll. 130–4: The sergeants, who are dangerous men, Are not afraid of tormenting us. All that bunch would go to hell To plead their case with Lucifer, In order to accomplish their work.

A character in *Les Premiers* is disguised as a pilgrim in order to fool any 'paillard garson sergent' whom he may meet; he can then 'give it' to the *sergent* on the head when his back is turned (ll. 222–8; cf. *Les Menus Propos*, ll. 20–1). *Les Rapporteurs* denounces *sergents* as *ivrognes*, *gourmands*, and *larrons* (ll. 134–55). The *sergent* was clearly one of the group of *métiers* toward which the *sots* felt the most rancor.

This evidence of popular antagonism toward the *sergent* is contradicted by the only role in which a representative of the *métier* appears on stage. In *Les Povres Deables*, Le Sergent assists La Reformeresse in summoning and exacting tribute from the 'poor devils' who owe her money. The language of Le Sergent is conveyed with realism through the vocabulary of his calling: 'faire ses sommations', 'prinses de corps', 'ajourner a ban', 'être en forfaicture'. The rest of the portrait contradicts the traditional conception of the *sergent* in the *sottie*, for Le Sergent shows himself to be merciful toward those summoned; he pleads for them and succeeds in getting them excused. Furthermore, to one of them, L'Avocat, he gives advice on how to 'make it' in the world – advice on how to take money from both parties in a lawsuit, how to take money 'de toutes mains' (l. 169). Although dishonest, Le Sergent is made to act out of charitable motives in order to satirize the unscrupulous legal practices of the day. This attitude toward Le Sergent may indicate that *Les Povres Deables* was written for the Connards of Rouen (which seems likely; see l. 345: 'tout plaisant conard'), who were probably connected with the Basoche of Rouen. As the *sergent* was a type of legal officer, the Connards might be more sympathetic toward him than would non-Basoche *sots*. In addition they would be familiar, as future lawyers, with the underhanded methods that he recommends.

The discrepancy between this characterization and the satiric remarks about *sergents* in other plays introduces one of the secondary problems that concerns satire in the *sottie*, and in the comic theater as a whole, the problem of the medieval attitude toward the legal profession. Although the medieval comic theater has traditionally been thought of as hostile to the entire legal profession, there is evidence that such a view is an oversimplification, that the attitudes expressed in the comic plays could vary from antagonism to sympathy. It might seem out of place to discuss the various attitudes toward the legal profession in the context of satire of the bourgeoisie, but it can be argued that *légistes* can rightly be treated as a kind of bourgeois. Alter has shown that 'C'est toute la profession des hommes de loi qui présente, sans équivoque, des caractères bourgeois, tant en son

développement historique que par la nature de son activité.'¹⁵⁶
The *sottie* also seems to consider *gens de pratique* as types of bourgeois: in *Satyre*, for instance, they are associated with *usuriers*
(l. 225). Nor is it out of place to discuss members of the legal
profession in the context of *folie*, for the character Folie claims
that she is clearly to be found 'Dessoubz les chapperons fourrez
[des avocats]' (*La Folie des Gorriers*, l. 112). The legal profession
is a favorite satiric object in the *sottie*, and satiric remarks about
judges and lawyers, or characters representing them, abound.
The following plays in particular deal with the legal profession
(and may have been written by Basochiens): *Les Rapporteurs*;
Les Sotz fourrez; *Les Sotz qui remetent*; *Le Monde, Abuz*; *Les
Béguins*; *Tout le Monde*; *Les Sobres Sots*; *Le Cry de la Bazoche*;
La Folie des Gorriers; *Les Premiers*; *and Les Povres Deables*.¹⁵⁷

It is difficult to generalize about the treatment of the legal
profession in these plays, for the lawyer is the source of diverse
types of humor. Sometimes he is the brunt of good-natured
ridicule, as when young lawyers, apprentices, and students are
characterized as 'sots nouveaulx', who do nothing but 'cracher
gloses et loix / Ausi dru que mouches de boys' (*Les Sobres Sots*,
ll. 359–60: 'spit glosses and laws / As thick as flies'; see also
ll. 350–67). Much more frequent, however, is the type of satiric
attack, characterized by the intensity of its invective, that is
found in the role of Sot Corrompu, in *Le Monde, Abuz*. Representing judges (and perhaps the entire legal profession), Sot
Corrompu is accused of the vices of Ambicion, Faulceté, Haus-
térité, and Corruption (instead of Vérité, Equité, Misericorde,
etc.). Such satiric attacks on the legal profession have led scholars
to claim that anti-legal satire is both frequent and acerbic in
medieval farces and *sotties*. Petit de Julleville in particular believed
that such satire formed one of the most important elements of the
medieval comic theater.¹⁵⁸

However, Howard Graham Harvey, who is himself a lawyer,
argues that lawyers and law officers receive 'a treatment strikingly
different from that accorded other powerful social groups.
Their appearance or mention is comparatively infrequent in these
plays, and when they are mentioned, it is with marked restraint.'¹⁵⁹
In his opinion, the comic playwrights attack the legal profession

timidly or not at all, while they attack the representatives of the other privileged classes, the nobles and the clergy, with the utmost violence and malice.[160] Harvey's first line of argument is, then, that the intensity of satire of the legal profession has been overestimated. But he also attempts to show that more attention should be given to evidence of Basoche authorship in many of the existing plays: the amount of this evidence has been underestimated, he argues. If satiric attacks are in reality fewer than previous critics have claimed, according to Harvey, much more numerous are allusions to the practices of the legal profession, to events in the lawyer's world, and to the personal lives of members of the profession, allusions which would have had little point for persons outside the inner circle, but which would have amused an audience in the Grand'Salle of the Palais de Justice.[161]

While Harvey has increased our understanding of many farces, moralities, and *sotties* (his analysis of *Pathelin* is particularly helpful), nonetheless his view of the medieval comic theater is affected by a certain bias with which he approaches the plays. He remarks, for example, that 'in several *sotties* there are a few negligible remarks about lawyers',[162] whereas at least one-fifth of the plays offer a significant amount of legal satire. Similarly, Harvey argues that *Le Monde, Abuz* offers 'a little satire' of the judiciary, 'but it is entirely traditional, harmless, and without point'.[163] Why Harvey judges the satire of Sot Corrompu to be negligible in comparison with the satire of other groups is not made clear: satire of the judge appears to be as outspoken as that of the others – after all, he is accused of abandoning the virtues of Vérité, Equité, Juste Vouloir, and Misericorde (see ll. 1015–46).

The value of Harvey's study of legal satire in the medieval comic theater is decreased by the author's desire both to find evidence where it may not exist and to put aside satiric elements that should be taken into account. Nonetheless, his study has a definite validity: he has shown that, in many plays, satire of the legal profession in the comic theater is more traditional and milder than previous scholars claimed; that some references to judges and lawyers are directed only against seigniorial and ecclesiastical tribunals of the lowest order; and that law clerks probably wrote and performed many of the plays, in particular the *sotties* – they were plays by a clan (Harvey's term), for a clan. But in the end we must remember that the medieval comic theater frequently had a large and popular audience, not just the law clerks of the Palais de Justice.

While satire of *légistes* in the medieval theater may be milder than previously claimed, nonetheless it is shaped by certain traditional attitudes toward the legal profession. A kind of alliance of all classes was formed in the face of certain offensive traits of the *légiste*. This alliance resulted in a complexity of satiric treatment which constitutes, according to Alter, 'le monument satirique le plus vaste et le plus permanent qu'une profession ait jamais connu'.[164] The satire of *légistes* is chronologically the last type of professional satire to develop in the Middle Ages, and the only type that grows in intensity throughout the Middle Ages and into the sixteenth century, while in the later period new criticisms appear, the result of conditions proper to that century. These various satiric themes are linked by one underlying vision of the *gens de loi*: they are unscrupulous in their greed.[165]

Like merchants, lawyers and judges are accused primarily, in the *sottie*, of two vices: avarice and deception. Money is the primary goal of the *légiste*, and *tromperie*, or any form of lie, is the means to that goal. However, the goal and the means have become so intertwined in the minds of the *sots*, that it is difficult for them to say whether the lawyer is *rusé* for the sake of money, or whether his wealth is a consequence of his deep-seated dishonesty. In *Le Monde, Abuz*, for example, 'Ambicion d'avoir de l'or, / D'offices' (ll. 1032–3) is closely tied to Faulceté. The charge of greed is frequently linked to the idea of the *pot de vin*, or the custom of bribing officials (often called paying *espices*). The judge in *Le Monde, Abuz* sees no need to hide the facts:

> Nous disons, sans que homme s'en tence,
> Que celluy qui plus baille argent
> A le droict si cler et si gent.
> . . .
> Diz: Qui a l'or en main tenu
> Soit diffiniment maintenu.

Ll. 182–8: We say, without anyone disputing, That he who gives the most money Is in the right, free and clear... Say: He who offers ready cash Should be definitely supported.

'O quel leurreur de chappons gras!' exclaims one of the *sots*. (L. 173: 'Oh what a decoyer [receiver] of plump chickens!') Lawyers are as grasping as judges, according to the *sots*: '[ils] ne font rien sans argent' (*Les Premiers*, l. 234). The *sots* called 'Rapporteurs', in the play by that name, report this amazing news:

> Les advocatz de maintenant
> Ne veullent plus prendre d'argent,
> Ilz font tout pour l'amour de Dieu.

Ll. 208–10: The lawyers of today Don't want to take money any longer, They do everything for the love of God. (See also *La Folie des Gorriers*, ll. 350–2.)

As we have seen, Le Sergent in *Les Povres Deables* gives advice to a lawyer who seems unable to pull in the same fees as his colleagues:

> Soys-moy un petit plus pillard,
> . . .
> Pren moy argent de ta partye;
> Sy tost qu'elle sera partye,
> Va moy signer le faict contraire,
> Petis et grand pouras atraire.

Ll. 162, 164–7: Be a little more grabbing.... Take money from your clients; As soon as they have left, Go sign the opposite statement, You will attract both great and small.

The entire passage is a résumé of dishonest methods used by lawyers.

Clearly the greed of the *légiste* is expressed primarily through his dishonesty. He does not work hard for the money he acquires; he brings it in fraudulently: he accepts bribes, alters testimony (*Le Cry de la Bazoche*: 'forger les témoins', ll. 278–9), and in general avoids the truth whenever possible (*Le Monde, Abuz*, ll. 1042–5). His profound corruption is indicated in an amusing way in *Le Cry de la Bazoche*. The *sots* are puzzled by the oath that judges must take when they assume office:

> On faict aux officiers jurer
> N'avoir baillé or ny avoir
> Pour office de juge avoir;

> Pour quoy, veu que toutes se vendent,
> A faire ce serment entendent?

Ll. 565–9: One makes officers swear Not to have given gold or wealth In order to get the office of judge; Why, seeing that all offices are sold, Are they asked to swear this oath?

Monsieur Rien has a ready explanation for this oath:

> Affin de s'accoustumer d'heure
> A avoir bonne bouche et seure
> Et ne descouvrir les secretz
> Qui sont cachez soubz leurs decretz.

Ll. 570–3: In order to get used early To having a firm, tight mouth And to not revealing the secrets That are hidden under their decrees.

No more ingenious statement of the duplicity of the *légiste* is to be found in the *sottie*.

Thus, satire of the legal profession, limited as it may be, reveals two of the recurring preoccupations of the *sots*: a belief in the corrupting effects of money and of the all-pervasiveness of *tromperie*. Over and over it has become clear that the *sots* distrust the power of money and those who have it. Avidity was deemed one of the principal causes of the ruses of the *légat* and of the *légiste*. Money becomes a danger when greed is aided by deceitfulness, when it is used by the unscrupulous.

Every type of satire studied so far has been rooted in the conflict of illusion and reality. This conflict is summed up in the idea of pretense: Pretense is found when a class or individual appears to fulfill the role allotted to it, while in reality betraying that role or usurping the role of another. The nobility pretends to live up to the ideals of chivalry while, in effect, it derogates from them by pillaging. The clergy's pretense is twofold: the lower clergy pretends to live in accord with religious principles; the higher clergy pretends to serve Mère Sainte Eglise. Both levels of the clergy are false to their estate, as is the bourgeois who cheats or the judge who accepts bribes. This theme of pretense was also suggested in the satire of powerful individuals. People in high places pretend to be serving their king and country, while in reality they 'Ayment leur proufit singulier'.[166] Sometimes the individuals who by their misconduct are responsible for public misery are clearly indicated by the *sots* (as in the case of the Amboise brothers). Frequently, however, references to powerful and self-serving individuals are veiled to such an extent that it is impossible today to determine beyond doubt who is being indicated.

Again and again the *sots* allude to certain individuals who they feel are the cause of popular miseries. In the complaints against these people, certain characteristics stand out: those whom the *sots* call by terms such as 'les gens nouveaulx', or simply 'les gens', are powerful, rich and ambitious, self-serving, and profoundly deceitful. That the *sots* blame their troubles on certain politically powerful people and not on themselves or on fate is clear from a number of their remarks. 'Et se Chascun se plaint, il n'a point tort', the *sots* of *L'Astrologue* tell us, 'et toult par le discort / Des principaulx.' (Ll. 12, 14–15: 'And if Everyman complains, he's not at all wrong, / ... / And all because of the discord / Of the important people.') It is these 'principaulx' who have ruined La Chose Publicque (in *Les Sotz fourrez*), a character described as having been ravished by certain members of the government:

> Sotz gouvernée m'ont contre nature
> Comme voyez...
> Et mise au bas totalement.

Ll. 203–6: *Sots* have governed me unnaturally, As you see... And ruined me totally. (Cf. ll. 288ff.)

These 'gens nouveaulx' are not only powerful but hypocritical, for Le Monde claims that

> En me monstrant signe d'amour
> De nuyt et jour vous me pillez.

Les Gens nouveaulx, ll. 289–90: While showing me signs of love, Night and day you pillage me.

Pou d'Acquest (ll. 108–15) prefers to call them 'flateurs de court', and he imitates their contorted way of speaking, a language fabricated in order to hide their thoughts (but which wins them honor at court). Similarly the bizarre and comical character, Les Gens, in *Mestier et Marchandise*, speaks in unintelligible gibberish:

> Qui sterna, ha, la,
> Fari planga, hardet, stella,
> My hard, fiol, berty, hardit (ll. 360–2).

This character is an imaginative satiric incarnation of the type of person that the *sots* blame for their troubles: Les Gens are powerful: 'ils ont la puisance si forte / De faire le Temps tel qu'il est' (ll. 335–6: 'they have such strong power / To make Time go as it does'); self-serving, and unscrupulous: 'Ilz en font a leurs apetis' (l. 33: 'They do with it [Time] as they wish'); and deceitful: Les Gens hide their faces by walking backwards, with a mask on the back of the head, and they hide their thoughts in the gibberish quoted above. These people are responsible for all the miseries that plague Mestier, Marchandise, and Le Berger, and until they change, everything will go 'vilainement'. Similarly the Gens Nouveaulx of the *sottie* by that name are seen as the cause of unhappiness for the lower classes:

> Peuple, d'avoir bien ne te attens
> Quand gens nouveaulx sont sur les rens:
> Toujours viendra pis que devant.

Ll. 339–41: People, don't wait to have any good When the New People are in the saddle: It will always be worse than before.

Other plays refer to this menacing, grasping group of individuals in terms that vary but which reflect the same condemnation. *Troys Pelerins et Malice*, for example, calls them 'mangeurs de lune'; in *Faulte d'Argent* they are 'privez loups', 'ung tas de broulleurs' (ll. 15 and 216); they appear in *La Croix Faubin* as the characters L'Un and L'Autre. Although these *brouilleurs* are not identified, it is nonetheless made clear that the *sots* will never have relief from their 'grans doleurs' until the 'broulleurs / Soient hors de bruit [reputation, recognition] non aultrement' (ll. 216–17).

These 'gens nouveaulx' are charged with acting in devious ways. 'Entreprises incongnues' and 'traysons secrettes' are continuously suspected by the *sots* (see *Le Jeu du Prince des Sotz*, ll. 281–3, 286, 301–5, and 327ff.). The 'gens nouveaulx' attempt to deceive through words (in *Les Gens nouveaulx*, for example, they assure Le Monde that he is 'logé en logis plaisant', while he knows that his lodging is first Mal, then Pire); by flattery; and by ruse (see *Troys Galans et Monde*, 284ff.). In *Les Esbahis*, Justice asserts that

> Plusieurs besongnes sont brassées,
> Tant en fait en dit que en penscée
> Dont je ne sçais rien bien souvent
> . . .
> Il est trop de fines gens.

Ll. 138–40, 144: A number of affairs are brewing, In words and deeds as well as thought, Of which I frequently know nothing... There are too many shrewd people.

La Bazoche predicts that one day many things will be discovered 'Qui sont au temps present cachées' (*Le Cry de la Bazoche*, ll. 130–4; see also ll. 142–5, 172, 334–40). The world has been overturned by 'bourdes' (lies, deceit), Folie herself tells us:

> Les petiz mis en grans estas,
> Et les grans du tout my aux bas.[167]

La Folie des Gorriers, ll. 327–8: The small fry put in high positions, And the great put down completely.

These lines suggest a vague but abiding anxiety regarding certain powerful, self-serving, and deceitful people. Such fears are more pervasive than these isolated lines would suggest, however, for a number of plays expand the theme of the machinations of the 'gens nouveaulx' until it constitutes the plot of an entire play, not simply one of the topics of conversation.

In these *sotties* that act out allegorically the threat of the 'gens nouveaulx', a pattern is used that has been observed in the structural analysis of certain *sotties*, one that consists of two or three *sots* confronted by an antagonist. Sometimes the group of *sots* represents the 'gens nouveaulx', the evil-doers; sometimes they represent their victims and accusers. Here is a clear indication of the ambivalence of the *sot*, an ambivalence that explains in part why the fool became a popular means of satire in the late Middle Ages.[168] Fools are most commonly those who are clearly vicious or wrong-headed. Yet the fool was also associated with the idea of simple, uncultured, even unfortunate people. As such he became the spokesman for popular complaints; he became a popular counterpart of the knight, insofar as he championed the cause of the troubled lower classes.

This double-edged conception of the *sot* leads to two types of *sottie*, both of which are allegories of lower-class fears. The first type are plays in which the *sots* represent the evil-doers, the 'gens nouveaulx'. The most rudimentary example of this type of allegory is the *sottie* by the name of *Les Gens nouveaulx*. The title summarizes the minimal action of the play: 'Farce nouvelle moralisée des gens nouveaulx qui mengent le monde, et le logent de mal en pire, a quatre personnaiges'. The characters are also minimal: three *sots* and Le Monde. This action and these characters form a pattern recurring in other plays. The threat of the 'gens nouveaulx' is here acted out in its simplest form: the 'gens nouveaulx' explain their desire to govern the world and to change everything in it; they take the world on an allegorical journey[169] that goes from bad to worse, and in the end they are revealed as self-seeking and hypocritical. The 'gens nouveaulx' are symbolically defeated by the satiric treatment they are given (satire constituting a form of public disapproval), and by the moral that Le Monde pronounces at the end, in which he exposes and condemns the *sots*.

This most simple statement of the threat of the 'gens nouveaulx' and of their symbolic defeat is the theme of other *sotties*. In *La Folie des Gorriers*, two *sots* try to succeed in the world by dishonest means. Their connection with folly is made explicit by their allegiance to a character named Dame Folie. Although for a time they seem on the point of succeeding, in the end the *gorriers* are ruined. Similarly, in *Les Sotz triumphans*, the *sots* want to learn to *tromper* and thus to rule the world. They in turn are deceived and defeated. The defeat of the 'gens nouveaulx' is most developed in the play *Troys Galans et Monde*, for in it a character is specifically created to vanquish the *galants* (i.e., 'gens nouveaulx'). The character is called Ordre, and the *sots* know him not at all. And although they refuse to recognize him or to accept his tutelage, he triumphs over them.

In the second type of allegorical *sottie*, the roles are reversed and the *sots* represent the world, the victim of the evil-doers, or simply that part that was important in the *sottie*, the 'bas estats'.

Now the 'gens nouveaulx' are played by a single adversary, called Les Gens, Grosse Despense, or a similar name. *Mestier et Marchandise* and *Pou d'Acquest* offer the clearest development of this type of allegory. The character called Les Gens, in the first play, is branded as the cause of all the miseries of the three estates, Mestier, Marchandise, and Le Berger. He is all false men who act in a sinister way, who conspire in a language that only they understand, and who cause the breakdown of society. In the end, Les Gens is not simply defeated, but changed into a carefree, unthreatening person – like the *sots* of the play. He is neutralized by being absorbed into the society of *sots*. This play thus offers one of the most original and hopeful variations on the theme of the defeated 'gens nouveaulx'. *Pou d'Acquest*, written about the same time, shows how different can be the spirit in which the threat of the 'gens nouveaulx' is treated. In this play, the cause of the fools' troubles, Grosse Despense, who governs 'toutes gens somptueus' (l. 206), is not overthrown or neutralized. Instead the *sots* appear to be ruined by her. The only weapon they have left is ridicule, which will turn out to be the principal arm of the *sottie*.

The ritualized acting-out of a threat and the neutralization of it through ridicule will be studied in more detail later. At this point we have a better idea of the nature of the threat as the *sots* conceived of it, and we are in a position to speculate on the identity of the 'gens nouveaulx', that is, which class or social group may have been represented by them. In general, a character such as the 'gens nouveaulx' could have represented any powerful, unscrupulous individual who was seen as playing a political or social role to which he was not entitled. Satire of the higher clergy in the *sottie* is built largely on this theme. More specifically, though, it seems likely that the 'gens nouveaulx' represent a new and growing class of merchants and lawyers in the fifteenth and sixteenth centuries, which I shall call for convenience the higher bourgeoisie. Stated succinctly, the theory generally accepted by economic historians today sees the late Middle Ages and Renaissance as a period of growing economic activity on a large scale (banking, exchange, loans, industrial investment, etc.), an economic growth which was in the hands of a business élite (about 2 percent of the population). In contrast to this élite, most bourgeois were part of the more populous class of shopkeepers, artisans, and wage workers.[170] Pirenne has summarized the growth of capitalist commerce in this way: 'Si le commerce local demeure asservi à la réglementation minutieuse des corporations de métiers et au protectionnisme étroit de l'économie urbaine, le grand commerce leur échappe et n'obéit qu'à l'individualisme capitaliste.'[171]

This separation of the bourgeoisie into two groups began in the fifteenth century, and by the sixteenth it was a *fait accompli*. Thus, in this period two castes can be distinguished: the *patriciat* (the higher bourgeoisie) and the *petite bourgeoisie* – a *major bursa* and a *minor bursa*, in the words of L'Astrologue. In particular, the development of the capitalist mode of production in industry and, to a lesser extent, in agriculture, produced a widening gap between capital and labor, rich and poor. This division within the bourgeoisie led to conflicting interests. The lower bourgeoisie tried to maintain the *status quo*, thus becoming more and more the guardian of tradition, while the higher bourgeoisie attempted to acquire new and greater social, economic, and political powers. The result was a pronounced class tension.[172] Perhaps what was most galling to the lower bourgeoisie was the awareness of the growing economic disparity between the rich merchant class and themselves. Poverty that may be cheerfully accepted in itself (and the *sots* often do accept it), becomes oppressive when compared with great wealth. The Rapporteurs express this resentment against the élite of the bourgeoisie when they exclaim: 'Que de gens qui ont trop d'avoir, / Que de gens qui ont trop de biens!' (ll. 53–4).

The widening gap between the two parts of the bourgeoisie was visible not only in standard of living, but also in political power. In the fifteenth century, the less prosperous portion of the bourgeoisie was reduced to impotence as a political force, and the capitalist élite had little reason to fear it. The reverse was not true, however. Opposition to this élite could be expressed only verbally, that is, by means of one of the few arms that the lower bourgeoisie could still use against the higher: the power of public ridicule, of dramatic satire. Popular theater of this period bears witness to the exacerbation of social conflicts.[173] Until now, however, this conflict between two parts of the bourgeoisie has not been observed in the *sottie*, because it was transmuted into indirect representation by means of the 'gens nouveaulx'.

The *nouveau riche*, especially the kind who was seen flaunting his wealth and power at the court, corresponds strikingly with the satiric image of the 'gens nouveaulx' in the *sottie*. Both the higher bourgeoisie and the 'gens nouveaulx' were seen as individuals who had attempted to rise above their proper estate. The sixteenth-century merchant class was extremely fluid, with trade and industry serving as the chief means by which men moved up in the social hierarchy (whereas the Church had offered this mobility during an earlier period). As the financial and commercial élite rose in wealth and power, it acquired many of the attributes of the *noblesse*; it bought the lands of the aristocracy; it usurped the role of the nobility in the royal councils; finally, more and more often members of this élite attained legal *anoblissement*. Under Louis XI, for example, individual ennoblings seem to have been legion; as a political and economic policy, the king surrounded himself with *roturiers* or recently ennobled bourgeois.[174]

Unlike the nobleman, the priest, or the peasant, the *gros bourgeois* did not occupy a traditionally established place in the social hierarchy. Whereas the other classes were seen as socially necessary, even divinely ordained, the members of the higher bourgeoisie were late-comers to the composition of medieval society. As such they seem to have been viewed as superfluous, as social climbers *par excellence*, since they did not fit into the three traditional classes. They were illegitimately encroaching on these classes, especially the nobility, whenever they attempted to become part of them. Furthermore, the economic interests of the lower classes were involved, for a non-noble who became ennobled no longer paid taxes. Thus, the envy and rancor felt by the *sots* toward the 'gens nouveaulx' is intense. A *sot* sums up their protests in *Tout le Monde*:

> Tout le Monde, a le faire court,
> Par Marchandise vient en biens
> Et a honneur.

Ll. 97–9: Everybody, to be brief, By means of commerce comes into wealth And honor.

> Par argent plus que par combatre
> Tout le Monde est faict gentillatre.

Ll. 138–9: By money, more than by combat, Everybody is made a little gentleman. (Cf. *Les Veaulx*, ll. 297–9.)

The attitudes of the *sots* toward the higher bourgeoisie are complex. The fools resent and perhaps envy the social mobility of the *gros bourgeois*; they resent his wealth and style of living, they distrust his methods of acquiring a lofty position. They see the bourgeoisie as having become corrupt at the top, of having lost its traditional values of economy and industry, of honoring display and 'conspicuous consumption' instead of practicality and good sense. A number of *sotties* preach this morality of prudence, which has since been called 'la morale petite bourgeoise': *Deulx Gallans et Sancté* and *Folle Bobance* are the two clearest statements of the values of hard work and thrift.

Above all, the suspicion runs through the *sotties* that the 'gens nouveaulx', or the *gros bourgeois*, act in unscrupulous ways. And the *sots* were probably not exaggerating. They lived at a time in which, according to Lucien Febvre, 'la politique et la morale apparaissaient en plein divorce'.[175] The history of the fifteenth and sixteenth centuries abounds in 'hommes nouveaulx', who, like Jacques Cœur, 'fondèrent leur prosperité sur la spéculation, le monopole, l'abus du crédit.... Il est évident que, dans la poursuite de la fortune, on ne s'embarrasse plus guère de la morale traditionnelle.'[176] The means by which one became rich – traffic in raw materials and grains,[177] the exploitation of mines, control of the wool trade and of navigation, and, above all, the buying, selling, and exploiting of public offices – all these means are viewed by the *sots* as profoundly devious and immoral. Furthermore, the wealthy bourgeois was believed to profit from the greatest man-made disaster to strike the lower classes: war. Monsieur Rien, in *Le Cry de la Bazoche*, points out that peace is abhorred by wealthy and powerful people, because they do not make any money from peace; war is preferable to peace 'A gens qui veulent s'advancer' (l. 489). (Wartime profiteering was a satiric subject long before George Bernard Shaw.)

If war was one of the principal ways to wealth, so was traffic in public offices. New offices were created whenever the government needed money, so that the total number of *charges* under Louis XI rose to the extraordinary figure of 64,000. The Etats Généraux of 1484 discussed the problem of those who buy offices wholesale, that is, in lots, and sell them retail. Public outcry against the widespread corruption resulted at times in investigatory commissions (parodied in *Les Sotz fourrez*) and in purges, such as the great purge of 1522. The results were meant to be superficial, however, since it was in the king's short-term financial interest to continue the sale of offices (in fact, the purges were designed to provide vacant offices which could be resold).[178] Therefore, the system of offices didn't change with the purges: only the office-holders changed.

Public offices were the easiest road to social advancement, but it was a rocky road, for the periodic purges ruined fortunes and sometimes led to the execution of the formerly fortunate. Public protest seems to have been satisfied by the periodic purges, although they were unaccompanied by reform. Thus, the trials of great and wealthy men, who were eventually unmasked and ruined, were a periodic public spectacle. The lower levels of society came to see the higher bourgeoisie not only as powerful, ambitious, and unscrupulous, but also as living precariously. The world – the new world they had tried to build for themselves – could come down on them (as it does in *Le Monde, Abuz*), and could crush them. The 'gens nouveaulx' of the *sotties* mirror this image of the bourgeois élite, for not only are they powerful, ambitious, and unscrupulous, but they live on the edge of disaster. *Pou d'Acquest* alludes to their precarious position:

> Tel cuydoit bien avoir credit
> En aulcun lieu, a tout gasté.
> Pour ce qui s'est par trop hasté
> De monter, il est cheu a val.

Ll. 120–3: So-and-so believed he had credit In a certain place; he has lost all. For having too much haste To rise, he has fallen low.

Les Esbahis pretend to be surprised by 'gens de court'

> Qui ont tant broué sur le gourt
> Et puis après les vis deffaire.

Ll. 154–6: Who have schemed so deviously And then afterwards we saw them undone.

According to *La Folie des Gorriers*, merchants come into positions of power 'Soubz le dangier d'estre decapité' (l. 406); in *Tout, Rien, et Chascun*, we are told that the great often go 'de Tout à Rien'.

Thus, the striking similarities between the popular view of wealthy and powerful men and the characterization of the 'gens nouveaulx' leads to the hypothesis that this satiric character was intended to represent the élite of the bourgeoisie. Seen in this light, the *sottie* becomes an expression of a class antagonism that existed in the fifteenth and sixteenth centuries, a conflict between two groups of the bourgeoisie. The *sottie* gives voice to the anger and anxiety of the lower classes in the face of the rapid and unruly rise of the higher bourgeoisie and the showy life and unscrupulous maneuvres that were attributed to it. As we have seen, class antagonism in the *sottie* takes the form of satiric allusions to certain powerful trouble-makers. It is also embodied, more dramatically, in certain evil characters, such as the 'gens nouveaulx', who make an allegorical journey leading to their downfall. The enactment of the Rise and Fall of the Higher Bourgeoisie is not allegorical, but also ritualistic, for the plays use ritual, the repetition of certain elements (costume, plot structure, language, characterization) in certain ways, for certain effects.[179] Consequently, the ritualized satire of the *sottie* can best be understood in terms of the class antagonisms, anxieties, and attitudes it was developed to express.

These attitudes are important not only for what they reveal about popular culture in the late medieval period, but also for their dramatic role in shaping the plays, both in terms of plot and characterization, and also in terms of costume (and clothing in general), and of language. In the following chapter these attitudes and how they are expressed, are looked at in more detail.

5

The theme of social hierarchy in the *sottie*

Women, important individuals, priests, and pope; knight, laborer, and *gros bourgeois*: the *sottie* makes specific charges against each. Underlying and structuring these accusations are certain attitudes toward social hierarchy, order and disorder, and the nature and causes of society's ills. Each individual, social class, or group is satirized because it fails to live up to an implicit ideal. (The attitudes expressed in the *sottie* are both prescriptive – concerned with a normative description of the ideal society – and diagnostic, for they suggest the causes of the ills of society.) The study of satire in the *sottie* can now be completed by a summary of those ideals which such satire reflects.

It has been seen, in the preceding chapter, that the most severe criticism is made of those who attempt to move from one social rank to another, or (what amounts to the same thing) who usurp the prerogatives and powers of another estate. This criticism is universal, it is made in regard to both commoner and clergy, king and *vilain*. Consequently, the *sots* appear to be profoundly non-egalitarian, for they believe in a necessary and beneficial social hierarchy. Of course they were people of their times in recognizing the leveling effect of death:

> Autant les povres que les riches
> Emporteront apres leur mort.

Les Menus Propos, ll. 363–4: The poor will carry away as much As the rich after their death.

Yet only one overt expression of egalitarian sentiment is made in all the plays, a line spoken by a Galant, in *Troys Galans et Monde*, who is trying to persuade Le Monde to surrender its wealth. In an attempt to fool the supposedly naïve Monde, the Galant claims that 'Nous sommes tous d'Eve et d'Adam' (l. 328). Le Monde is not convinced that this makes them equal. Neither were the *sots*.

The lesson of the *sotties* is rather the moral offered by *Folle Bobance*: '(Que) Chascun maintienne son estat' (l. 550). One must not try to *contrefaire* another estate, for one's 'nature' is defined by the social condition into which one is born. Only a fool (in the derogatory sense) tries to change his estate, and he will consequently suffer ridicule: 'Chascun le monstre au doyt (*doigt*)' (*Folle Bobance*, l. 384). So important is a stable society to the *sots* that they offer this prayer:

> Face Justice gouverner
> Chascun et garder ses estas.[1]

Ll. 372–3: Make Justice govern Everyman, and keep him in his Estate.

It is in the light of this conception of social hierarchy that the supposedly anti-authoritarian attitude of the *sots* must be re-interpreted. Some scholars have argued that the *sottie* is antagonistic to authority, whether ecclesiastical, military, scholastic, or judicial. Porter, for example, defines the primary desire of the *sots* as to 'accabler de reproches, avec un haut degré d'impunité d'ailleurs, leurs supérieurs'.[2] Bowen places this supposed anti-authoritarianism in a larger context, for she views it as 'un phénomène qui est peut-être particulièrement du moyen âge et qui est certainement très français'.[3] Above all, it is Mikhail Bakhtine who has developed most consistently the view that the *sottie*, as a form of carnival literature, enacted the 'abolition provisoire de tous les rapports hiérarchiques'.[4]

My study of the *sotties* has found that the plays do not question the validity or the necessity of a social hierarchy, through either their satire or their parody of such a hierarchy. They do oppose those members of society, in authority or not, who either misuse their estate for selfish gains, or attempt to usurp the role of another estate. Similarly, parody of the Church or of the monarchy does not advocate, *prima facie*, the abolition of those institutions. Parody is not necessarily destructive: children parody, animals parody, without intending the overthrow of what they laugh at.

The Catholic Church was parodied for centuries – frequently by its own members, and in a profoundly religious society. The parodic inversion of the Church, in the Fête des Fous, the parodic kings and popes of the *sottie*, were not necessarily meant as incitement to overthrow those rulers. If the *sots* indeed desired to abolish even temporarily 'tous les rapports hiérarchiques', as Bakhtine claims, they would presumably have created, theatrically, an egalitarian society. Instead, the *sottie*, far from being a non-authoritarian, non-structured, 'free' society, is a detailed reproduction of contemporary royal, aristocratic, and ecclesiastical organizations.[5]

The *sottie* reveals a belief in the necessity of social hierarchy, a belief that is fundamental to its conception of society – so fundamental that it expresses itself in many ways and on many levels. This belief leads the *sots* to distrust anyone who attempts to change society: the structure of society is given as eternal and immutable. Thus, the *sotties* are not 'reforming' in the sense of advocating social change. If the state of society is portrayed as bad, the *sots* nonetheless have little hope that man can improve it. Le Monde, pillaged in the past, will be so in the future:

> Ainsi, je suis de tous assaulx,
> Pillé des vieulx et des nouveaulx.

Les Gens nouveaulx, ll. 218–19: Thus I am assaulted on all sides, Pillaged by the old and the new.

Consequently, innovators are feared and condemned. The villains of the *sottie* are the 'new men' who try to change things: the *sots* of *Le Monde, Abuz* are condemned for attempting to build a new world:

> Maistre, en brief nous pretendons
> Muer ce Monde d'autre sorte.[6]

Ll. 375–6: Master, in brief we claim to change This world into another kind.

The world can only go 'de mal en pire' (a favorite phrase of the *sotties*, enacted allegorically in *Les Gens nouveaulx*). Huizinga has succinctly summarized this pessimism of the late Middle Ages:

Pour les hommes de ce temps, le monde semblait aussi bon ou aussi mauvais qu'il pouvait l'être....L'idée d'un effort conscient pour l'amélioration et la réforme des institutions politiques et sociales n'existait pas.... Même quand on crée une nouvelle forme sociale, on la considère d'abord comme le rétablissement de la bonne vieille loi, ou comme une réparation des abus.[7]

If the *sots* do not believe in a linear historical 'progress', they do posit a superhuman, cyclical fatality that they believe (or perhaps only hope) will sooner or later bring back peace and prosperity. The *sottie* frequently expresses a cyclical view of history:

> Ne savés vous pas
> Qu'après la pluye vient le beau temps?
> Tout viendra bien.

Mestier et Marchandise, ll. 34–6: Don't you know That after the rain comes the nice weather? All will turn out well.

> Le Temps a nous retournera,
> En la fin, je n'en doubte point.

Les Sotz triumphans, ll. 265–6: Time will come back to us, In the end, I have no doubt. (Cf. *Faulte d'Argent*, l. 8, and *Satyre*, ll. 1 and 11.)

But the Wheel of Fortune can be equally unfriendly:

> Voit-on pas, après ris et chantz,
> Muer joye en dueil et couroux?[8]

Faulte d'Argent, ll. 13–14: Don't we see, after laughter and song, Joy change into sadness and anger?

Happier times, if they come, will be given by God – like the millennium in Christian eschatology – independently of human will or action.[9]

The *sots* refer to that point on the cycle characterized by peace and prosperity by the vague, but for them emotionally potent, term, 'Bon Temps'. Like many of the desires (and anxieties) of the *sots*, this concept becomes embodied in an allegorical character, who appears on stage in four *sotties*: *Satyre*, *Faulte d'Argent*, *Le Jeu par Jehan Destrées*, and *Les Sotz qui remetent* – and is referred to in many more (see in particular *Le Cry de la Bazoche*, *Les Béguins*, *Les Maraux*, and *Les Croniqueurs*).[10] (All of these desires are particular manifestations of the *actant Objet*, as developed by A. J. Greimas, in *Sémantique structurale* and elsewhere.) Put most simply, Bon Temps in the *sottie* represents a joyful period that once existed, a long time ago, and which periodically returns, although briefly. There is in the *sottie* a distinct nostalgia for a

Golden Age, an ancient *paradis terrestre*: the Sobres Sotz, for example, hope that soon

> on veroyt le temps rigoureulx
> Revenir a son premyer estre.[11]

Les Sobres Sots, ll. 31–2: we would see the unfavorable time Return to its first state.

This ancient period of peace and joy is a kind of utopia, and as such constitutes the opposite of the satirical world of the *sottie*, for satire presents the defects and abuses of a real world, while in utopia the joys and virtues of an ideal world are imagined.[12] The two modes, utopia and satire, are linked in the saturnalian festival, of which the Fête des Fous was a variety.

Bon Temps is clearly the friend of the lower classes. Evidently seeing themselves not simply as fools but as representatives of the people, the *sots* feel that Bon Temps has no business living anywhere but with them. The character Bon Temps promises to stay with Peuple Francoys (*Satyre*) or to return shortly to the people (*Faulte d'Argent*). Consequently, the joys that Bon Temps offers are those generally considered to be popular pleasures: free-flowing wine,[13] abundant food (with white bread: 'Dehors pain bis!': *Folle Bobance*, l. 253), dancing and singing, clean clothes, and a soft bed. The rather simple, physical pleasures attributed to the 'innocent' are the joys of which the *sots* dream.[14] In this respect, *folie* and joyous living are connected: Mère Folie is the widow of Bon Temps in *Les Béguins*.

'Bon temps avrons', exult the *sots* of *Folle Bobance*: fine perfumed sheets (over fine perfumed women); golden rings set with pearls and rubies; and especially *banquets* and *boissons*. Yet in the same play these joys, that so resemble those generally attributed to Bon Temps, are condemned as wasteful, even sinful. They are condemned, and at such length – 225 lines of details – that one suspects that the *sots* were vicariously enjoying those pleasures while detailing them: such energy in describing forbidden joys suggests an ambivalent attitude toward the pleasures of Bon Temps. The problem for the *sots* was that such pleasures were both part of their conception of happiness and also morally condemned. The ambivalence expressed toward pleasure is a function not only of the fact that those pleasures are frivolous and wasteful (from the *petit bourgeois* point of view), but also of the fact that they were earthly, not spiritual, pleasures and as such were condemned by the Church. To the extent that some *sots* look for their reward on earth, not in an after-life, their attitude exemplifies Renaissance values.

The plays point out that the 'enemies' of Bon Temps are also the 'enemies' of the people. Avarice is seen as a formidable deterrent to Bon Temps and to the pleasures that money buys; war is another foe (e.g., *Faulte d'Argent*, ll. 182–3; *Satyre*, ll. 262–3; and *Tout le Monde*, l. 25). A further obstacle to good times is governmental repression of the *compagnies joyeuses* (see *Les Béguins*, ll. 101–2). Finally, the 'gens nouveaulx' who were seen as the cause of popular miseries are, consequently, also seen as the enemies of Bon Temps: in *Faulte d'Argent*, the *sots* speak of the 'privez loups' (ll. 15–18) and of the 'broulleurs' (ll. 214–17) as those who prevent the Gallans from rejoining Bon Temps.

Although the type of utopia called Bon Temps is depicted in the *sottie* in only a vague and rudimentary manner, yet this concept reveals a connection with major satiric themes of the *sottie*. It is linked to the question of progress and to the view of history as cyclical; it reflects the themes of war, money, and the threat of the 'gens nouveaulx'. In addition, it serves as an implicit criticism of society as it then existed, for Bon Temps – order, peace, prosperity – was everything that society was not. If we now examine the underlying cause (according to the *sots*) for the absence of Bon Temps, we find again the longing for a necessary and stable social hierarchy.

The theme of most of the *sotties* is, in one form or another, *tromperie*: it underlies the satire of various *états* and *métiers*; it is an integral part of the conception of the *sot*; it expresses itself in certain *jeux de scène* (for example, in *Trote Menu*, in *Les Coquins*, and in *Les Esveilleurs*) and, as we shall see, in certain uses of costume and language.[15] Moreover, the importance of the idea of *tromperie* in the *sottie* is revealed in the vocabulary of the plays. A proliferation of terms conveys that idea: *Le Jeu du Prince des Sotz*, for example, offers 13 different ways to say *trompeur*, *tromper*, or *tromperie*: 'fins varlez', 'jouer de passe passe', 'brasser un faulx bruvaige', 'faillir a son sens', 'jouer de fins tours', 'piper', 'faire un tas de mynes', 'rompre la foi promise', 'aller oblique sentier' (or 'n'aller pas la droicte voye'), 'la falace', 'propose divers', and 'fixion'. Other plays give 'gabbeur', 'rapporteur', 'musart', and a series of words made up of 'bailler' plus object, all of which signify *tromper*.[16] This alone indicates how important is the theme of *tromperie* for an understanding of the *sottie*. Ultimately it becomes the key to the plays' themes of class conflict and of threat to the social hierarchy.

The *sots* live in a confused world; they have difficulty knowing anything with certainty. This bewilderment is illustrated, in *Les Esbahis*, by a series of questions about *trompeurs*, all of which begin with 'Que scavez-vous si...' (ll. 105–26). The discrepancy between what people seem to be, or ought to be, and what they really are, is expressed in *Le Jeu du Prince des Sotz* in this way:

> Je voy les plus grans empeschez
> Et les autres se sont cachez:
> Dieu vueille que tout vienne a bien.
> Chascun n'a pas ce qui est sien;
> D'affaires d'aultruy on se mesle.

Ll. 301–5: I see the greatest people blocked, And the others have hidden themselves: May – God willing – everything work out well. Everyman does not have what is his; People are interfering in the affairs of others.

The idea of social confusion is reiterated again and again in *Le Monde, Abuz*, l. 584: 'C'est le fons dont [le Monde Nouveau] sera fundé.' ('It's the basis on which the New World will be founded'; see ll. 585–8, 598–9, 600–1, *et passim*.)

The essential *tromperie*, the deception which most concerns the *sots*, is any attempt to undermine the stable social structure which they desire. If the only valid social arrangement is hierarchical and unchanging, then all who rise socially must do so illegitimately – by means of *tromperie*. The *sots* express a social reality by their use of the term *tromperie*, for the plays were written in a time of increasing social mobility, a period when a growing capitalism was making it possible to acquire great wealth and thereby to move up the social scale without concern for moral principles. Coming from and speaking for that level of society which did not share the opportunities offered by the growth of capitalism and industry, the *sots* condemn the new social order as one founded on *tromperie*, which they see as the cause for the disintegration of society's traditional framework.

This explains in part the strange 'advice' that several *sotties* offer on how to succeed in the world, which advice must be ironic, for when followed, as in *La Folie des Gorriers*, it leads, treacherously, to the ruin of the proselytes. The *sots* of that play point out that

> Brief, il nous fault estre gorriers
> Se nous voulons plus hault monter.

Ll. 45–6: In brief, we must be *gorriers* [dandies, fops], If we want to rise higher.

They believe that they will rise in society by appearing to be rich, by throwing around borrowed money (which will never be repaid), in other words by the methods of 'le temps qui court' (*Le Roy des Sotz*, l. 354; see also *Chascun, Plusieurs*, ll. 232–47; and *La Croix Faubin*, ll. 311ff.). This is a commentary on the values and methods of the *nouveaux riches* of the period and their life-style, at least insofar as the popular audience of the *sottie* conceived of them.

This ironic[17] advice given by several *sotties* reflects one type of *tromperie*, the deception found in public behavior, in how an individual acts in society. At this level, the actions of the *sot trompeur* are directed at deceiving others. The idea that deception is the route to wealth and power – to changing one's 'estat' – begins with one of the earliest *sotties, Mestier et Marchandise,* and finds its fullest development in *La Folie des Gorriers* (see above, p. 209): Dame Folie is in effect telling the *sots* not to act like fools, but rather like the great men of their times (ll. 472–6).[18] *Mestier et Marchandise* summarizes this conflict of values:

> Cuydes vous sçavoir les valleurs
> Du temps qui court? Pour et afin
> De le vous dire, qui n'est fin,
> Caut et inventif, bref et court,
> Y ne scayt riens du temps qui court.

Ll. 149–53: Do you think you know the values Of the present day? I'll tell You directly: whoever is not shrewd And deceitful, clever and quick, Doesn't know anything of the present day. (See also *Les Sotz triumphans*, ll. 239ff. and 258.)

The *sots* see themselves as awakening a sleeping world to this danger posed by the 'gens nouveaulx' (see *Le Monde, Abuz*, ll. 108 and 343). Their task is difficult, for the number of *trompeurs*, of 'gens nouveaulx', can never be known – their very method is to hide their method. Consequently, the *sots* suspect the existence of secret powers and underhanded dealings among governmental leaders. *Tout le Monde*, which speaks of 'lettres closes' and of 'maincte grand finesse' committed by 'puissances cachées', is one of the most emphatic statements of this paranoid view of power.

This first type of dissimulation occurs in the public sphere; but dissimulation runs so deep, according to the *sots*, that it is found also on the private level of existence. The *sot trompeur* becomes deceptive not only in his dealings with others, but in his very nature, so that one never knows the reality of another person. In the end the *sot trompeur* loses touch with his own identity (see below, p. 153). Often the distinction between pretense and reality is blurred. *Les Maraux*, for example, presents two *misérables* who believe themselves rich and happy, or at least on the verge of so being; they are prisoners who believe in their imminent freedom; they are *soldats cassés* who see themselves as heroes; cowards who brag about prowesses which the audience would recognize as that popular scourge, pillaging: they live in illusion to the point of forgetting their poverty and imprisonment. A similar conflict of appearance and reality is found in the character Triboullet, in *Le Roy des Sotz*, a man who believes himself to be one of the 'gens de bien', until he is shown to be a 'sot vilain pugnès', 'tueur de poux', and simply *fou*.

The *sots* of *Folle Bobance* not only act deceptively (by spending money they do not have), but more importantly they try to appear to be what they are not; they imitate (*contrefaire*) great lords, in the hope that this facade will bring them 'les grans honneurs' (ll. 129–31 and 285–6). But they themselves are so taken by appearances that they are easily fooled by Dame Folie. (A similar role is played by Folie in *La Folie des Gorriers*. Although her name – her true nature – is written on her sleeve, the *sots* cannot read.) *Les Povres Deables* summarizes, in a series of proverbs, this conflict between reality and appearance:

> Tel semble estre bonne personne
> Qui est un tres mauvais pinard.
> Tel est fin et qui mot ne sonne
> Qui est un tres rusé regnard.

Ll. 341–4: So-and-so seems to be a good person But is a very bad scoundrel; So-and-so seems astute and close-mouthed, But is a very crafty fox.

Thus, as the fundamental theme of the *sottie* is that of a fixed social hierarchy, so the desire to change one's estate is the fundamental type of *tromperie*. Ultimately, the fundamental type of *folie* in the *sottie* is that from which the 'gens nouveaulx' suffer: a madness that drives them to deceive others in a frantic attempt to rise socially. Two means are favoured by these *trompeurs* in their attempts to upset society's structure: money and clothes. By the late Middle Ages both have become important tools of the *parvenus* – and, similarly, of the *gens nouveaux* of the *sottie*. Consequently, the theme of social structure molds the conception of both money and clothes, as they are expressed in the *sottie*.

In the *sottie* money takes on several of the characteristics of a taboo object.[19] First, it is the object of ambivalent feelings. It reveals a double meaning, which is essential to any taboo object, for 'taboo' means both sacred and forbidden, unclean; both what is most desired and what is most repulsive.[20] Second, money is believed to have a mysterious power to corrupt those who come into contact with it. This corruption works like an infection, for it spreads from the original possessor to those whom he in turn wishes to corrupt.

The desire for money is expressed, in the *sottie*, more indirectly than is the condemnation of it. In two ways the *sots* indicate their valuation of money: they lament their own poverty (half of the references to money in *Les Menus Propos* refer to the poverty of the *sots*); and they desire the objects and pleasures that money buys (see pp. 142–3, above). Yet the condemnation of money and of those who have it is a recurring theme of the *sottie*. In this respect, the plays participate in a venerable medieval satiric tradition, for love of money is condemned throughout the medieval period, both in Latin and in the vernacular.[21] In the *sottie*, however, it is not so much love of money that is condemned, as the social effects of money. In ten plays,[22] these social effects are one of the dominant themes. The idea that the basis of social interaction is economic is expressed clearly in *Les Brus* and *Mestier et Marchandise*: 'Car vous congnoises par expres / Que l'argent faict partout la voye' (*Mestier et Marchandise*, ll. 318–19: 'For you know clearly / That money opens every door').[23] Everything has a price, anyone can be bought – prostitutes of course (*Les Brus*), but also government officers (*La Mère de Ville*, l. 265). *Tout le Monde* is one of the most outspoken expressions of the theme of the corrupting power of money: 'Car aujourd'uy tout se marchande' (l. 101), the *sots* point out: nobility can be bought, Church offices are for sale. The Church uses money to harm both strong and weak (l. 206). The phrase 'par argent' recurs hypnotically throughout the play.

Because money is essential to social mobility, it is linked in the minds of the *sots* with *tromperie*. *Troys Pelerins et Malice* (ll. 246–7) connects money with those 'mangeurs de lune' who create disorder in government and society as a whole: 'argent / Les maintient en leur entregent' (the social position they have achieved). *Le Cry de la Bazoche* is explicit in describing the means by which these *trompeurs* maintain their lofty social status: the king's finance ministers, for example, lend their master's money at interest, for private gain (see ll. 367–71; ll. 357–82 are a further discussion of various unethical ways to grow rich). Wealth is invariably associated, in the minds of the *sots*, with 'tricherye'. With a greater sense of drama, Gringore has his *sots* stop talking about the connection between *tromperie* and money in order to act it out. From the opening lines of *Le Jeu du Prince des Sotz*, the *sots* are discussing the two principal ways to grow powerful: money and secret maneuvers. These tactics are then put into action by Mère Saincte Eglise and her two counselors, Sotte Occasion (who tries to buy the support of the *sots*), and Sotte Fiance (who tries to deceive them with words). Mère Sotte herself does not hesitate to use money to 'mutiner princes, prelatz' (l. 370). There is no mistaking the connection between social ambition, money, and deception.

In these ways the *sotties* reveal a distinct malaise in the face of the growing wealth of increasingly industrialized and capitalist society. Several factors contributed to this attitude. Since the *sots* most commonly represented the lower classes, who, as has been seen, were not participating in the economic prosperity enjoyed by the higher bourgeoisie, it is likely that their fear of money was mixed with envy. Their fear was also tied to conservative social values, to a desire to preserve an older, unchanging social structure. Such attempts at historical 'social psychology' must remain speculative, however, for all the *sottie* says clearly is that money is intimately bound up with falsehood, so that it undermines the stable social structure which the *sottie* accepts as the valid one.

The dandies of *La Folie des Gorriers* are told they should borrow without repaying; they should deny having borrowed and return *bourdes* for their creditor's money – all this in order to procure costly clothes. The theme of clothes in the *sottie* ultimately reveals, as does the theme of money, an ambivalent attitude on the part of the *sots*: clothing was viewed both favorably, as a means of delineating the various social strata, and unfavorably, as liable to become a further means of *tromperie*. Consequently, clothing in general and costumes in particular express once again the two fundamental themes discussed above: the desirability of a stable social hierarchy, and the threat to such a hierarchy posed by social climbers, by *trompeurs*.

In the late medieval and Renaissance period sumptuary laws were enacted on the principle that clothing was an effective means of social demarcation: the way an individual dressed indicated his social level. By regulating the dress of various levels of society, these laws were meant to draw a line between the diverse elements of the Third Estate, and furthermore to separate these elements from the nobility. An example of the ferocity of these laws is a parliamentary *arrêt* of October 20, 1559, which forbids artisans to wear 'chausses chiquetées et bouffantes de taffetas' – on pain of hanging or strangulation.[24] Similarly, costume is used iconographically in the *sottie*, as a symbolic representation of a character's place in the social hierarchy. Conversely, one's costume could be used to show not what one is, in terms of estate, but what one pretends to be. Clothes are useful in maintaining social distinctions; yet clothes are also used as a potent and prevalent means of pretense, thereby undermining those very distinctions: clothes both reveal and deceive.

In addition to this widespread conception of the social role of clothing, the iconographic use of clothes in the *sottie* is tied to the nature of theatrical costume. The costume of the fool made his role, or at least one level of it, immediately known to the audience – its iconographic function, or function as 'sign', was clear. One play, *Le Roy des Sotz*, indicates that its *sots* wore objects added to the basic fool's dress in order to symbolize an outstanding characteristic of that person (Coquibus, for example, wears a basket on his back in which there are rats: he is 'rapporteur'). Similarly, in *La Folie des Gorriers*, Folie points out that her 'habit' indicates who she is (ll. 163–5). But costume is more commonly used in the *sottie* to suggest the outstanding traits or nature of a group than of an individual. In *Les Sotz qui remetent en point Bon Temps*, Tout is dressed in rags to indicate the pitiful state of the people. Bon Temps is similarly dressed, for he also represents the misery of much of the nation: the expression 'remettre en point' of the full title refers to the symbolic act of giving Bon Temps new clothes, thereby restoring the nation to a period of joy. The theme of *Mestier et Marchandise*, that of the instability of the period, is also symbolized by the various costumes worn by Le Temps. The play could in effect be subtitled 'Le Jeu des costumes', for Le Temps wears five different ones, and Les Gens, two: a costume of 'diverses couleurs' is meant to indicate national instability; red clothes symbolize war; armor means civil strife; the trappings of a 'galant' represent the return of good times (ll. 399ff.).[25]

In addition to representing the state of society as a whole through the costumes of Bon Temps and Tout, the *sottie* frequently indicates a smaller social grouping, a class or profession, by means of costume. For example, Tout le Monde, in the play of that name, indicates that he represents all estates by wearing a costume composed of elements symbolic of each (see ll. 81–2).[26] In *Le Jeu du Prince des Sotz*, the prince verbalizes what the costume of Mère Sotte conveys visually:

> Pour en parler reallement,
> D'Eglise porte vestement,
> Je veuil bien que chascun le notte.

Ll. 607–9: To speak truthfully, Of the Church she wears the habit, I want everyone to note that.

In the *sotties*, the person becomes what his costume indicates about him – one is what one wears. Thus, if Margot 'estoit attournee, / On l'appelleroit daimoiselle' (*Les Menus Propos*, ll. 149–50). Professions as well as estates are symbolized by a particular type of clothing or part of a costume: lawyers, for instance, are often referred to by their fur hats (*Les Menus Propos*, ll. 349–50; and *La Folie des Gorriers*, l. 112).

This is the first function of dress in the *sottie*: to indicate, in a schematic, traditional way, the estate, profession, or characteristics of a person. Socially it is an ordering function, for dress becomes a means of assigning each person to his place. This place, moreover, is the most important aspect of an individual; a character is defined by the position in society that he occupies. Appearance and identity (essence) seem to be related in the iconographic function of dress.

The use of dress to represent one's place in the social hierarchy can be abused, however, for when a person tries to change his social status by imitating the dress of another class, clothing then constitutes a means of *tromperie*. In the remark about the Church vestment of Mère Sainte Eglise quoted above, the prince is unaware as yet that Mère Sotte has usurped that costume. In social climbing, Folle Bobance tells us, appearance is everything:

> Se ung homme est remply de science
> Et n'est gourrierement vestu,
> De tout le monde c'est l'usance,
> Ne sera prisé ung festu.
> . . .
> Estre gorrier, gentil et frisque
> Tout le monde luy faict honneur.

Ll. 161–4 and 177–8: If a man is very knowledgeable And not foppishly dressed, It's the custom of everybody, That he will not be valued as much as a piece of straw.... If he is foppish, agreeable and gallant, Everybody honors him. (See also *Pou d'Acquest*, l. 24.)

Consequently, clothes are crucial for social climbing.[27] This explains the determination of the 'gorriers' to procure, by any means, the finery that will give them the appearance of nobility and wealth. 'Or estez vous gens d'apparence', Folie remarks ironically (*La Folie des Gorriers*, l. 247), when she sees the 'gorriers' decked out, so conveying the idea of finery as falseness. (The term 'gorrier' was generally given to those who dressed in such finery, but it could also refer to courtiers.) And with new clothes comes a new morality (or rather immorality):

> Et, au lieu de toutes vertuz,
> Soyez mesdisans et flatteurs.

La Folie des Gorriers, ll. 271–2: And instead of all the virtues, Be back-biters and flatterers.

Thus, the connection between clothes, social status, and *tromperie* is clear in the *sottie*.[28]

Given this view of clothes as a means of deception, it is not surprising that the use of disguises is a favorite dramatic technique in the *sottie* (see pp. 48–9, above). A number of plays revolve around the use of disguises: one or more *sots* enter wearing a costume representing a particular estate (usually the nobility or the Church); they are forced to remove that costume, revealing the costume of the *sot* underneath. Although this use of disguise has been interpreted as a satiric attack on the members of the clergy or the nobility, in effect it is neither the nobility nor the clergy *per se* who are satirized, but those who impersonate them. *Troys Pelerins et Malice* states quite explicitly this condemnation of disguise:

> Il est de trop lache courage
> Qui se contrefaict et desguise.

Ll. 58–9: He is very cowardly Who changes his appearance and disguises himself.

A similar condemnation of those who are 'en leurs habitz desguisez' is found in *Les Premiers* (l. 311). It is through the dramatic technique of removing the disguise to reveal the *sot* beneath that the *sottie* satirizes those who use clothes to deceive others.

Ultimately, this ambivalence of clothing is a reflection of the conflict between illusion and reality which exists at all levels in the *sottie*. In at least one instance the demarcation between reality and illusion breaks down and for a short time the *sots* become confused as to where reality begins and illusion ends. Significantly, this breakdown is set off by a change of clothes. In *La Folie des Gorriers*, two *sots* identify so completely with what they wear that when they don new clothes their perceptions of their own identities fluctuate and break down, in a sort of comical identity crisis. A few lines will give an idea of the scene:

> Le Second.   Plus regarde, et moins me congnoys;
>   Je ne suis plus moy, se me semble.
> Le Premier.   Je ne sçay a qui je ressemble;
>   Je ne suis point.
> Le Second.   Dea! Qui peust ce estre?
> Le Premier.   Je ne suis ne varlet ne maistre,
>   Et ne sçay se je suis ou non...
>   Point ne suis moy certainement.
> Le Second.   Mais qu'en ditz tu, par ton serment?
>   Suis je?
> Le Premier.   Tu es. Et moy? Non, rien...
> Le Second.   Je suis moins que toy la moitié...
> Le Premier.   Dea! Tu es toy ny plus ny moins;
>   Mais moy, c'est aultre personnaige (ll. 425–65).

In this *sottie*, clothes are so vital to a person's self-image that if the exterior changes, the underlying identity is also modified. The disintegration of society resulting from a confusion between exterior and interior, between appearance and reality, is mirrored in the break-down of the identities of the two *sots*. The *sottie*, developing in a time of great social flux, reflects that situation through the theme of clothes; the plays express both a view of society in a state of change, and a fear of that change.

Instability, change – even the very idea of movement – all are defined as *folie*. The character Folie describes herself as 'Detestant les choses estables' (*La Folie des Gorriers*, l. 585), as being 'A tous vens toujours variable' (Sotte Folle in *Le Monde, Abuz*, l. 560; cf. *Mestier et Marchandise*, ll. 138–40). *L'Astrologue* makes it clear that the constituent parts of society ('les éléments') do not cause wars and catastrophes; rather it is their 'mouvements' (changes) that are at fault. Chascun expresses the feelings of all the *sots* when he exclaims: 'Au deable le mouvement!' (*L'Astrologue*,

l. 277, *et passim*). For movement and change are for the *sots* synonyms of disorder, which they adamantly reject. The pilgrims, who are popular spokesmen in *Troys Pelerins et Malice*, verbalize this view of disorder: 'Nous ne voulons poinct de Desordre' (l. 222). What the world needs, conversely, is order. This is the advice given to an ailing Monde by the doctor who has just examined its urine:

> Ainçois pense aux abusions
> Qui se font tous les jours chez toy.
> Mects y ordre selon la loy,
> Car je prens bien dessus ma vie
> Que tu n'as autre maladie.

Le Monde, ll. 268–72: Therefore think of the abuses   Which are done every day in the world.   Put order in your house, according to the law,   For I swear on my life   That you have no other malady.

'Mects y ordre': this prescription is followed to the letter by *Troys Galans et Monde*, in which Ordre personified rushes in when he sees 'd'aulcuns folyer, / Ou d'aultres regiber ou mordre' (ll. 342–3: 'some act foolishly, / Or others kick or bite'). (Similarly, Sancté scolds the *sots* in *Deulx Gallans et Sancté* for their disorderly behavior: 'Vous ne tenés nulle ordonnance', l. 176.) If Ordre were always with the world, he himself tells us, 'Il n'aroyt soulcy ne ennuy' (l. 350).

Thus, the concern for preserving a structured society is an expression of a larger concern with order and disorder. Economic change and its accompanying social mobility, ideological change and the break-up of traditional values concerning social structure – these two types of change in the late medieval period are reflected in the all-pervasive theme of the *sottie*, that of order and disorder.

The theme of order and disorder runs through the conception that the *sottie* offers of money, of clothes, and of *tromperie*; it also underlies certain uses of language in the plays. The subject of language in the *sottie* would require more pages than have already been written, so I will restrict my discussion to some of the ways that language in the *sottie* expresses fundamental attitudes toward change and disorder, toward illusion and reality.[29]

The *sots* evidently see language as having a relation to the 'real world', for they frequently attempt to verbalize their experience of reality when they want to 'raconter les nouvelles'. Their thirst for news is great:

> Et je te supply par amours,
> Dy quelque chose de nouveau![30]

Le Prince des Sots, ll. 184–5: And I beg you by your love, Tell me something new!

An entire play, *Les Esbahis*, is structured on the exchange of news; the *propos décousus* also frequently take this form. The *sots* wish to 'raconter le monde' when they exchange news, to put into words what they have seen and experienced.[31] But the language of the *sots* shows not only a desire to reproduce their experience *verbatim*, as it were, but also to give it a semblance of order, of structure. Enumeration and repetition are two of the principal ways used to make words appear to be predetermined and therefore more or less predictable and ordered.[32] In enumerating all the constituent parts of some category – kinds of fools (in *Les Sobres Sots*), for example, or kinds of threads (in *Le Pelerinage*) – a *sot* is attempting to 'capture' or 'exhaust' a subject, to name all its possible manifestations, so that no new ones can appear.

Similarly, the repetition of a word or line structures a passage: with each repetition the words seem less spontaneous, more inevitable. Refrains, which occur frequently in many *sotties*, are examples of the structuring use of repetition. As Garapon points out (*Fantaisie*, p. 71), 'la répétition d'un même refrain entraîne inévitablement, chez le spectateur, l'idée d'une schématisation': variety and detail are suppressed, in favor of the reiteration of one idea. Thus, the repetition of the line 'Y pleust a Blays [*Bloys*], le Temps est rouge', in *Mestier et Marchandise*, structures the discussion about the nobles in revolt against Charles VII; each repetition increases the force of the line and makes the revolt seem imminent.

Given the preoccupation of the *sottie* with order and structure, it is not surprising that repetition is the most common use of language in the plays (according to Garapon's chart; *Fantaisie*, p. 102). Garapon noted twice as many examples of repetition in the *sottie* as the three other types of 'verbal fantasy' that he describes (jargon, *propos sans suite*, and enumeration).[33] Moreover, he found that repetition is much more prevalent in the *sottie* than in the other comic dramatic genres. In particular, the *sotties* abound in the form of repetition called refrains. In *Les Gens nouveaulx*, for example, the identity of the *trompeurs* is established through two refrains repeated no fewer than ten times: 'Somme, nous sommes gens nouveaulx', and 'Ainsi serons nous gens nouveaulx.' In addition to scattered lines, another form of refrain appears in the rondeau, the most common poetic *forme fixe* of the *sottie*. (In the eight lines of a rondeau, the fourth line is a repetition of the first, and the first two lines become the last two.) *Les Esveilleurs* offers no fewer than 10 rondeaux in its 137 lines. It is significant that the very plays that deal with the threatening 'gens nouveaulx' are those that offer a great number of refrains and rondeaux – no fewer than one-fourth of the lines in *Mestier et Marchandise* are rondeaux.

Another form of repetition common in the *sottie* is a series of words formed on the same root word (usually called *annominatio* in medieval rhetoric),[34] as in this example from *Les Coppieurs*:

> Pour larder lard en larderie
> Tant qu'en lardant le lardé rie,
> Je larde lardons bien lardez (ll. 32–4).[35]

In addition to expressing the pleasure of verbosity, this comic procedure is yet another method of using language to structure a passage. The various derivatives become echoes of an underlying unity, producing an almost monotonous predictability. It is worth noting that the majority of the passages cited in note 35, above, deal with words expressing deception or unpredictability ('larder' and 'corner' are synonyms for *tromper*, and the *sot* or *fol* was an unpredictable, illogical being), as though fluctuating phenomena could be fixed by means of the repetition of a common element.

Yet another use of language as a structuring device is the proverb. The *sots* frequently express their thoughts by means of proverbs, a procedure that varies from an isolated dictum to the bout of proverb-speaking that closes *Les Cris de Paris*. The proverb is a way of summarizing experience, of drawing a lesson, at least implicitly. Commonly, the fools' proverbs have to do with their two most unhappy experiences, poverty and deception. For example, the *sots* of *Les Gens nouveaulx* sum up the periods of good times and hard with the proverb 'Car apres la nuyt vient le jour' (l. 32). The machinations of powerful people are exposed in the proverbs that *Pou d'Acquest* offers, such as:

> Tel cuide souvent menasser
> Qui est frappé de son cousteau.

Ll. 74–5: Often a man who thinks to threaten Is struck with his own knife.

These proverbs attempt to simplify and to summarize the flux of changing, varied experiences.

Proverbs are a type of metaphorical image (the proverb quoted above presupposes an immediately apparent similarity between night and hard times, for example). As such they lend themselves to allegory: the *sots* make proverbs the basis of allegory by taking literally what was meant figuratively (they might plunge the stage into darkness, if they could, to symbolize the advent of hard times). In *Les Gens nouveaulx*, to take an example from the plays, the proverbial expression 'aller de mal en pire' is reified: 'Mal' and 'Pire' become places to which Le Monde is forced to go. *Troys Galans et Monde* is built on three such allegories, for three metaphors are taken literally and acted out. Other examples are to be found in *Les Esveilleurs*, *Les Sotz qui corrigent*, *Mestier et Marchandise*, and *Pou d'Acquest*.

Bowen has described this process as 'un jeu verbal–physique',[36] since it combines both words and actions. But the process is also an attempt to contain experience in the limited, fixed form of a proverb. When in addition this proverb is acted out, the underlying idea becomes even more fixed: the various unfortunate events of life are first summarized simply as 'mal'; this idea is then made concrete through reification in a place named Mal. Thus proverbs illustrate the tendency, observed in several kinds of language in the *sottie*, to use words in order to delimit and fix the phenomena of experience.

The various kinds of enumeration and repetition and the use of proverbs in the *sottie* take on new meaning if viewed in the light of the fundamental theme of the plays, that of order and disorder. These uses of language are less an example of 'gratuité fantaisiste', in Garapon's words (*Fantaisie*, p. 98), than an expression of an ordering need.

What most scholars refer to as the 'verbal fantasy' of the *sottie* – puns, absurd images, disconnected ideas – turns out to be not an original, creative use of language, but a traditional one. Even medieval 'fantasy' was not the creation of an individual, but was collective and traditional. An illustration of this process is to be found in the strange images that occur in some plays and which would seem to be the most likely instances of 'verbal fantasy' in the *sottie*. They are found notably in *Les Menus Propos* (and its offshoot, *Estourdi*), and to some extent in *L'Astrologue*, *Les Rapporteurs*, and *Les Gens nouveaulx*. These images are generally of two types. The first is a form of absurdity related to the rhetorical technique of the 'world upside-down',[37] which dates from antiquity. It consists simply of having things do the opposite of what they normally do: lambs run after wolves (*Les Menus Propos*, ll. 127–8); birds fly without wings (*Les Gens nouveaulx*, l. 41).

This technique becomes satirical in intent when someone is indirectly criticized by having his character or behavior described as opposite to what it really is. In *Les Rapporteurs*, for example, it is reported that 'Moynes ne parlent plus aux dames' (l. 179), and that 'Seigneurs ne seront plus gouteux' (l. 224). Some images combine both the absurd and the satiric, as in the discussion in *L'Astrologue* of fish that are born from the earth rather than from the sea – a pun on 'maquereau' (mackerel or pimp) is the link between the absurd, inverted image and the satiric gibe. Both types of images, the absurd and the satiric, occur in *Les Gens nouveaulx*. Les Gens make outrageous promises to change the world, in order to prove that they are indeed 'gens nouveaulx'. They will work miracles: lawyers will no longer be grasping, nor 'gens d'armes' cowardly, nor monks lecherous. Such language is intentionally and satirically divorced from reality; it is the language of the illusory promises of politicians of all times.

Far from reveling in the pleasure of fantastic images, however, the *sots* sometimes see them as another method of deception.

That is, when they come from the mouths of *trompeurs*. Like money and clothes, words can become a weapon of the evildoers. In *La Folie des Gorriers* 'dissimulleurs' are condemned for hiding their thoughts 'soubz faincte loquence' (l. 99); the same charge could be made of Sotte Fiance, in Gringore's *sottie*; and the most extreme example of gibberish as a screen for one's thoughts is the language of Les Gens, in *Mestier et Marchandise*.

The suspicion that unscrupulous people are subverting the desired ordering use of language is summarized in the theme of infidelity to one's word. Breaking one's word symbolizes the potential unreliability of language; and this theme runs like a leitmotiv through many of the plays. *Les Coquins*, for example, is structured on the game of whether or not the *sots* can keep their word: does one's word mean anything anymore? In *L'Astrologue* an ounce of *foi* (in this case faithfulness to one's word) is included in the medicine that Chascun needs.

As disorder is seen as affecting social structure and traditional beliefs, as clothes and money are used more and more often to subvert ordered society, so language too ultimately suffers from the inroads of disorder. Words, in the mouths of the 'gens nouveaulx', can become a means to hide reality, rather than a means to order fluctuating experience. Thus, in its view of language, as in that of money and clothes, the *sottie* reveals the same fundamental concerns with fixity and change, with order and disorder, with appearance and reality. One final question now remains to be asked concerning the *sottie*: why did these attitudes, and their ambivalence, find a useful vehicle for expression in Dame Folie and her family of *fous*?

6

The importance of folly in the *sottie*

Dieu gard tous bons sotz assoctez
Qui soctie veullent nourir.

La Feste des Roys, ll. 1–2

Me dis tu que dame Folie
Est morte? Ma foy, tu as menty;
Jamais si grande ne la vy,
Ne si puissante comme elle est.

Les Sotz nouveaulx, ll. 146–9

The idea of *folie* fascinated the late Middle Ages: so important had the concept become that the Church 'promoted' Folie from her minor place as one of the 12 qualities that make up the human soul, to first place among the chorus of human weaknesses.[1] As we have seen, paralleling this development in medieval thought is the increased importance of the *fou* or *sot* in the theater. The *sot* had become more and more useful as a dramatic device for acting out certain social conflicts. Therefore, a study of satire in the *sottie* and of the attitudes that underlay it must include a consideration of the nature and place of *folie* in those plays.

One reason for the popularity of Folie and her troupe of fools is suggested by the characteristics attributed to them. The most complete description of Folie is given by the lady herself, in a type of *curriculum vitae* in *La Folie des Gorriers* (see in particular ll. 88–157 and 563–608): she details where she was born, and whom she frequents; her age, and her exploits. She does not hide her negative side, for she is 'Manteresse par flacterie', 'Toute plaine d'abusion', and she detests anything stable. Above all, she is eternal and universal. Yet this is not all there is to Folie; she is not simply arrogant, malicious, and deceiving (as Swain describes her in *Fools and Folly*, p. 108). She also reveals to the audience the truth about the 'gorriers' (in *La Folie des Gorriers*); and she is frequently *justicière* (Mère Sotte in many *sotties* plays a role similar to La Justice in *Les Esbahis*). In the end, she simply gives people what they deserve.

The character of the *fou* in the *sottie* is similarly complex.[2] He too is seen as lacking in common sense, yet he is also a truth-speaker. The *sot* is a striking example of the medieval fool's freedom to criticize.[3] Perhaps the fool, being a kind of 'innocent', was seen as closer to nature and its truths, as in the case of Le Badin, who can hardly read, but who nonetheless knows the secret of life (*Les Troys Galans et un Badin*, ll. 49–50). In any case, the fool could get away with his outrageous truth-telling because of the mask of *folie* (see above pp. 66–8). He could criticize, mockingly, anyone and everyone, as Malostru claims: 'Je copie [ridicule] cy Dieu et le monde' (a refrain in *Les Coppieurs*, ll. 9, 18, *et passim*).

The theme of the *sot révéleur de vérité* runs through a number of *sotties*: in *Le Gaudisseur et le sot*, for example, it is the *sot* who comments on the boasts of the Gaudisseur, and who establishes the truth. A more complex variant of the truth-speaker is found in *Les Cris de Paris*. The *sot* seems to be commenting on the conversation of two 'gallans' by means of his 'cris'; these hawker's cries do in effect comment on what the 'gallans' really mean, but in a comic manner, since the commentary takes the form of advertisements for cakes and vegetables. At the end of the play the *sot* insists on the truth, although the 'gallans' believe that '[il] n'a guère de sens en la teste' (l. 235). In *Le Jeu du Prince des Sotz*, it is likewise the three *sots* who reveal that Mère Sainte Eglise is only Mère Sotte (see also *Les Rapporteurs*, ll. 134–45 and 158ff.).

Yet there is nothing stern or humorless about the fool's truth-telling. On the contrary, he lets fall the most outrageous criticisms in a spirit of *gaieté*. The *sots* never tire of rejoicing. *Gaudeamus* became the motto and rallying cry for any fool or fool society,[4] for Gayecté is the 'cher filz tresaymé' of the Prince des Sotz (*Le Jeu du Prince des Sotz*, ll. 200–1). Haulte Follie brings 'Deduit, Joye, Soulas' both to her *sots* and to the audience that watched their *folâtries*.[5] This penchant for merry-making is undoubtedly one of the reasons for the popular success of the fool (his poverty also suited him to the role of popular spokesman). Yet, as we have seen, the view of joy and pleasure in the *sottie* is not simple. At times the *sots* are criticized for their frivolity, as by Sancté in *Deulx Gallans et Sancté*, when she rebukes them for carrying on with 'trop de léesse' (l. 126). In the end they seem to accept her point of view. Similarly, in *Le Monde, Abuz* and *Folle Bobance*, a life of gaiety and pleasure is shown to be ruinous.

The *sot* lends himself to the expression of such ambivalence, for as a dramatic character the fool was multiform. That is, we are dealing not with one Fool but with several varieties of them. The characteristics of the *sot* generally fall into opposites: one fool is ignorant or even stupid, while another shrewdly reveals the truth about a person or situation; one fool celebrates pleasure, while another is condemned for his frivolity. Consequently, a *sot* was at hand, to the dramatist, to embody almost any point of view, any value; but above all fools were capable of embodying a conflict between opposing values.

Thus, contradictory characteristics oppose one type of fool to another, or they oppose a fool at one moment to what he is later. The conflict of *trompeur/trompé* is one of the principal pairs of contradictions. In the preceding analysis of the threat posed by certain devious individuals (see Chapter 4), some fools played the role of well-intentioned, simple people who were deceived by other fools (by 'les gens nouveaulx'). In effect, the fool deceiver is a more common character than the fool deceived, although a play sometimes combines both functions in the same fool: in *Les Sotz triumphans* the *sots* attempt to deceive, but are in turn deceived. From a certain point of view the *sot trompeur* is always seen as deceived by his own foolish pretentions.[6] *Le Jeu du Prince des Sotz* divides the two types of fools into distinct camps in order to oppose them in the most dramatic manner. In any case, whether embodied in one fool or many, the conflict *trompeur/trompé* was an inherently dramatic one, which the authors of the *sotties* exploited to the full.[7]

In addition to the *trompeur/trompé* type, other conflicts were exploited dramatically. The disorderly fool, for example, was countered by the orderly one. 'Gallans' seem to be particularly prone to disorderly conduct, for twice they are repressed by an authority of some sort (in *Troys Galans et Monde* and *Deulx Gallans et Sancté*). In each case the 'disorder' of the *sots* consists of acting entirely according to their own whims, thereby disregarding propriety or morality: 'Vous ne faictes rien / Synon a vostre volonté' (*Deulx gallans et Sancté*, ll. 132–3). Not only are they unable to obey authority, but they are unable even to agree among themselves on a concerted course of action (see *Troys Galans et Monde*, l. 289). Similarly, the 'gens nouveaulx' proclaim their unruly individuality: 'Chascun a par soy se regente' (l. 7). Although the lack of constraint that leads to disorder is criticized and eventually suppressed by such characters as Ordre and Sancté, nonetheless the attitude of the *sottie* toward wilfullness is ambivalent. The individual will is sometimes (though rarely) recognized as a reliable guide to action. Le Premier Sot of *Les Sotz escornez* observes, simply, that 'Obeyr n'est pas tousjours bon' (l. 320; cf. *Les Sobres Sotz*, ll. 75–6). Of course such remarks, in the mouths of fools, may be meant to be ironic. Are we to believe a 'gallan' when he argues

> Ce qu'on faict volontairement
> Vault mieulx qu'a force mile foys.

Troys Galans et Monde, ll. 21–2: What one does by one's own will Is worth a thousand times more than what one does by force.

It is frequently difficult to know how seriously a fool was meant to be taken.

This complex nature of the fool enabled the authors of the *sotties* to develop the three roles of evil-doer, accuser, and victim (see above, pp. 53–5) in a way that no other satiric theater has been able to do. The fool had the remarkable ability to represent any and all of the roles. He of course embodied the role of accuser (truth-speaker) to an extent never seen again in Western culture, for he alone was given the right to speak his mind openly. The *sottie* is the logical literary development of this right. But in addition the *sot* was foolish – he stood for all the misguided, wrong-headed, silly, self-destructive behavior that mankind could devise. That is not all, though, for the *sot* also spoke for the simple-minded, the naïve (in the original sense), the meek of the earth, and for this reason he came to stand for the downtrodden – the victims – of society. Thus these three primary roles not only account for the characteristics of the *sottie* as satiric drama; they also make it possible for us to determine the fundamental characteristics of the *sot* himself. Each of the roles is the result of one of the facets of the fool: he is basically truth-speaker, wrong-headed, and lowly. All other characteristics are secondary and grow out of these three.

Ultimately these characteristics fall into two very broad types: those that are praiseworthy, and those that are condemned. The evil-doers are those fools whose *folie* is destructive to themselves and to society, whose madness is 'Toute plaine d'abusion' (*La Folie des Gorriers*, l. 563). These are the various *gens nouveaux*, the *sots* of *Le Monde, Abuz*, Mère Sainte Eglise and her unscrupulous counselors – all the *sots* whose machinations threaten the stable order of society.[8] It is striking that these fools are sometimes associated with devils: L' Arbre de Folye, in *Le Monde, Abuz*, has in it 'quelque dyablerie' (l. 239; references to devils in this play are numerous: e.g., ll. 246, 263 and 276ff.). La Femme in *L'Arbaleste*, whose husband is a *sot*, remarks:

> Qui en a de plus sot congneu
> Se n'est pas le deable d'enfer?[9]

Ll. 323–4: Who has known a man more foolish If not the devil of hell?

This type of fool's sinful ways (and undoubtedly also his love of earthly pleasure) placed him outside the Church, even in opposition to religion; and these characteristics he shared with the devil. Opposing these fools are the 'wise' fools, the victims and their allies, the accusers, who are sometimes designated by clearly praiseworthy names (Ordre, Sancté), or simply by general ones (Le Monde, Chascun). At times, not just one but a group of wise *sots* opposes the evil-doers, as in *Mestier et Marchandise*. Sometimes, but rarely, the trouble-makers are themselves converted, neutralized, or transformed into wise fools, as happens to Les Gens in *Mestier et Marchandise*, and to the three *pèlerins* who first follow Malice, only to chase him away in the end (*Troys Pelerins et Malice*).[10]

Within the context of a particular play, the distinction between wise and foolish fools is not always immediately evident due to the combining of more than one role in a particular fool or to the shift from one role to another. The great potential for irony that existed in the fool was exploited by writers of the fifteenth and sixteenth centuries (Erasmus is the best example), as has often been pointed out by modern critics. The *sots* themselves never tire of telling us that he who seems *sage* is in reality *fou*, and vice versa. The character Monsieur Rien, who symbolizes the falseness of all appearances, claims that he can make a wise man of a fool, or at least the fool will seem so ('il le semblera', *Le Cry de la Bazoche*, l. 240). *Folie* is, according to Foucault, 'comme la punition comique du savoir et sa présomption ignorante';[11] and the Sobres Sotz tell us as much:

> Tout homme qui s'estime sage,
> Il doibt estre fol reputé.

Les Sobres Sotz, ll. 372–3: Every man who believes himself wise, He must be reputed a fool.

For this reason the number of fools in the world is incalculable – the supposedly sage must be included in their number.[12]

This makes the *sottie* a profoundly ironic form of drama. In *Les Rapporteurs*, the *sots* speak the truth (about *sergents*, churchmen, etc.) by saying the opposite of what they mean. Such irony is undoubtedly common in the *sotties* (though not always discernible today). While condemning worldly pleasures, for instance, the sots seem, ironically, to be praising them. Much of what the *sots* say is capable of a double meaning, for the *sot* voices contradictory views of money and poverty, joy and sobriety, constraint and freedom. The *sot* was able to express such ambivalence dramatically because he was an inherently ambivalent character: wise or foolish, stable or unpredictable, carefree or stern, conservative or socially ambitious, licentious or moralistic, and at times all of these. The ambivalence of the *sot*, rather than any particular characteristic, was what made him peculiarly adapted to expressing the changing and conflicting values of the late Middle Ages.

The irony of the fool also allows the playwright to side-step responsibility for his satire in a time of variable, unpredictable, and often severe repression. For who takes a fool seriously? Indeed, who can tell what a fool means anyway? Thus the fool could both ridicule his enemy by calling him a fool, and avoid the consequences by playing the fool himself. The *sottie* veils its message not only through the ironic point of view that it adopts but also through the use of allegory. The evil-doer is used to symbolize a line of conduct or philosophical position, while the accuser and victim embody the opposite position. The conflict over that conduct or position is then acted out allegorically. Consequently, many of the characteristics of allegory are found in the *sottie*. As Fletcher has pointed out, it belongs, with other forms of allegory, in the area of 'epideictic rhetoric, the rhetoric of praise and ceremony, since it is most often used to praise and condemn certain lines of conduct or certain philosophical positions'.[13] The division of fools and of their characteristics into opposing camps is particularly suited to dramatizing symbolic power-struggles between ways of life, modes of conduct, or social groups.[14] In addition, the *sottie*, like other forms of allegory, acts out these struggles for power only in an unclear fashion (as we have seen in the case of the 'gens nouveaulx'). 'Enigma', again according to Fletcher, 'appears to be allegory's most cherished function';[15] the ironic character of the fool made his point of view particularly enigmatic.

This irony is not only allegorical, but satiric. Satiric allegory, as a sub-genre, has been neglected by literary scholars.[16] Both satire and allegory are concerned with conflicts between groups, specifically between their conduct or attitudes; both satire and allegory are used to criticize and condemn. In addition, both are ritualistic.[17] The ritualistic confrontation with and defeat of an antagonistic force, as in the triumph over the evil-doers in the *sottie*, is both a form of symbolic aggression, and a reaffirmation of group values. Elliott develops the thesis that satire originally was a ritual, one which was meant to injure or even kill the offender (we still speak of 'blistering' satire). He maintains that 'all satire "kills", symbolically at any rate'.[18] This hypothesis is clearly applicable to the use of satire in the *sottie*, in particular to that of the evil-doer, the dangerous fool – the *trompeur*, the *gens nouveaux.* Although the power of satire that Elliott describes had become symbolic long before the late Middle Ages, satire remained an attempt to triumph over a threatening group, philosophy, or line of conduct. It may have been merely a symbolic triumph, yet when the popular culture is under hopelessly powerful attack, in the words of Fletcher, 'this secret mental survival is better than none at all'.[19] Consequently, the fool became more and more useful as a means of satire in the late Middle Ages, first because of his liberty to criticize, but also because his triple nature allowed him to embody all three roles in the rituals of condemnation and affirmation.

If satire was originally and fundamentally a curse, as Elliott maintains, then the words of the *sottie* could be used to 'curse' a variety of enemies, whether group (the churchmen of *Les Sotz ecclesiasticques*, for example) or individual (a particular churchman, the Pope, in *Le Jeu du Prince des Sotz*). Above all, the *sottie* was suited to cursing those whom the popular classes saw as their enemies in the late fifteenth and early sixteenth centuries. The duality of the fool allowed him to embody the rising members of the bourgeoisie (in the form of Les Gens, the Gens Nouveaulx, etc.), while at the same time it was other fools who unmasked and defeated these *trompeurs*. By splitting the ranks of the fools into two camps (the evil-doers on one side, the accusers and victims on the other), the *sottie* succeeded in working out a fantasy of triumph over popular enemies.[20] The victory over powerful but unspecified enemies is in effect more common than any other single theme of the *sottie*. Therefore, the remarkable popularity of the *sottie* as a dramatic form in the late Middle Ages cannot be entirely understood without reference to the social conflicts that it acts out.

The *sottie* was peculiarly adapted not only to a time of growing class conflict, but also to one of generally changing values. It was most popular in a period of economic and cultural transition, a period which the multiform fool could best embody.[21] Conversely, the decline and disappearance of the *sottie* can be explained not solely by the traditional argument that tastes change, and that styles of popular spokesmen vary. More importantly, the class conflict which the *sottie* expressed was changing. Perhaps the rise of the bourgeoisie was such that by the seventeenth century popular theatrical expressions of fear and opposition were no longer permitted; or it is likely that the bourgeois values that the *sottie* attacked – innovation, opportunism, materialism, social mobility in particular – had been so widely accepted that they were no longer a source of overt conflict, no longer constituted the object of satire. (Both audience and author must agree on the undesirability of the object of satire.) However it may be (and future studies will undoubtedly provide more information on class evolution and conflict in the Renaissance), neither the popularity of the *sottie* in the fifteenth and sixteenth centuries, nor its decline by the beginning of the seventeenth, can be understood if detached from the context of class conflict in which it occurred.

The fool became a spokesman for popular satirical attitudes because of his duality of fool condemned, fool praised, a duality which allowed him to express ambivalence at a time of fluctuating and conflicting values. His duality further made it possible for him to dramatize a ritualistic conflict with a vaguely perceived threat to popular values; he acted out a symbolic triumph over that threat, thereby reaffirming those values. Ultimately, the *sot* came to be the symbol for the period of change – of order and disorder – in which he was an increasingly popular dramatic character. In a time when appearance could be relied on less and less, when people were frequently not what they seemed, the variable, inconsistent fool came stage front to epitomize the sense of flux, of illusion. As such, he is by nature theatrical, for the theater is fundamentally illusion – which is, as Michel Foucault has pointed out, 'au sens strict, la folie'. Theater is illusion; *folie* is illusion; in a time of change all three were incorporated in the *sot*. And as all three are intrinsic to society, so, in one form or another, is the *sot*. This, then, is the lasting value of understanding the *sottie*.

Appendix

The following table contains the title of each play as it appears in the earliest edition; the short title used in this study; the date, probable or certain, when possible to indicate one; and the most accessible modern edition. When a date is hypothetical, the source of the hypothesis is indicated in parenthesis.

The works referred to in this table are the following:

(A)   Aubailly, *Monologue*
(B)   Bossuat, *Deux moralités inédites*
(C)   Cohen, *Recueil*
(D)   Droz, *Trepperel*
(F)   Fournier, *Théâtre*
(L)   Lecocq, *Histoire du théâtre en Picardie*
(Le R)   Le Roux de Lincy and Michel, *Recueil de farces*
(M)   Maxwell, *French Farce*
(P)   Picot, *Recueil général*
(Ph)   Philipot, *Six farces*
(T)   Tappan and Carrington, 'Deux pièces comiques'
(V)   Viollet-le-Duc, *Ancien Théâtre*

SHORT TITLE	FULL TITLE	DATE	EDITION
L'Astrologue	*Sottie nouvelle de l'Astrologue*	1498 (P)	Picot, I
Le Bateleur	*Farce du Bateleur*	c. 1555 (Ph)	Philipot
Les Béguins	*Sottie jouée a Geneve en la Place du Molard*	Feb. 22, 1523	Picot, II

SHORT TITLE	FULL TITLE	DATE	EDITION
Les Brus	Farce nouvelle de troys Brus et deulx Hermites	c. 1536 (P)	Picot, III
Chascun, Plusieurs	Moralité de Chascun, Plusieurs, le Temps qui court, le Monde	end of 15th century (A)	Le Roux de Lincy, III, no. 2
Les Coppieurs	Sotie nouvelle tres-excellente des Coppieurs et Lardeurs qui sont copiez et farcez	before 1488 (D)	Droz
Les Coquins	Farce nouvelle des Coquins	c. 1480 (C)	Cohen
Les Cris de Paris	Farce nouvelle tres-bonne et fort recreative pour rire des cris de Paris	c. 1540? (P)	Picot, III
La Croix Faubin	Moralité novelle de la Croix Faubin	mid-15th century (A)	Tappan
Les Croniqueurs	Sotye nouvelle des Croniqueurs	May 1515	Picot, II
Le Cry de la Bazoche	Pour le cry de la Bazoche	March 5, 1549	Picot, III
Deulx Gallans et Sancté	Farce des deulx Gallans et une Femme qui se nomme Sancté	c. 1485? (P)	Picot, I
Les Esbahis	Farce nouvelle des Esbahis	1480–92 (C)	Cohen
Estourdi	Sotie et farce nouvelle de Estourdi et Coquillart	after 1460 (D)	Droz
Les Esveilleurs	Farce nouvelle tres-bonne et fort joyeuse des Esveilleurs du Chat qui dort dont ilz s'en prennent par le nez et sont farcez	1480–92 (C)	Cohen
Faulte d'Argent	Farce nouvelle de Faulte d'Argent, Bon Temps et les troys Gallans	1480–92 (C)	Cohen
La Feste des Roys	Sotie nouvelle pour porter les presens a la Feste des Roys tresbonne	uncertain	Droz

SHORT TITLE	FULL TITLE	DATE	EDITION
La Folie des Gorriers	Farce nouvelle nommée la Folie des Gorriers	c. 1465 (P)	Picot, I
Folle Bobance	Farce nouvelle tres-bonne de Folle Bobance	c. 1500 (P)	Picot, I
Fragment for three characters	[No title]	c. 1420 (P)	Picot, I
Fragments for six characters	[No title]	1517 (P)	Picot, II
Le Gaudisseur et le Sot	Nouvelle farce du Gaudisseur qui se vante de ses faitz et ung Sot luy respond au contraire	c. 1450 (D)	Droz
Les Gens nouveaulx	Farce nouvelle moralisée des Gens Nouveaulx qui mengent le Monde et le logent de mal en pire	c. 1461 (P, F)	Picot, I
Le Jeu du Capifol	Moralité du Ministre de l'Eglise, Noblesse, le Laboureur, Commun	beginning of 16th century (A)	Le Roux de Lincy, II, no. 23
Le Jeu du Prince des Sotz	Le Jeu du Prince des Sotz et de Mère Sotte	Feb. 25, 1512	Picot, II
Le Jeu par Jehan Destrées	Jeu extraordinaire fait [par] Jehan Destrées et joué la Nuyt des Roys mil IIIIᶜLXXII	1472	Lecocq
Les Maraux	Farce nouvelle des Maraux enchesnez	after 1479 (C)	Cohen
Les Menus Propos	Les Menus Propos	Feb., 1461 (P)	Picot, I
La Mère de Ville	Farce nouvelle de la Mère de Ville	c. 1540 (P)	Picot, III
Mestier et Marchandise	Farce de Mestier, Marchandise, le Berger, le Temps, et les Gens	1440 (F)	Fournier
Le Monde	Seconde Moralité	Feb. 14, 1524	Picot, II
Le Monde, Abuz	Sotise du Monde, Abuz	1507? (P)	Picot, II
La Moralité de 1427	Moralité faict en foulois pour le chastiement du Monde	1427	Bossuat

SHORT TITLE	FULL TITLE	DATE	EDITION
Le Pelerinage	*Farce du Pelerinage de mariage*	Oct., 1556 (P)	Picot, III
Le Pelerin et La Pelerine	*Farce joyeuse et recreative du Pelerin et de la Pelerine*	*c.* 1557 (P)	Picot, III
Pou d'Acquest	*Farce nouvelle de Marchandise et Mestier, Pou d'Acquest, le Temps qui court et Grosse Despense*	reign of Charles VII (F)	Fournier
Les Povres Deables	*Farce nouvelle des Povres Deables*	*c.* 1520 (M)	Le Roux de Lincy, I, no. 15
Les Premiers	*Sotie nouvelle des Premiers Gardonnez*	before 1488 (D)	Droz
Le Prince des Sots	*Farce nouvelle fort joyeuse du Prince des Sots*	1480–90? (C)	Cohen
Les Rapporteurs	*Sotie nouvelle des Rapporteurs*	*c.* 1480 (D)	Droz
La Reformeresse	*Farce de la Reformeresse*	*c.* 1540 (P)	Picot, III
Le Roy des Sotz	*Sottie nouvelle du Roy des Sotz*	*c.* 1545 (P)	Picot, III
Satyre	*Satyre pour les habitans d'Auxerre*	1530 (P)	Picot, II
Les Sobres Sots	*Farce moralle et joyeusse des sobres Sots entremellez avec les Syeurs d'Ais*	Carnival of 1536 (P, F)	Picot, III
Les Sotz ecclesiasticques	*Sotie nouvelle tresexcellente des Sotz ecclesiasticques qui jouent leurs benefices au content*	April, 1511 (D)	Droz
Les Sotz escornez	*Sotie nouvelle des Sotz escornez tresbonne*	beginning of 16th century (D)	Droz
Les Sotz fourrez	*Sotie nouvelle des Sotz fourrez de malice*	*c.* 1480 (D)	Droz
Les Sotz nouveaulx	*Les Sotz nouveaulx farcez couvez / Jamais n'en furent de plus folz /*	*c.* 1513? (P)	Picot, II

SHORT TITLE	FULL TITLE	DATE	EDITION
	Si le deduict veoir vous voulez / Baillez argent ilz seront voz		
Les Sotz qui corrigent	Sotie nouvelle des Sotz qui corrigent le magnificat	before 1488 (D)	Droz
Les Sotz qui recueuvrent	Sotie nouvelle des Sotz qui recueuvrent leur mortier	after 1480 (D)	Droz
Les Sotz qui remetent	Sotie nouvelle des Sotz qui remetent en point Bon Temps	end of 16th century (D)	Droz
Les Sotz triumphans	Sotie nouvelle et fort joyeuse des Sotz triumphans qui trompent chacun	c. 1475 (D)	Droz
Tout le Monde	Moral de Tout le Monde	c. 1535 (P)	Picot, III
Tout, Rien, et Chascun	Farce nouvelle très bonne, moralle et fort joyeuse de Tout, Rien, et Chascun	beginning of 16th century (A)	Viollet-le-Duc, III, n. 56
Les Trompeurs	Sottie nouvelle des Trompeurs	c. 1470 (D) c. 1530 (P)	Picot, III
Trote Menu	Sotie nouvelle tresbonne et fort joyeuse de Trote Menu et Mirre Loret	end of 15th century (D)	Droz
Troys Galans et Monde	Farce joyeuse de troys Galans, le Monde qu'on faict paistre et Ordre	c. 1445? (P)	Picot, I
Les Troys Galans et un Badin	Farce nouvelle de troys Galans et un Badin	c. 1571 (P, F)	Picot, III
Troys Pelerins et Malice	Farce morale de troys Pelerins et Malice	1523 (P)	Picot, II
Les Veaulx	La Farce des Veaulx jouée, devant le Roy en son entrée a Rouen	c. 1485 or 1550 (A, P)	Le Roux de Lincy, III, no. 33
Les Vigilles de Triboullet	C'est la farce ou sotie des vigilles Triboullet	c. 1455 (Ph) c. 1480 (D)	Droz

Notes

INTRODUCTION

1 The words *folie* and *fou* are difficult to translate into English, as they had a number of different meanings in the Middle Ages: they could mean 'foolish', 'crazy', or just 'simple-minded'. In addition both *fou* and *sot* could refer to the jester. These two terms are largely synonymous in late medieval literature and for the purposes of this study will be used interchangeably. See also the discussion of the word *sottie* below, p. 5.

2 Eugène Viollet-le-Duc (ed.), *Ancien Théâtre françois*, 10 vols. (Paris: Jannet, 1854–7), vol. II, p. 215. Translations will be provided for those lines from the *sotties* which may not be easily understood by someone knowing modern French.

3 *Tiers Livre*, ed. Pierre Jourda (Paris: Garnier, 1962), ch. xxxVIII. Similar lists are part of the following *sotties*: *Folle Bobance, Le Jeu du Prince des Sotz, Les Sotz triumphans*, and *Les Trompeurs*.

4 Francis Douce, *Illustrations of Shakspeare, and of Ancient Manners: with Dissertations on the Clowns and Fools of Shakspeare* (London: Longman, Hurst, Rees, and Orme, 1807), vol. II, p. 304.

5 Georges Doutrepont, *La Littérature française à la cour des Ducs de Bourgogne* (Paris: Champion, 1909). See also the list of works on the court fool in E. K. Chambers, *The Mediaeval Stage* (London: Oxford Univ. Press, 1903), vol. I, p. 387. The court fools were 'artificial', that is, they played at being fools; they were fools by profession, not by nature.

6 Léon de Laborde, *Les Ducs de Bourgogne*, 3 vols. (Paris: Plon, 1849–53), vol. III, p. 538.

7 Ll. 238–9. A list of the plays and their sources is given in the appendix. For convenience I have given each *sottie* a short title based on the title found in the manuscript or incunabulum, when one is given, or on the principal characters, when no title is given in the original text. The plays will be referred to in this study by their short titles. The appendix also gives the complete title, the most accessible modern edition, and, if possible, the date.

8 *Histoire de la folie* (Paris: Plon, 1971), p. 31.

9 *The Fool: His Social and Literary History* (London: Faber & Faber, 1935), p. xi.

10 The present study is concerned with theatrical manifestations of the *sot* in France. For studies of related forms in Belgium and Germany, cf. J. Stetcher, 'La Sottie française et la sotternie flamande', *Bulletins de l'Académie royale des Sciences, des Lettres et des Beaux-arts de Belgique*, 2nd series, 43 (1877), 388–432; and Joël Lefebvre, *Les Fols et la folie* (Paris: Klincksieck, 1968).

11 *La Sottie en France* (Nogent-le-Rotrou: Impr. Daupeley-Gouverneur, 1878). Eugénie Droz's introduction to the first volume of the *Recueil Trepperel*, 2 vols. (Paris: Droz, 1935) discusses the *sottie*. See also Barbara Swain, *Fools and Folly during the Middle Ages and the Renaissance* (New York: Columbia Univ. Press, 1932). Other writings on the *sottie* will be discussed in the course of the study.

12 The best recent study is that of Jean-Claude Aubailly, *Le Monologue, le dialogue et la sotie* (Paris: Champion, 1976). See also Barbara Goth, *Untersuchungen zur Gattungsgeschichte der Sottie* (Munich: Fink, 1967); and Ida Nelson, *La Sottie: Jeu du gay vouloir* (Paris: Champion, 1974).

13 Mikhail Bakhtine discusses the attitudes he perceives in the *sottie*, considered simply as one of many types of carnival literature, in *L'Oeuvre de François Rabelais et la culture populaire au Moyen Age et sous la Renaissance*, trans. Andrée Robel (Paris: Gallimard, 1970). While we both approach the *sottie* from the point of view of class attitudes, his findings and mine are quite different, as will be seen toward the end of this study.

1 THE PLAYS

1 The etymology of the word *sottie* is uncertain, according to the *Dictionnaire étymologique de la langue française* (3rd edn, 1964). The Vulgar Latin form *sottus* (9th century) has been suggested by the *Nouveau Dictionnaire étymologique du français* (1971). Miraulmont's hypothesis, that a pun on *saut/sot* is the root of *sottie* and its variants, is more fanciful than likely (*Les Mémoires de Pierre de Miraulmont escuyer* (Paris: Claude La Tour, 1612), p. 656).

2 *La Comédie et les mœurs en France au Moyen Age*, 4th edn (Paris: Cerf, 1886), p. 69. See also Petit de Julleville, *Les Comédiens en France au Moyen Age* (Paris: Cerf, 1885), pp. 32 ff.

3 Cambridge, Mass.: Mediaeval Academy of America, 1949, p. xi.

4 See *Recueil général des sotties*, ed. Emile Picot, 3 vols. (Paris: Fermin–Didot, 1902–12).

5 'La Farce et la sotie', *Zeitschrift für romanische Philologie*, 75 (1959), 89–90. See also Droz, *Trepperel*, p. lxviii. For an excellent discussion of the problem of medieval genres in general, see 'Littérature médiévale et théorie des genres', by Hans-Robert Jauss, *Poétique*, 1 (1970), 79–101; and Paul

Zumthor, 'Classes and Genres in Medieval Literature', in *Medieval French Miscellany*, ed. Norris J. Lacy (Lawrence: Univ. of Kansas Press, 1972), pp. 27–36.

6 *Fools and Folly*, p. 92.

7 Gustave Cohen, *Le Théâtre comique au XVe siècle et dans la première moitié du XVIe siècle* (Paris: Centre de Documentation Universitaire, 1940), p. 5.

8 François and Claude Parfaict are most likely referring to this situation when they write: 'Le Prince des Sots donna la permission aux Clercs de la Bazoche de jouer des *Soties* ou *Sotises*, en échange il reçut de ces derniers celle de représenter des farces' (*Histoire du théâtre françois, depuis son origine jusqu'à présent* (Paris: Mercier & Saillant, 1745), vol. II, p. 98).

9 Cohen has argued that *Pathelin* was in effect a *sottie*; see *Théâtre comique*, pp. 158 ff.

10 See Porter, 'Farce et sotie', p. 90; and Parfaict, *Histoire*, vol. III, p. 106.

11 *Trepperel*, p. lxvii.

12 'Towards a Definition of Farce as a Literary "Genre" ', *Modern Language Review*, 56 (1961), 558. The differences that Grace Frank perceived between the farce and the *sottie* are similar to those that Bowen points out: farces, according to Frank, 'are mostly stories of human frailty, rather than satires of society' (*Medieval French Drama* (Oxford: Clarendon Press, 1954), p. 246).

13 'Farce et sotie', pp. 120–1.

14 *French Farce and John Heywood* (Melbourne and London: Melbourne Univ. Press, 1946), p. 20. Barbara C. Bowen also points out differences in general structure, tone, and kind of action presented by each genre, in *Les Caractéristiques essentielles de la farce française et leur survivance dans les années 1550–1620* (Urbana: Univ. of Illinois Press, 1964), pp. 6–9. An excellent résumé of scholarly opinion, and of differences between the farce and the *sottie*, is given in Aubailly, *Monologue*, pp. 280–5.

15 Howard Graham Harvey, *The Theatre of the Basoche* (Cambridge, Mass.: Harvard Univ. Press, 1941), p. 174. Cf. *Journal d'un bourgeois de Paris sous le règne de François Ier (1515–36)*, ed. Ludovic Lalanne (Paris: Renouard, 1854), p. 13. Droz also recognizes this order (*Trepperel*, p. lxv).

16 *La Poésie du XVe siècle* (Paris: Lamier, 1886), p. 25. See also Petit de Julleville: 'Un petit tableau d'une scène triviale de la vie journalière' (*Comédiens*, p. 31).

17 'Satyre' appears in the title of only one *sottie*, that of Roger de Collerye (Picot, *Recueil général*, vol. II, pp. 357–72). Before the use of the term 'farce', comic playwrights frequently used 'jeu', 'dict', or 'debat'.

18 *Journal d'un bourgeois de Paris sous le règne de François Ier*, ed. V.-L. Bourrilly, new edn (Paris: Picard, 1910), gives us further evidence of this meaning of 'farce', when it speaks of three 'joueurs de farces' who were arrested, in 1516, 'pour avoir joué... entre autres choses, que mère Sotte gouvernait en cour, et qu'elle tailloit, pilloit et desrobboit tout' ('for having played...

among other things, that Mother Sotte was governing at the court, and that she was taxing, pillaging, and stealing everything') (pp. 39–40). In other words, they were playing a *sottie*.

19 Picot, *Recueil général*, vol. III, pp. 150–1; Harvey, *Theatre*, p. 108; and Maxwell, *French Farce*, p. 145.

20 Most of the following remarks on the *sottie* are speculative since, as Zumthor has pointed out, 'Plus encore que pour les autres parties du corpus poétique médiéval, nous sommes, en ce qui concerne le théâtre, victimes de l'état fragmentaire de notre documentation' (*Essai de poétique médiévale* (Paris: Seuil, 1972), p. 433). Howard Brown has discussed the 'fragmentary condition of the evidence' concerning performances in *Music in the French Secular Theater* (Cambridge, Mass.: Harvard Univ. Press, 1963), p. 13.

21 Harvey, *Theatre*, p. 9.

22 Petit de Julleville, *Répertoire du théâtre comique en France au Moyen Age* (Paris: Cerf, 1886), p. 306; see also p. 312.

23 Droz, *Trepperel*, p. xii.

24 Droz and Félix Lecoy have shown reason to doubt some of Cohen's datings and localizations. See the following reviews: Félix Lecoy, *Romania*, 71 (1950), 513–30; Eugénie Droz, *Bibliothèque d'Humanisme et Renaissance*, 11 (1949), 296–303; and U.T. Holmes, Jr, *Speculum*, 24 (1949), 563–6.

25 Droz, *Trepperel*, ll. 29–40.

26 *Caractéristiques*, pp. 62–3.

27 *Recueil*, p. xxi.

28 'Notes sur quelques pièces du *Recueil de farces inédites*', *Romania*, 76 (1955), 342–73.

29 'Les plus récentes datations d'anciennes farces françaises', *Bulletin d'Humanisme et Renaissance*, 25 (1963), 325–36.

30 *Recueil général*, vol. I, p. 138.

31 Emmanuel Philipot (ed.), *Six farces normandes du Recueil La Vallière* (Rennes: Plihon, 1939), p. 45; Droz, *Trepperel*, p. 185.

32 Picot, *Recueil général*, vol. III, pp. 5 ff.; Droz, *Trepperel*, p. 30. Similarly, seven different dates have been suggested for *Le Bateleur* (see Philipot, *Six farces*, pp. 43–4).

33 The remaining fourteenth-century works are: *Maitre Trubert et Antroignart*, and *Le Dit des quatre offices de l'hotel du Roy*, by Deschamps; and the three moralities in the manuscript Chantilly 617, discovered by Gustave Cohen (see *Théâtre comique*, p. 49).

34 Gustave Cohen, 'Le Théâtre à Paris et aux environs à la fin du XIVe siècle', *Romania*, 38 (1909), 587.

35 Frank, *Drama*, p. 267.

36 Petit de Julleville, *Répertoire*, p. 323.

37 Harvey, *Theatre*, p. 201. See also Petit de Julleville, *Comédiens*, p. 123.

38 *Recueil général*, vol. I, pp. xx–xxi. Malherbe speaks of the 'pois pillés'

(probably a troupe similar to, or part of, the Enfants-sans-souci) at the Hôtel de Bourgogne at the end of 1625 (*Oeuvres*, ed. Ludovic Lalanne, 5 vols. (Paris: Hachette, 1862–9), vol. IV, p. 94). See also Picot, *Sottie*, p. 7.

39 *Theatre*, p. 201.

40 Marcelin Defourneaux, *La Vie quotidienne au temps de Jeanne d'Arc* (Paris: Hachette, 1952), pp. 117–18. Doutrepont has discovered that Maître Mouche (the name of a *sot*) and his *compagnons* appeared before Philippe le Bon in 1434, in Brussels (*Littérature*, p. 352).

2 THE ORIGINS AND PLAYERS OF THE *SOTTIE*

1 'Les Commencements du théâtre comique en France', *Revue des Deux Mondes*, 99 (June 15, 1890), 883. E. K. Chambers has argued that the 'germ of the *sottie*' is to be found in the work of Adam de la Halle, specifically in *Le Jeu de la feuillée* (*Mediaeval Stage*, p. 381).

2 Gustave Cohen, *La 'Comédie' latine en France au XIIIe siècle*, 2 vols. (Paris: Les Belles Lettres, 1939). See also Edmond Faral, *Les Jongleurs en France au Moyen Age* (Paris: Champion, 1910), p. 226.

3 *La Poésie du Moyen Age*, 2 vols. (Paris: Hachette, 1895), vol. II, pp. 249 ff. See also Maurice Wilmotte, *Etudes critiques sur la tradition littéraire* (Paris: Champion, 1909).

4 Faral, *Jongleurs*, pp. 226–8.

5 Petit de Julleville, in his discussion of the *sot* in *La Passion de Troyes*, pointed out that the *sot* 'n'a aucun lien avec la pièce: c'est une superfétation.... Les vers bouffons qu'il débite sont écrits en marge et d'une autre main' (*Les Mystères*, 2 vols. (Paris: Hachette, 1880), vol. II, pp. 412–13).

6 *Comédiens*, p. 3.

7 Ed. W. Foerster, *Romania*, 2 (1873), 315–25. For passages in the *sotties* that probably involved acrobatics, see *Les Coppieurs*, ll. 106–20, and *Le Bateleur*, ll. 15–20 (see p. 28, below).

8 *Mediaeval Stage*, p. 381.

9 *Ibid.* pp. 300 and 314; Petit de Julleville, *Comédiens*, p. 40; Jacques Heers, *Fêtes, jeux et joûtes dans les sociétés d'Occident à la fin du Moyen Age* (Montreal: Institut d'Etudes Médiévales, 1971), p. 128. For a bibliography of works on the Fête des Fous, des Innocents, de l'Ane, des Conards, etc., see Alfred de Martonne, *La Piété du Moyen Age* (Paris: Dumoulin, 1855), pp. 202–5. A summary of the Feast of Fools can be found in *La Revue des Revues*, 25 (1898), 400, by F. Loliée.

10 See Chambers, *Mediaeval Stage*, pp. 275 and 318.

11 Other possible references to the Feast occur in *Le Prince des Sots*: 'N'est-il pas aujourd'huy la feste / Que nous devons tous folloyer?' (ll. 180–1), and in *Les Sotz ecclesiasticques*: 'Il est la saison qu'on folloye' (l. 43).

12 Heers has attempted to establish the evolution of the terms given to the Feast: the Fête des Fous was the last of the series, following the Fête des Innocents and de L'Ane (*Fêtes*, pp. 127–8).

13 Karl Young, *The Drama of the Medieval Church* (Oxford: Clarendon Press, 1933), p. 104.

14 See Cohen, *Théâtre*, p. 6; and Chambers, *Mediaeval Stage*, p. 329.

15 For a theory which traces the origins of the Feast from Antiquity, see Joseph S. Tunison, *Dramatic Traditions of the Dark Ages* (1907; repr. New York: Burt Franklin, 1970), pp. 56–7.

16 Chambers, *Mediaeval Stage*, p. 294.

17 *Ibid.* p. 295.

18 'Dieu a déposé les puissants de leur siège, et il a élevé les humbles.' See *Deposuit* in Charles Du Cange, *Glossarium mediae et infimae latinitatis* (Paris: Firmin—Didot, 1842).

19 Chambers, *Mediaeval Stage*, p. 279; see also Petit de Julleville, *Comédiens*, p. 34. Bakhtine lists the dates of attempts to suppress the Fête des Fous extending over nine centuries (*Rabelais*, p. 86).

20 *Epistola de Reformatione Theologiae* (*Opera omnia*, i, 121). Quoted by Chambers, *Mediaeval Stage*, p. 292. Cf. Swain, *Fools and Folly*, p. 71. A noted English clergyman, Robert Grosseteste, Bishop of Lincoln, also condemned the Feast of Fools, in 1244.

21 Clergymen who had attempted to abolish the Feast were the subject of an insulting *jeu*, performed in Troyes, in 1445 (Defourneaux, *Vie quotidienne*, p. 48).

22 Adolphe Fabre, *Les Clercs du Palais*, 2nd edn (Lyon: Scheuring, 1875), p. xix.

23 *Church*, p. 110.

24 Petit de Julleville, *Répertoire*, p. 330; Chambers, *Mediaeval Stage*, p. 296.

25 *Recueil général*, vol. i, pp. iv–v.

26 *Caractéristiques*, p. 7.

27 Lambert C. Porter, *La Fatrasie et le fatras* (Geneva: Droz, 1960). See also W. F. Patterson, *Three Centuries of French Poetic Theory*, 2 vols. (New York: Russell & Russell, 1966), vol. i, pp. 123–4 and 147–9; Robert Garapon, *La Fantaisie verbale et le comique dans le théâtre français du Moyen Age à la fin du XVIIe siècle* (Paris: Armand Colin, 1957), p. 28; and Hans-Robert Jauss, 'Littérature médiévale', pp. 86–7, for a discussion of the fatrasie.

28 *Poésie du Moyen Age*, p. 249.

29 *Fools and Folly*, p. 92.

30 'Farce et sotie', p. 98; *Fatrasie*, pp. 94–5. See also Leonard E. Arnaud, *French Nonsense Literature in the Middle Ages: The 'Fatras' and its Later Evolution* (New York: New York Univ. Press, 1942); and Ernest Langlois, *Recueil d'arts de seconde rhétorique* (Paris: Leroux, 1902), in particular p. 192.

31 'Farce et sotie', p. 98.

32 Henri Chatelain, *Recherches sur le vers français au XVe siècle: Rimes, metres et strophes* (Paris: Champion, 1908), p. 222; Arnaud, *Nonsense Literature*, p. 15: 'nowhere does a *fatras* appear in the sotties'.

33 'Fatrasie et coq-à-l'âne', in *Mélanges Guiette* (Antwerp: Nederlandsche boekhandel, 1961), pp. 5–18.

34 'J'appellerais "fatras" ce processus de dissociation, considéré comme un mode particulier du langage, par opposition à la "fatrasie", genre littéraire comportant en tant que tel des aspects non proprement linguistiques: versification, mélodie, en certains cas élocution dialoguée' (*ibid.* p. 11).

35 *Ibid.* pp. 11–12.

36 *Ibid.* p. 16.

37 Heers, *Fêtes*, p. 142.

38 Emile Magnin, 'Ancien Théâtre françois', *Journal des Savants* (1858), 406; Harvey, *Theatre*, p. 174.

39 Chambers, *Mediaeval Stage*, p. 373.

40 Cohen, *Théâtre comique*, p. 8; see above, p. 20.

41 Swain, *Fools and Folly*, p. 78; see also Petit de Julleville, *Répertoire*, p. 399; and Aubailly, *Monologue*, pp. 477–9.

42 For a discussion of the etymology of this term, see Charles Magnin's review article of Lenient, *La Satire en France au Moyen Age*, in *Journal des Savants* (1859), 602.

43 Petit de Julleville, *Comédiens*, p. 249; also bibliography, pp. 256–61.

44 Brown, *Music*, p. 23; Petit de Julleville, *Comédiens*, pp. 232ff.; Cohen, *Théâtre comique*, p. 8.

45 Petit de Julleville, *Répertoire*, p. 106.

46 Harvey, *Theatre*, p. 17, n. 12.

47 *Ibid.* p. 14; Petit de Julleville, *Comédiens*, p. 97; Fabre, *Clercs*, p. 133.

48 For a history of the Enfants-sans-souci, see Walter Dittmann, *Pierre Gringore als Dramatiker* (Berlin: Ebering, 1923), Appendix: 'Die pariser Enfants-sans-souci zu Gringores Zeit', pp. 259–333. See also Petit de Julleville, *Comédiens*, pp. 148–91; Jean Frappier, 'Sur Jean du Pont-Alais', in *Mélanges Cohen* (Paris: Nizet, 1950), pp. 133–46; and Cohen, 'Triboulet, acteur et auteur comique du dernier quart du xve siècle', *Revue d'Histoire du Théâtre*, 6 (1954), 291–3.

49 Porter, 'Farce et sotie', p. 90.

50 'Ancien Théâtre', p. 266. A. Darmesteter and Adolphe Hatzfeld also assert that 'Les deux sociétés étaient rivales', in *Le Seizième Siècle en France*, 15th edn (Paris: Delagrave, 1928), p. 148.

51 Harvey, *Theatre*, pp. 24–5; and Fabre, *Clercs*, pp. 136–53. Miraulmont believes quite categorically that 'Le Prince de Sots est l'un de ses supposts [du Roi de la Basoche]' (*Mémoires*, p. 656).

52 *Arrêt du 15 mai 1476;* see Petit de Julleville, *Comédiens*, p. 101.

53 Harvey, *Theatre*, p. 175; Aubailly, *Monologue*, pp. 370–3.

54 Second Epistre du coq à l'asne', *Les Epistres*, ed. Georges Guiffrey (Paris: Morgand & Fatout, 1881), vol. III, p. 352 (my italics). Marot's connection with the Enfants-sans-souci and his sympathy for them are shown in a series of poems written between 1512 and 1515 (see Harvey, *Theatre*, p. 223, n. 48). See Marot's 'Epistre pour la Bazoche', ed. Guiffrey, vol. III, pp. 352–3.

55 *Comédiens*, p. 153.

56 Viollet-le-Duc, *Ancien Théâtre*, vol. VII, p. 177.

57 *Oevres complètes de Pierre de Bourdeille, seigneur Brantôme*, ed. Ludovic Lalanne, 11 vols. (Paris: Renouard, 1864–82), vol. IV, p. 10.

58 Gustave Cohen, 'Rabelais et le théâtre', *Revue des Etudes rabelaisiennes*, 9 (1911), p. 49; Malherbe, *Oeuvres*, ed. Lalanne, vol. IV, p. 94.

59 Vol. II, p. 198.

60 *Tableau historique et critique de la poésie française et du théâtre français au XVIe siècle*, new edn (Paris: Charpentier, 1843), p. 173. Similar opinions have been expressed by Charles Lenient, in *La Satire en France au Moyen Age*, 4th edn (Paris: Hachette, 1893), p. 334 ('de jeunes et joyeux désœuvrés, fils de famille pour la plupart'); Darmesteter and Hatzfeld, *Seizième Siècle*, p. 148; Victor Hallays-Dabot, *Histoire de la censure théâtrale en France* (Paris: Dentu, 1862), p. 6; and Paris, *Poésie du Moyen Age*, vol. II, p. 250.

61 *Comédiens*, pp. 150 and 154. Brown believes also that these were 'the Bohemians of their day, and companions to François Villon. No doubt adventurers, young students chafing at the academic bit, even thieves and murderers occasionally joined the sots for a bit of fun and a role in a play' (*Music*, p. 29).

62 *Poésie du Moyen Age*, p. 250.

63 *Theatre*, p. 27.

64 'Ancien Théâtre', p. 267.

65 *Clercs*, p. 147.

66 *Drama*, p. 250.

67 *Recueil général*, vol. I, p. xvii.

68 *Jongleurs*, p. 248; see also p. 250.

69 *Caractéristiques*, p. 13.

70 Harvey, *Theatre*, p. 27. See in particular ch. 3, in which Harvey discusses various textual indications of the Basoche origins of some *sotties*.

71 Petit de Julleville, *Comédiens*, pp. 113–14.

72 Fabre, *Clercs*, pp. 5ff.

73 Petit de Julleville, *Comédiens*, p. 103; see also Fabre, *Clercs*, pp. 138–42; Cohen, *Théâtre comique*, p. 8.

74 Petit de Julleville, *Répertoire*, pp. 330–5.

75 *Oeuvres*, ed. Guiffrey, vol. III, pp. 623–4; cf. Petit de Julleville, *Comédiens*, p. 115.

76 Fabre, *Clercs*, pp. 136–53; Petit de Julleville, *Comédiens*, pp. 100ff.; Miraulmont describes the steps taken by 'la Censure de la Cour' in order to

force the 'Clercs Bazochiens' to perform their *jeux* 'avec la modestie requise' (*Mémoires*, pp. 652–3).

77 Harvey, *Theatre*, p. 177.

78 Brantôme: 'qu'il falloit qu'ilz [les sots] passassent leur temps, et qu'il [le roi] leur permettoit qu'ilz parlassent de luy et de sa court, non pourtant desreglement mais surtout qu'ilz ne parlassent de la Royne, sa femme, en façon quelconque; autrement, qu'il les feroit tous pendre' (*Vies des dames illustres françaises et étrangères* ('Anne de Bretagne'), ed. L. Moland (Paris: Garnier, 1920), pp. 10–11).

79 Jehan Bouchet, *Epistres morales et familières du Traverseur* (Poitiers, 1545, in-fol.), vol. I, fol. 32d.

80 We have records of such payments in 1512, 1513, 1517, 1525, 1531, and 1534. See Fabre, *Clercs*, pp. 143–4; and Harvey, *Theatre*, p. 227. An example of these payments is given in Archives nationales, sect. jud., vol. X, 1512, 1513, fol. 120: 'le Parlement ordonnance chaque fois trente livres parisis pour être remises aux tresoriers de la Bazoche, pour leur aider à payer les frais de leurs spectacles'.

81 See Lenient, *Satire au Moyen Age*, p. 341.

82 Picot, *Recueil général*, vol. II, pp. 265–73.

83 Other references to censorship or punishment occur in the following plays: *Faulte d'Argent*, l. 205; *Les Maraux*, ll. 365–6; *Le Monde, Abuz*, l. 959; and *Le Cry de la Bazoche*, ll. 67–8 and 140–1.

84 Chambers, *Mediaeval Stage*, pp. 384–6. Le Monde, in *Troys Galans et Monde*, calls a *sot* 'mimin à sonnetes' (l. 190). For a discussion of the relation of the monk's hood to the fool's headgear, see the remarks of Guiffrey, on the 'Second Epistre du coq à l'asne' of Marot (*Les Epistres*, ed. Guiffrey, vol. III, p. 353, n. 1).

85 Cohen, *Théâtre comique*, p. 5.

86 Gustave Cohen in *Le Théâtre profane*, vol. II of *Le Théâtre en France au Moyen Age* (Paris: Rieder, 1931) reproduces an illustration of the costume of the *sot* in Plate XLV. The most thorough and detailed collection of illustrations is to be found in Douce, *Clowns and Fools of Shakspeare*. For other sources of illustrations, see Chambers, *Mediaeval Stage*, p. 384; Picot, *Recueil général*, vol. I, p. xix; M.-J. Rigollot, *Monnaies inconnues des Evêques des Innocens, des Fous* (Paris: Merlin, 1837), pp. 73, 166, *et passim*.

87 Chambers, *Mediaeval Stage*, pp. 384–5.

88 *Théâtre comique*, p. 5.

89 Chambers, *Mediaeval Stage*, p. 386.

90 Rabelais refers to a 'Fou à marotte' in his list of fools (*Tiers Livre*, ch. XXXVIII). Other references to the *marotte* are found in *Les Sotz ecclesiasticques* (ll. 68–70), and in *Les Vigilles de Triboullet*, where the bauble of the famous fool is described as working miracles: 'Sa marotte faisoit miracle, / Elle esprouvait le triacle, / Contre poison et tout venin' (ll. 148–50); cf. ll. 160–2.

3 THE *SOTTIE* AS DRAMA

1 Cf. Bowen, *Caractéristiques*, p. 8; and Frank, *Drama*, p. 245.

2 'Bynete', in *Le Bateleur*, although appearing in a popular song of the period, may have been a pleonasm formed from the verb *biner*, which gives the noun *binet* (in modern French, *second labour*, second plowing), a term with erotic overtones in the Middle Ages. See Halina Lewicka, *La Langue et le style du théâtre comique français des XVe et XVIe siècles*, 2 vols. (Paris: Klincksieck, 1960), vol. I, p. 117; E. Philipot, *Six farces*, pp. 43–76. Aubailly shows that the seemingly proper names of the *sots* in *La Moralité de 1427* are all ways of saying 'fool'.

3 'Doribus' was coined at the end of the fifteenth century from the expression (*poudre*) *d'oribus*, the humorous name of a drug that supposedly contained gold. It became the nickname of any hawker of patent medicine (Lewicka, *Langue*, vol. I, pp. 282–3).

4 One miscellaneous type of name, which is partly individual, partly generic, is that of a proper name based on a species of animal. Only two examples of this onomastic procedure appear in the plays: Rossignol and Perrocquet. It is significant that they are both the names of birds. Cf. also the farce entitled *La Pipée*.

5 See Picot, *Recueil général*, vol. II, pp. 120–2.

6 For a lexical analysis of names of this type, see Lewicka, *Langue*, vols. I and II.

7 *Ibid.* vol. I, pp. 109, 133, and 174.

8 Randle Cotgrave, *A Dictionarie of the French and English Language* (London, 1611; repr. Colombia, S.C.: South Carolina Univ. Press, 1950).

9 Rabelais has Panurge consult the Triboulet of François I on marriage (*Tiers Livre*, ch. XLV). For a discussion of the name, history, and roles of Triboulet, see Cohen, *Recueil*, p. xxviii; and the article, 'Triboulet', pp. 291–3; also Picot, *Recueil général*, vol. III, p. 205; and especially Droz, *Trepperel*, pp. 217–19.

10 *Les Vigilles de Triboullet*, ll. 131, 202, 243, and 277. Cohen discusses Maître Mouche, in 'Maître Mouche, farceur et chef de troupe au XV siècle', *Revue d'Histoire du Théâtre*, 6 (1954), 146–9. Another example of a real name that was also a fool's name is that of Jehan l'Espine du Pont-Alletz (Songecreux): see Picot, *Recueil général*, vol. II, pp. 115–20.

11 This kind of name could be considered as belonging either to the category of names made up of a personal trait, or to that of group names, since fools were viewed as a section of society. The *sots* are discussed here as a separate category in part because of their importance to the *sottie*, in part also because the terms applied to them present certain peculiarities.

12 *Mediaeval Stage*, p. 5.

13 Aubailly suggests that the term *galant* became popular later than *sot*. For

an excellent discussion of the various names used for fools, see *Monologue*, pp. 350–66.

14 According to Aubailly, the *badin* was 'le simple d'esprit "par nature". . . . défini face à la société par un rapport d'exclusion – inferiorité', and the *sots* could be defined 'à l'égard de la société par un rapport d'exclusion – supériorité, justifié par la possession d'une véritable sagesse qui leur permet d'ouvrir sur cette société dont ils se détachent, un œil critique et objectif' (*Monologue*, pp. 354–5). See also Petit de Julleville, *Comédie*, pp. 281–6.

15 *Recueil général*, vol. III, p. 206.

16 Lewicka gives a thorough analysis of these words in *Langue*, vol. I: 'La Dérivation dans les textes comiques'. See, in particular, pp. 216 and 281–3. She also recognizes the connection between *sot* and *trompeur* in names like Coquillart.

17 Picot, *Recueil général*, vol. II, pp. 206 and 207.

18 Lucien Febvre, *Le Problème de l'incroyance au XVIe siècle*; *La Religion de Rabelais* (Paris: Albin Michel, 1942), p. 11.

19 *Art et science de rhétorique métrifiée* (Toulouse: Nicolas Vieillard, 1539). Quoted in Petit de Julleville, *Comédie*, pp. 65–6.

20 Not counted are two unusually long plays of over 1,500 lines, *Le Monde, Abuz*, and *La Moralité de 1427*. Picot has suggested that the exceptional length of *Le Monde, Abuz* may indicate that it took the place of both the *sottie* and the morality of a theatrical production (*Recueil général*, vol. II, p. 1).

21 Dramatic construction in these *sotties* contrasts sharply with that of the Renaissance play, whose assumption was 'that a drama is the setting forth of an action whose full course and dénouement the audience can foresee from the beginning', according to Darnell Roaten, in *Structural Forms in the French Theater. 1500–1700* (Philadelphia: Univ. of Pennsylvania Press, 1960), p. 161.

22 This type of construction is not limited to the *sottie*: in *Le Povre Jouhan*, the *sot* comments on the actions of the other characters in a forthright way. For further discussion of this procedure in the farce, see Swain, *Fools and Folly*, p. 95.

23 Paul Zumthor, 'Classes and Genres', p. 32. For other examples of this kind of textual syntax, see *Les Troys Galans et un Badin*, *Les Sobres Sots*, *Les Rapporteurs*, and *Les Croniqueurs*.

24 See also Brian Jeffery (ed.), *Chanson Verse of the Early Renaissance*, 2 vols. (London: Brian Jeffery, 1971–6).

25 Brown, *Music*, p. 61.

26 Where the number of voices used in a song can be established, trios are particularly common: 'the three-part setting may be considered the customary one for secular polyphonic compositions in the theater' (*Ibid.* p. 101). The fact that *sots* usually come in groups of three may be tied in some plays to the musical structure of the songs they sing. The arrange-

ments of the songs were more likely simpler than the sophisticated poly-phonic treatments of the 'theatrical *chansons*'.

27 According to Brown, *Music*, p. 146.

28 A similar use of refrains is to be found in the farce and morality also; e.g., *Obstination des femmes* and *Le Pâté et la Tarte*.

29 My analysis agrees with the findings of Paul Zumthor with regard to medieval literary forms in general: 'it is impossible to detach the inter-pretation of individual texts from a history of forms' ('Classes and Genres', p. 35).

30 Tr. Laurence Scott, 2nd edn (Austin and London: Univ. of Texas Press, 1968). An excellent analysis of roles in the *fabliau* can be found in 'Func-tions and Roles in the Fabliau', by Mary Jane Schenck, in *Comparative Literature*, 30: 1 (Winter 1978), 22–34.

31 Scholars have not been able to agree on the different 'types' of *sotties*. Aubailly's classification, 'sottie–jugement', 'sottie–action', etc., is one of the best. Each of these types can be shown to be a particular configuration of the three roles. For example, the 'sottie–journal' is a play in which only the accusatory role is represented on stage, in which the accuser verbalizes the other two roles. Aubailly's groups 1, 2, and 3 (*Monologue*, pp. 366–68) are not at the same level of abstraction as the roles outlined here. Group 1 (*les sots contestataires*) is a particular manifestation of the accusatory function; but groups 2 and 3 are both kinds of wrong-headed-ness. Finally, Aubailly's groups make no provision for the role, distinct from the previous two, of victim.

32 A. J. Greimas, *Sémantique structurale; recherche et méthode* (Paris, Larousse: 1966).

33 For a discussion of this question, see Picot, *Recueil général*, vol. I, p. vii, and vol. III, p. 205; Droz, *Trepperel*, pp. lxvi–lxviii; Harvey, *Théatre*, p. 174; Porter, 'Farce et sotie', p. 93; and Aubailly, *Monologue*, pp. 286–91.

34 See Félix Gaiffe, *Le Rire et la scène française* (Paris: Boivin, 1931), pp. 16 and 25; and Henri Bergson, *Le Rire* (Paris: PUF, 1969).

35 A different system of classifying the *sotties*, one based on the kind of action involved, is given by Aubailly, in *Monologue*, pp. 287–321.

36 The plays that are almost entirely constructed of *jeux de scène* are *Trote Menu* and *Les Esveilleurs*. The following plays are a mixture of *jeux* with other types of comedy: *Les Coppieurs*, *Les Coquins*, *Le Roy des Sotz*, *Les Sotz nouveaulx*, *Troys Galans et Monde*, and *Les Vigilles de Triboullet*.

37 Not all scholars of the medieval theater have found this type of humor inaccessible. Peter Conroy believes, on the contrary, that our times share with the Middle Ages 'an appreciation of vulgar, scatological comedy and of fast-talking gyp artists, but also many secrets of the theatrical essence which transcend the rigidity and literal-mindedness of intervening times'. ('Old and New in Medieval French Farce', *Romance Notes*, 13 (Winter 1971), 342–3).

38 *Le Rire*, pp. 34–5.

39 *Fantaisie*, p. 10.

40 See Zumthor, 'Fatrasie', pp. 11–12 and 16–17. Picot is undoubtedly referring to *Les Menus Propos* when he defines one type of *sottie* as 'une fatrasie divisée en couplets et récitée en public par des sots ou des badins' (*Recueil général*, vol. I, p. vi).

41 *Fantaisie*, pp. 55–6.

42 *Ibid.* p. 56.

43 For examples of plays which are in large part *sotties de bande*, see *Les Sotz qui corrigent*, *Les Sotz qui remetent*, *Les Sobres Sots*, *Les Coppieurs*, and *Les Veaulx*.

44 Droz, *Trepperel*, p. lxvii. Porter, like Droz and Picot, divides the *sotties* into 'primitive' and those 'à allusions politiques' ('Farce et sotie', pp. 92–3), the latter having 'un sens', 'de vrais thèmes'. See also Petit de Julleville, *Comédie*, p. 278; and Eugène Lintilhac, *La Comédie: Moyen Age et Renaissance*, vol. II of *Histoire générale du théâtre en France*, 5 vols. (Paris: Flammarion, 1904–10), p. 180.

45 Other plays that are *proverbes en action* or a similar form of general satire are *Les Esbahis*, *Faulte d'Argent*, *Le Monde*, *Les Sotz fourrez*, *Les Sotz qui corrigent*, *Les Sotz qui remetent*, *Tout le Monde*, and *Les Trompeurs*; and, in part, *Les Esveilleurs*, *Mestier et Marchandise*, *Pou d'Acquest*, and *Les Troys Galans et un Badin*.

46 For other examples of this type, see *Les Brus*; *Les Cris de Paris*, *Le Cry de la Bazoche*; *Folle Bobance*; *Les Maraux*; *La Mère de Ville*; *Le Monde, Abuz*; *Le Pelerin et La Pelerine*; and *Le Pelerinage* (the institution of marriage); *La Reformeresse*; *Les Sobres Sots*; and *Les Sotz qui recueuvrent*; in part: *Les Esbahis*; *La Feste des Roys* (the satire of religion); *Les Sotz qui corrigent*; *Tout, Rien, et Chascun*; and *Troys Galans et Monde*.

47 *Comédie*, p. 358.

48 In contrast to *Le Jeu du Prince des Sotz*, another play in this category which has been attributed to Gringore, *Les Croniqueurs*, is specific satire at its least theatrical. The play satirizes individuals verbally, not through the kind of dramatic action that *Le Jeu du Prince des Sotz* employs.

49 Other examples of this type of satire are *L'Astrologue*, *Les Béguins*, *Mestier et Marchandise*, *Pou d'Acquest*, *Les Rapporteurs*, and *Troys Pelerins et Malice*. It is of course always possible that we are no longer able to recognize specific allusions in other *sotties*.

50 'Classes and Genres', pp. 35–6.

4 SATIRE IN THE *SOTTIE*

1 *Les Origines de la satire anti-bourgeoise en France*, 2 vols., I: *Moyen Age – XVIe siècle* (Geneva: Droz, 1966).

2 Samuel Macon Carrington, Jr, 'The Elements of Humor and Satire in the

Medieval Farces and *Sotties*', doctoral dissertation, Univ. of North Carolina, 1963. (*Dissertation Abstracts*, 26, 3946–7.)

3 'The Nature of Satire', *Univ. of Toronto Quarterly*, 14 (Oct. 1944), 76. This definition is similar to that of Samuel Johnson (*Rambler*, 22, June 2, 1750), who wrote that satire was born of an unholy cohabitation of wit and malice.

4 *Psychocritique du genre comique* (Paris: Corti, 1964), pp. 70–1. See also p. 38, where Mauron distinguishes between 'l'esprit tendancieux' and 'l'esprit inoffensif'. Lenient has defined satire solely according to its literary form in *La Satire en France au XVIe siècle*, 2 vols., 3rd edn (Paris: Hachette, 1886), p. xi.

5 This 'object of attack' is sometimes called the 'subject' of satire. To avoid confusion, the term 'object' or 'object of satire' will always be used to mean that which is satirized.

6 See Walter Kaiser, *Praisers of Folly; Erasmus, Rabelais, Shakespeare* (London: Victor Gollancz, 1964), p. 61, for a discussion of the 'mask of folly' in the work of Erasmus. Bakhtine summarizes the complex implications of the mask in *Rabelais*, pp. 49–50. Abel Lefranc discusses the use of the mask of folly by Rabelais in the Introduction to *Pantagruel* (vol. III of *Oeuvres de François Rabelais*, Paris: Champion, 1922), p. lxviii.

7 *Fools and Folly*, p. 112.

8 *Recueil général*, vol. II, pp. 107–8.

9 French trans. by Pierre de Nolhac (Paris: Garnier–Flammarion, 1964), p. 44. See also p. 45: 'les Dieux ont réservé la vérité aux fous'. A strongly-worded and lengthy reaffirmation of the fool's right to criticize everyone is developed in *La Moralité de 1427*, ll. 883ff.

10 Porter, 'Farce et sotie', p. 101.

11 For a discussion of the differences between the farce and the *sottie* with regard to satire, see Bowen, *Caractéristiques*, p. 271.

12 *Epistres du Traverseur*, vol. I, fol. 32.

13 Porter, 'Farce et sotie', p. 95; Droz, *Trepperel*, p. lxvii.

14 *Satire en France au Moyen Age*, p. 373. See also Gustave Attinger, *L'Esprit de la commedia dell'arte dans le théâtre français* (Paris: Publications de la Société d'Histoire du Théâtre, 1950), p. 86: the *sot* is 'le porte-parole autorisé de la critique des institutions, des classes et des hommes'; and Darmesteter and Hatzfeld, *Seizième Siècle*, p. 150: the *sotties* 'flagellaient audacieusement toutes les sottises des hommes depuis le peuple jusqu'au roi'.

15 *Recueil général*, vol. I, p. iii; see also Harvey, *Theatre*, p. 28.

16 *Comédie*, p. 6.

17 *Trepperel*, p. lxx.

18 See Lenient, *Satire au Moyen Age*, p. 326.

19 *Origines*, p. 212.

20 See Zumthor, *Essai*, p. 447; and Gaiffe, *Rire*, p. 36: the theater is 'une

adaptation directe et constante avec les besoins et les habitudes du public'.

21 See Defourneaux, *Vie quotidienne*, p. 46.

22 *Origines*, p. 178.

23 See Brown, *Music*, p. 39; and Picot, *Recueil général*, vol. I, pp. 13, 137, 198. *Troys Galans et Monde, L'Astrologue*, and *La Folie des Gorriers* are probably the work of *basochiens*; see also Aubailly, *Monologue*, pp. 371-2.

24 'Satire', p. 77.

25 Picot, *Recueil général*, vol. II, p. 327.

26 Brown, *Music*, p. 40; see also pp. 11 and 111.

27 *Comédie*, p. 120; see also p. 117.

28 Bakhtine, *Rabelais*, p. 98 (Bakhtine's italics).

29 *Origines*, p. 178.

30 *Ibid.* p. 112; see also p. 148.

31 *Theatre*, p. 176.

32 See Alter, *Origines*, p. 138.

33 *Ibid.* p. 146.

34 Lenient, *Satire au Moyen Age*, p. 4.

35 Brown, *Music*, p. 11.

36 *Origines*, p. 146.

37 *Satire au Moyen Age*, p. 255.

38 See Alter, *Origines*, pp. 176-7. Gringore's case is a complex one, for although he seems to have been of bourgeois origins, it has been argued by Charles Oulmont that he wrote for the people: 'Pour que personne ne doute que la Sotie est écrite pour le peuple, Gringore s'exprime familièrement: il met dans la bouche des acteurs des jurons, lui qui n'a pas coûtume d'en user dans ses œuvres' (*La Poésie morale, politique et dramatique à la veille de la Renaissance; Pierre Gringore* (Paris: Champion, 1911), p. 286).

39 *Theatre*, pp. 176-7; cf. Alter, *Origines*, p. 212.

40 Droz, *Trepperel*, p. lxx.

41 Harvey, *Theatre*, p. 234; Swain, *Fools and Folly*, pp. 4-5.

42 See Lenient, *Satire au Moyen Age*, p. 317; see also *Satire au XVIe siècle*, p. 6: 'la médisance console de la faiblesse, le rire tempère les abus de la force'.

43 *Comédie*, p. 361.

44 *Ibid.* p. 71; Carrington, 'Elements of Humor', p. 76.

45 *Satire au Moyen Age*, p. 4.

46 F. E. Lumley has summarized the position of various writers who support or oppose the idea of satire as a means of social progress in *Means of Social Control* (New York: Century Co., 1925), pp. 251-5.

47 'Satire', p. 79.

48 *Comédie*, p. 360.

49 Two scholars of literature and music believe otherwise, but they are in the minority. See Brown, *Music*, p. 131: 'the various classes of French society had never before been so close to each other' as in the first quarter

of the sixteenth century; and Gaston Paris, *Poésie du Moyen Age*, pp. 21–2 (dealing with cultural divisions of society rather than economic ones).

50 Henri Pirenne, *La Fin du Moyen Age* (Paris: Alcan, 1929; repr. 1931), ch. 7: 'Les Nouvelles Tendences économiques', p. 151.

51 *Ibid.* p. 147.

52 *Les Institutions de la France au XVIe siècle* (Paris: PUF, 1948), p. 10.

53 *History of the Renaissance* (Salt Lake City: Univ. of Utah Press, 1963), Book I: *Economy and Society*, p. 121.

54 I have adopted the two criteria that Alter proposes for distinguishing the bourgeois from the non-bourgeois: (1) a bourgeois must be 'd'origine roturière'; and (2) he must be involved in the exchange of goods produced by another, the supervision of that exchange, the administration of the economic and political life tied to that exchange, and the practical or theoretical defense of the conditions favorable to that exchange (*Origines*, pp. 9–10).

55 Marcel Françon, in *Notes sur l'esthétique de la femme au XVIe siècle* (Cambridge, Mass.: Harvard Univ. Press, 1939), has analyzed the notion of the people and their collective part in the creative process (in particular, in poetry and music). He agrees with Pirenne and Zeller that the late Middle Ages and early Renaissance experienced a greater and greater separation between social groups, 'des antagonismes de plus en plus violents entre maîtres et ouvriers' (p. 22).

56 Ruth Mohl has made a detailed survey of this literature and of the varying concepts that contributed to the medieval idea of *état* in *The Three Estates in Medieval and Renaissance Literature* (New York: Columbia Univ. Press, 1933).

57 An impassioned plea for recognizing the importance of Labour is to be found in the *Moralité novelle de la Croix Faubin*, in D.W. Tappan and S.M. Carrington, 'Deux pièces comiques inédites du manuscrit BN fr. 904', *Romania*, 91 (1970), 169–88.

58 *Three Estates*, p. 277.

59 *Ibid.* p. 6.

60 See Alter, *Origines*, p. 21.

61 *Ibid.* pp. 15–24, for a lucid account of the evolution of the term 'bourgeois' in the Middle Ages.

62 Mohl, *Three Estates*, p. 80.

63 *Origines*, p. 16.

64 *Des Ordres*, in *Oeuvres*, 1610; cited by Gaston Zeller, *Institutions*, p. 37.

65 These characters appear in the following plays: Le Commun, in *Le Jeu du Capifol*; Sotte Commune, in *Le Jeu du Prince des Sotz*; Chascun, in *L'Astrologue*; *Chascun, Plusieurs*; *Tout, Rien, et Chascun*; and *Les Sotz triumphans*; Sot Ignorant, in *Le Monde, Abuz*; La Chose Publicque, in *Les Sotz fourrez*; and Peuple François, in *Satyre*.

66 *Les Sotz triumphans*, ll. 73–4.

67 *Satire au Moyen Age*, p. 367.

68 These roles were probably played by men, as these lines from *Les Coppieurs* indicate:

> Vous en jourez très bien la femme
> Vous avez le corps tant faictifz
> Les yeulx rians, le nez traitifz;
> Il semble que (vous) soyez fardé (ll. 186–9).

See also ll. 192–4.

69 These characters appear in the following plays: three *pèlerines* in *Le Pelerinage*, one in *Le Pelerin et La Pelerine*; three prostitutes in *Les Brus*, and La Fille esgarée in *Les Povres Deables*.

70 The *sotties* that discuss women and marriage to a significant extent are: *Les Cris de Paris*; *Le Monde, Abuz*; *Le Pelerin et La Pelerine*; *Le Pelerinage*; *Les Sobres Sots*; and *Les Troys Galans et un Badin*.

71 See Bowen, *Caractéristiques*, pp. 29–30ff.

72 See also ll. 184–93, 415–24; and in *Les Cris de Paris*, ll. 72–3, 170–2. Although the official subject of *Les Cris de Paris* is marriage, there is little satire specifically of women. This is the only *sottie* that criticizes both sexes equally, and for the same faults.

73 Another side of the connection between Folie and women's clothes is indicated in this statement from *La Folie des Gorriers*, ll. 116–18: Folie gets into women's heads 'Et leur faitz porter telz habiz, / Quant je vueil que l'on se soubmecte, / Qu'ils font leur chasteté suspecte' ('And makes them wear such clothes / When I want them to submit, / That they raise doubts about their chastity').

74 *Origines*, p. 89.

75 Ed. Lalanne, pp. 13–14. See Lintilhac, *Comédie*, pp. 29–31. Also Lucien Dubech, *Histoire générale illustrée du théâtre*, 5 vols. (Paris: Librairie de France, 1931–35), vol. II, pp. 120–1. The oldest remaining satiric revue, *Le Jeu de la feuillée* (which Gustave Cohen has argued may be a *sottie*), had set the tone with its satire of real townspeople.

76 *Theatre*, p. 33.

77 *French Farce*, p. 156. She may also have been satirized in *Troys Pelerins et Malice*, for at the time of the play she had become the focal point of popular recriminations. In a *sottie* played in December 1516, she was accused of pillaging the state and the government for her own benefit (see Picot, *Recueil général*, vol. II, p. 299).

78 Mohl, *Three Estates*, p. 367.

79 Details on the troubles caused by war are given in every history of the period. In particular the following works have been consulted: Georges Duby and Robert Mandrou, *Histoire de la civilisation française*, 2 vols. (Paris: Colin, 1958); see in particular vol. I, p. 185; Eugene F. Rice, Jr, *The Foundations of Early Modern Europe (1460–1559)* (New York: Norton, 1970), p. 100; and Defourneaux, *Vie quotidienne*, pp. 185ff. and 221–30.

80 *Taille* was also the name of a tax. References to war are to be found in many other *sotties*; see in particular *L'Astrologue*, ll. 270–83; *Les Gens nouveaulx*, ll. 167–70; *Les Menus Propos*, ll. 101–2; *La Moralité de 1427*, ll. 1408ff.; *Les Rapporteurs*, ll. 214–16; *Les Sotz qui remetent*, ll. 221–2; *Les Troys Galans et un Badin*, ll. 18–19, 105–8. It is striking that the two provinces in which the *sottie* flourished, Normandy and the Ile-de-France, are those which had little respite from war.

81 An excellent résumé of the difficulties this prejudice caused Louis XI is the article 'Louis XI, la noblesse et la marchandise', by Gaston Zeller, in *Annales: Economies, Sociétés, Civilisations*, I (1946), 331–41. See also Rice, *Foundations*, p. 56.

82 Zeller, 'Louis XI', p. 333; Rice, *Foundations*, p. 62.

83 Rice, *Foundations*, p. 99.

84 Defourneaux, *Vie quotidienne*, pp. 209–10.

85 The English knight Talbot would remind the *sots* that 'Si Dieu estoit gendarme il seroit pillard' (quoted by Kilgour, p. 26; see below, n. 86).

86 *The Decline of Chivalry as shown in the French Literature of the Late Middle Ages* (Cambridge, Mass.: Harvard Univ. Press, 1937); in particular pp. 21–5.

87 P. 387; my italics.

88 A long, violent tirade against the *gendarmes* who cause such miseries is to be found in the *Bergerie de Mieulx-que-devant*, which Aubailly calls a political morality (*Monologue*, p. 339), in particular the lines 39–150 (Viollet-le-Duc, *Ancien Théâtre*, play no. 57). See also *La Moralité de 1427*, ll. 1421ff.; and *La Croix Faubin*, ll. 318–45.

89 Popular antagonism toward the *gendarme* is expressed indirectly by such linguistic creations as 'gendarmatique', 'gendermerel' (*sic*) (*La Mère de Ville*, ll. 149 and 224), words 'à nuance franchement péjorative' (Lewicka, *Langue*, pp. 316–17; see also p. 355).

90 Zeller, *Institutions*, p. 298.

91 Kilgour, *Decline*, p. 25.

92 Defourneaux, *Vie quotidienne*, p. 213.

93 *L'Art militaire et les armées au Moyen Age en Europe et dans le Proche Orient*, 2 vols. (Paris: Payot, 1946), vol. I, p. 432.

94 Zeller, *Institutions*, p. 303.

95 A recently published sermon, dating from the year 1396, articulates this contradiction between the ideal and reality: 'or notez et considerez quantes persecucions sont faictes aux povres innocens, aux povres gens de ville par my le royaume par les gens d'armes qui le royaume doivent deffendre' ('Un sermon français inédit attribuable à Jacques Legrand', *Romania*, 93 (1972), 460–78: p. 474).

96 Duby and Mandrou, *Histoire*, vol. I, p. 197.

97 Rice, *Foundations*, pp. 99–100.

98 Another summary of the situation, a less ironic one, was given by a

delegate from the nobility to the Etats Généraux of 1484, when he proudly reminded the assembly that it was the knights who fought and the people who paid (quoted by Alter, *Origines*, p. 144).

99 The Lady was addressed as a Lord in Provençal courtly poetry (*midons*), a procedure that the *sots* may have been alluding to, thereby intensifying their parody of courtly genres.

100 See in particular *Le Jeu du Prince des Sotz*, ll. 202–13; *Les Brus*, ll. 28–9; *Les Maraux*, l. 90; and *La Feste des Rois*, ll. 179ff.

101 Similar boastings that recount pretended knightly prowesses are to be found in: *Les Sotz nouveaulx*, ll. 191–246; and *La Folie des Gorriers*, ll. 21–30. Charles Mauron has offered a psychoanalytic explanation of these braggings: 'La vantardise et le récit d'exploits imaginaires sont courants chez les enfants et l'on connaît assez le rôle des soldats dans leurs jeux' (*Psychocritique*, pp. 84ff.). The parody of noble deeds was a favorite procedure of a related medieval dramatic form, the *monologue dramatique* (Aubailly, *Monologue*, pp. 137ff.).

102 Bergson, *Le Rire*, p. 94.

103 Petit de Julleville, *Répertoire*, p. 390.

104 *French Farce*, pp. 145–6.

105 *Comédie*, p. 211; see also p. 227.

106 The abbots of *Le Jeu du Prince des Sotz* are the counterparts of the nobles of that play: they represent *sots* more than clergy, and their only function is to desert their king while accepting the advances of Mère Sainte Eglise. Sotte Fiance and Sotte Occasion are personified abstractions, rather than satirical clergymen. On the other hand, it is likely that L'Escumeur de Latin, in *Les Sotz qui corrigent*, is an ecclesiastic, for he corrects 'diable et Dieu', he preaches against stylish fashions in the manner of many *prédicateurs* of the period, and he tries to stop the revelries of the fools, as did the Church with regard to the Fête des Fous.

107 See in particular *Le Pelerinage*, *Le Pelerin et La Pelerine*, *Fragments* (Picot, *Recueil général*, vol. II), *Troys Pelerins et Malice*, and *Les Premiers*.

108 A minor charge, that of ignorance and incompetence, seems to be attributed to all levels of the hierarchy. Unlike the *sottie*, the farce sees incompetence as a major abuse, and the subject of the cleric unfit for the charge that he occupies or wishes to occupy is a favorite subject. See *La Farce de la Bouteille*; *Le Filz qui se fait examiner*; *Science et son clerc*; *Anerie et son clerc*; *Le Clerc qui fut refusé à être prêtre*; *Maître Jean Jenin, vrai prophète*.

109 See *La Confession Margot*, in which Margot has slept with a monk, a pilgrim, and a hermit.

110 Magnin, 'Ancien Théâtre', p. 268.

111 *L'Incroyance*, p. 288.

112 Other instances of anti-monastic satire are found in *L'Astrologue*, ll. 388–91; *Le Monde*, *Abuz*, ll. 700–23; *Les Povres Deables*, ll. 299–320; *Le Roy des Sotz*, ll. 137–40; and *Le Jeu du Capifol*.

113 An unusual charge is made in *Satyre* (ll. 133–40): *cordeliers* are accused of hoarding wheat and making a profit from it. Although stock-piling and speculation in grains was common in this period, I have no indication that Franciscan friars were particularly guilty of the crime.

114 *L'Astrologue*, ll. 372–5. Other references to simony occur in *Les Croniqueurs*, ll. 228–47; *Les Esbahis*, ll. 191–2; *La Folie des Gorriers*, ll. 147–8; *Le Jeu du Capifol, passim*; *Les Menus Propos*, ll. 233–4; *Les Rapporteurs*, l. 238; and *Tout le Monde*, ll. 203–6.

115 Augustin Renaudet has pointed out that 'la décadence de la discipline' permitted bishops to accumulate the revenues of several abbeys, and because of increased wealth and power these ecclesiastics became 'courtisans, hommes de guerre, diplomates', proud of the missions that the king entrusted to them (*Préréforme et humanisme à Paris, 1494–1517*, 2nd edn (Paris: Champion, 1953), p. 9).

116 *Comédie*, pp. 221–2, n. 2.

117 In *Le Roman de Fauvel* a similar reversal of roles occurs: prelates are busy counselling the king about temporal affairs and neglect their duties. In this case also the prelates are seen as hypocritical (see Mohl, *Three Estates*, pp. 52ff.).

118 See ll. 46–8, 280–7, 327–31, 343–4, 428–35, and 611.

119 See also *La Folie des Gorriers*: 'cristalline', 'precogité', ll. 189 and 196; and *Les Esbahis*, ll. 64–70.

120 Brown has analyzed these liturgies in detail in his study of music in the medieval French theater; see in particular pp. 173–7.

121 See Aubailly, *Monologue*, pp. 40–77. Religious parody in the *sottie* is related not only to the *sermon joyeux*, but also to certain carnival forms, which are, as Mikhail Bakhtine has pointed out, 'une véritable parodie du culte religieux'. He believes, furthermore, that these forms are 'résolument extérieures à l'Eglise et à la religion. Elles appartiennent à la sphère totalement à part de la vie quotidienne' (*Rabelais*, p. 15).

122 *L'Incroyance*, pp. 143–61.

123 *Ibid.* p. 277.

124 The contrast has frequently puzzled critics and historians. Gaiffe has attempted the following explanation: 'C'est sans doute parce que la foi était vivace et profonde, parce que l'on ne pouvait concevoir aucune possibilité de résister à l'autorité de l'Eglise, que, par une sorte de revanche ou de détente, de pareilles libertés pouvaient être tolérées' (*Rire*, p. 41).

125 *Ibid.* p. 40.

126 *Introduction à la Renaissance*, Sec. 12.

127 Febvre, *L'Incroyance*, p. 302.

128 See Renaudet, *Préréforme*, p. 609.

129 See Porter, 'Farce et sotie', p. 118.

130 *Théâtre*, p. 406.

131 See Lucien Febvre, 'Une question mal posée: les origines de la Réforme

française et le problème général des causes de la Réforme', *Revue Historique*, 161 (May–Aug. 1929), 21–9.

132 'Origines', p. 28.

133 Charles Mauron has argued that *le comique* 'corrige moins les mœurs qu'il ne guérit les angoisses' (*Psychocritique*, p. 96).

134 These characters appear in the following plays: Chascun, in *Les Trompeurs*, *Les Sotz triumphans*, and *L'Astrologue*; Le Monde, in *Troys Galans et Monde;* Tout, in *Les Sotz qui remetent;* and Tout le Monde, in *Tout le Monde.* See also Le Pain and Le Vin, in *La Croix Faubin.*

135 A summary of economic conditions in Europe in the Renaissance can be found in *History of the Renaissance*, by Emil Lucki. See in particular Book 1: *Economy and Society*, pp. 122ff. Although more study is needed to determine the nature of the medieval poor, F. Graus has argued that the urban poor were made up of all kinds of wage workers, from the servants of rich bourgeois to day laborers, and journeymen whom guild rules kept from becoming masters; also included were those who were 'outside society': thieves, cripples, prostitutes, and vagrants ('The Late Medieval Poor in Town and Countryside', in *Change in Medieval Society*, ed. Sylvia L. Thrupp (New York: Appleton-Century-Crofts, 1964), p. 317).

136 *Théâtre*, p. 61.

137 Rice, *Foundations*, pp. 53–4; see also Alter, *Origines*, p. 81.

138 Lucien Goldmann has analyzed this process in the first chapter of *Le Dieu caché* (Paris: Gallimard, 1955).

139 See the introduction to *Les Rapporteurs*, one of the plays richest in details of daily living in the late Middle Ages (Droz, *Trepperel*, p. 53).

140 Randle Cotgrave, in the article 'Four', gives an English version of this aspect of popular life: 'For while the bread bakes and the corne grinds, people have some leisure to tell how the world goes' (*A Dictionarie of the French and English Tongues*: London, 1611; repr. Columbia, S.C.: South Carolina Univ. Press, 1950).

141 See Defourneaux, *Vie quotidienne*, pp. 245–6; and Johan Huizinga, *Le Déclin du Moyen Age*, trans. J. Bastin (Paris: Payot, 1961), p. 11.

142 Sotte Folle, in the same play, gives an estimate which indicates a popular conception of the age of the world: 'Il y a de miliers plus de dix / Qu'il fut né' (ll. 373–4).

143 The plays which put such characters on stage are *La Folie des Gorriers*, *Folle Bobance*, *Les Gens nouveaulx*, *Mestier et Marchandise*, *Pou d'Acquest*, and *Troys Galans et Monde*; plays which allude to them are *Les Esbahis*, *Faulte d'Argent*, *Les Sotz fourrez*, and *Les Sotz triumphans*.

144 *Origines*, p. 157.

145 See *ibid.* p. 209.

146 *Ibid.* p. 127; see also Mohl, *Three Estates*, pp. 355–6.

147 Alter summarizes the general characteristics of anti-bourgeois satire in this period in *Origines*, pp. 74–5.

148 A number of individual *métiers* appear briefly in the *sottie*, as discussed above, pp. 39–40. Le Tavernier of *Les Coquins*, Le Vigneron of *Satyre*, and the various occupations that appear in *Le Monde* are not satiric roles. Marchandise and Mestier, while more developed dramatically than these roles, are no more satiric. For a discussion of Sot Trompeur, see Alter, *Origines*, p. 39.

149 The lack of references to usury in the *sotties* is striking, given the importance of this vice in other medieval satiric writings. Other than this reference in *Le Monde, Abuz*, there is an attack on usurers in *Satyre* (ll. 181–226), *Les Sotz qui remetent* (l. 241), and *L'Astrologue* (ll. 392–5). Generally the *sottie* seems to have accepted loans on interest as a normal business activity, for it does not condemn usury as it does *tromperie, avarice*, etc.

150 *Origines*, p. 115.

151 *Ibid.* p. 116.

152 See *ibid.* p. 129. Although some of the trades would seem to belong to the *artisanat* rather than to commerce, Alter has shown that the two appear as sister activities in medieval literature: 'Les artisans s'agglomèrent aux marchands, sans qu'il soit possible de distinguer nettement la part respective des deux genres' (pp. 51–2).

153 See *ibid.* pp. 36, 56 and 165. A curious exception to the general antipathy toward bakers and tavern-keepers is to be found in *La Croix Faubin*, where the characters Le Pain and Le Vin are given a very sympathetic treatment, probably because they stand for the working class as a whole (Tappan and Carrington, 'Deux pièces comiques'). Cf. Aubailly, *Monologue*, p. 338.

154 *Les Troys Galans et un Badin*, ll. 196–7; cf. *L'Astrologue*, ll. 574–7. Like the *sottie*, Renart places tavern-keepers at the lowest rung of the ladder: 'De trestous mestiers, c'est le pire' (*Renart le Contrefait*, ed. G. Reynaud and H. Lemaitre (Paris: Champion, 1914), vol. II, l. 26935).

155 Zeller, *Institutions*, p. 28.

156 *Origines*, p. 59.

157 The legal satire of the first eight plays listed is analyzed by Harvey, *Theatre*, pp. 177–201.

158 *Comédiens*, p. 95.

159 *Theatre*, p. 34.

160 *Ibid.* p. 221.

161 *Ibid.* p. 175.

162 *Ibid.* p. 177, n. 6.

163 *Ibid.* p. 184.

164 *Origines*, p. 63.

165 *Ibid.* pp. 166–70.

166 This line, from a letter describing a morality of Henry Baude, is quoted in Harvey, *Theatre*, p. 183, n. 12.

167 Other references to these devious individuals are to be found in *Faulte d'Argent*, l. 196, and *Troys Galans et Monde*, ll. 103–5.

168 Barbara Swain has also remarked on this ambivalence of the fool. She labels the divergent conceptions of the fool as the Fool condemned and the Fool critic, in *Fools and Folly*, p. 92. See also Aubailly, *Monologue*, pp. 350ff.

169 For a discussion of the journey as one of the two basic structures of allegorical writings, see Angus Fletcher, *Allegory: The Theory of a Symbolic Mode* (Ithaca, N.Y., Cornell, 1966), pp. 151–7.

170 Most of the following summary of economic changes is based on Rice, *Foundations*, pp. 41–4; and Pirenne, *Fin*, ch. 7: 'Les Nouvelles Tendances économiques'.

171 *Fin*, p. 144.

172 Rice, *Foundations*, p. 49. See also Alter, *Origines*, pp. 176 and 194.

173 For a discussion of the receptiveness of the theater to social change, see above, pp. 70–1). Alter summarizes satire of the higher bourgeoisie in the late Middle Ages in *Origines*, pp. 104–8.

174 Ruth Mohl has observed a similar concern with changes of estate in the sixteenth-century 'estats du monde': 'the diatribes against social climbers increase in number and volume' in this period (*Three Estates*, p. 332). See also Rice, *Foundations*, p. 57; Zeller, *Institutions*, pp. 12 and 17; and 'Louis XI', pp. 335 and 336.

175 *L'Incroyance*, p. 275.

176 Pirenne, *Fin*, p. 145. The ironic advice given by various *sots* on how to succeed in society reflects what they thought were the business practices of men like Jacques Cœur: 'Baillez bourdes en payment' (a refrain in *La Folie des Gorriers*, l. 337, *et passim*). See pp. 145–6, below.

177 The *sots* protest the hoarding of grain by speculators, in *Les Troys Galans et un Badin*: 'Monniers desrobent le bon grain' (l. 152).

178 Alter points out that this phenomenon, the selling of offices, 'exerce des effets sur l'évolution de la bourgeoisie tout entière. Il contribue à sa scission en deux groupes' (*Origines*, p. 202; see also pp. 198ff).

179 Robert C. Elliott, in *The Power of Satire: Magic, Ritual, Art* (Princeton: Princeton Univ. Press, 1960), has argued that the beginnings of satire were linked to ritual. His thesis is given further evidence by the satire found in the *sottie*.

5 THE THEME OF SOCIAL HIERARCHY IN THE *SOTTIE*

1 See also ll. 219–20: 'Qui Justice n'empecheroit, / Tel contrefait du gentilastre'; and *Chascun, Plusieurs*, ll. 191–4. Of course, the *sots* were not unique in their belief in a social hierarchy: medieval thought in general posited hierarchies of all types, human and animal, vegetal and mineral,

diabolic and angelic. Froissart, Chartier, Christine de Pisan (*Livre de la Paix*) and many other writers also advocated a stable social hierarchy.

2 'Farce et sotie', p. 121.

3 *Caractéristiques*, p. 33.

4 I interpret 'anti-authoritarianism' not as simply opposing a particular power-holder (Louis XII, for example), but as opposing the principle of authority and, consequently, the existence of a social hierarchy. Bakhtine's argument concerns primarily the carnival, but by extension the *sottie* as well, for he labels the *sottie* 'un genre extrêmement carnavalisé de la fin du Moyen Age' (p. 24). It was probably this attempt to extend the characteristics of the carnival to the *sottie* that resulted in the misinterpretation of the hierarchical attitudes of the *sots*.

5 Alan E. Knight has similarly observed in the *sottie* an 'image of the closed and rigidly hierarchical world of medieval society' ('The Medieval Theater of the Absurd', *PMLA*, 86: 2 (March 1971), 183–9. See also Elliott, *Satire*, p. 266.

6 See also ll. 360–74. Harvey argues that the lawyers and law clerks, to whom he attributes the authorship of many of the plays, were 'crusaders against a decadent social order. They were Renaissance men' (*Theatre*, p. 234). If this were true, it would be further evidence that the *sottie* was not under the control of the Basoche. In addition, Bowen has observed a similar resignation, or pessimism, in the farces (*Caractéristiques*, pp. 17 and 32). It seems that the medieval comic theater, and not just the *sottie*, 'reposait sur un grand fond de pessimisme' (Gaiffe, *Rire*, p. 47).

7 *Déclin*, pp. 45–6. Marc Bloch has made a similar summation: 'Dans les désordres ambiants, que nous qualifierons volontiers de bouillonnements d'adolescence, les contemporains, unanimement, ne voyaient que la décrépitude d'une humanité "vieillie". L'irrésistible vie, malgré tout, fermentait dans les hommes. Mais dès qu'ils méditaient, nul sentiment ne leur était davantage étranger que celui d'un avenir immense, ouvert devant les forces jeunes' (*La Société féodale* (Paris: Albin Michel, 1968), p. 133). An illustration of this attitude is found in *La Croix Faubin*, where Le Pain and Le Vin long for the return of 'Justice la vieille', who has been taken into captivity.

8 A very pessimistic view of the Wheel of Fortune is to be found at the end of *Tout, Rien, et Chascun* (ll. 241ff.).

9 Lucien Febvre has shown that this cyclical conception of history was held by political philosophers of the sixteenth century, as well as by the 'popular philosophers' of the *sottie*: 'L'histoire pour eux? Une succession de cycles, à qui donnait naissance le hasard ou, tout au moins, la mystérieuse influence des sphères célestes qui président à la formation des empires et des religions' (*L'Incroyance*, p. 392).

10 Bon Temps was also frequently mentioned in popular poetry and songs of the Middle Ages, with a variety of connotations. Picot has listed the

works, in the *Recueil de poésies françoises*, of Montaiglon and Rothschild, which deal with Bon Temps (*Recueil général*, vol. II, p. 268). Mohl discusses the traditional idea of the 'good old days' as it appears in the literature of the *états du monde* (*Three Estates*, pp. 39 and 257). For the song 'Bontemps reviendras-tu', sung in *Faulte d'Argent*, see Brown, *Music*, pp. 97 and 194. D'Hericault believes that Roger de Collerye gave his first name to the character Roger Bon Temps. See Roger de Collerye, *Oeuvres*, ed. Ch. d'Hericault, new edn (Paris: Jannet, 1855), p. viii.

11 See also *Le Cry de la Bazoche*, l. 46: 'Plus ne voyons le Bon Temps vieulx' ('We no longer see the Good Old Days').

12 Robert C. Elliott has summarized the historical relationship of the two modes in 'Saturnalia, Satire, and Utopia', *Yale Review*, 55 (1926), 521–36.

13 Wine in particular is as vital to the *sots* as to Rabelais's heros (see, for example, *Les Vigilles de Triboullet*, ll. 190–1).

14 See also *Les Troys Galans et un Badin*, ll. 308 and 310–11. A curious connection between childhood and Bon Temps is made in *Les Sotz qui remetent*, a play in which the character Bon Temps comes to live under the jurisdiction of Le Général d'Enfance. The joys of Bon Temps, as the *sots* conceive of them, do at times resemble the pleasures of childhood (but not always – see discussion of women, below).

15 *Tromperie* was of course one of the favorite themes of late medieval literature. But the fact that the general theme is not unique to the *sotties* does not prevent it from taking on special nuances in those plays.

16 See Lewicka, *Langue*, vol. I, p. 360.

17 Ironic in the sense that the plays seem to be advising what in effect they are either describing as social reality or condemning as vice.

18 Other *sotties* reiterate the idea of *tromperie* as the basis of social success: in particular, *Le Jeu du Capifol*, *Le Monde*, *La Mère de Ville*, *Le Cry de la Bazoche*, and *Le Jeu du Prince des Sotz* (based entirely on the theme of the ruses of the great and powerful).

19 A discussion of these characteristics is to be found in *Totem and Taboo*, by Sigmund Freud, trans. James Strachey (New York: Norton, 1950), pp. 20–2.

20 Fletcher discusses the ambivalent valuation of money as presented in psychoanalytic findings, in *Allegory*, p. 298.

21 See Mohl, *Three Estates*, pp. 324–42.

22 *Les Brus*, *Le Cry de la Bazoche*, *La Folie des Gorriers*, *Le Jeu du Capifol*, *Le Jeu du Prince des Sotz*, *Pou d'Acquest*, *Tout le Monde*, *Troys Pelerins et Malice*, *Mestier et Marchandise*, and *La Mère de Ville*.

23 *Les Brus* has the same lines (ll. 287–8, 293–4).

24 See Zeller, *Institutions*, p. 21. J. E. S. Quicherat records that, under Charles VII, 'on voulait la création d'un ministère de la mode'. Everyone was to dress, 'selon son estat', according to models worked out by the minister

(*Histoire du costume en France* (Paris: Hachette, 1875), p. 333; see also pp. 330–2).

25 Le Monde wears 'abillemens divers' in *Troys Galans et Monde* (ll. 109–12 and 132), but the meaning of the costume is unclear: it may represent the changing times, the various estates, or it may be a disguise. In *Chascun, Plusieurs, Le Temps qui court* wears a costume representing the estates of Noblesse, Eglise, Justice (evidently meant to represent the bourgeoisie), and Labour.

26 Similarly, France, in *Le Quadrilogue invectif* of Alain Chartier, wears a marvelous mantle representing the three estates (ed. Eugénie Droz (Paris: Champion, 1950), pp. 7–8).

27 Alter remarks that 'Dans son ensemble, le patriciat [the higher bourgeoisie] essaie de se distinguer du commun en imitant des manières de seigneur, et la satire en tient compte.' A bitter treatment is reserved, satirically, 'aux jeunes fats qui cherchaient dans la parure l'affirmation de leur supériorité par rapport à leurs pères bourgeois' (*Origines*, pp. 105–6).

28 The *morale petit bourgeois* further condemns the desire to imitate the dress of the upper classes as a desire for luxury. It is this luxury that is ruining the world, according to *Tout le Monde* (l. 230). Even the nobility is accused of dressing with 'trop grande pompe' (l. 229). Prodigality is defined in *Folle Bobance* as sartorial pomp (ll. 498–500), which is, in turn, a kind of madness: the three *sots* of the play serve Dame Folie by dressing in a costly manner.

29 An excellent analysis of the language of the *sotties*, especially in reference to techniques of dialogue, can be found in Aubailly, *Monologue*, ch. 4.

30 Numerous references to 'propos nouveaulx' are found in the *sotties*. See in particular *Les Vigilles de Triboullet*, ll. 49–50; *Les Troys Galans et un Badin*, l. 54; *Le Cry de la Bazoche*, ll. 26–7 and 170; and *Satyre*, ll. 274–6.

31 A number of scholars describe the language of the *sottie*, and of the comic theater as a whole, as the spoken language of the period, in particular of the lower classes: e.g., Droz, *Trepperel*, p. lxx; Bowen, *Caractéristiques*, p. 76; and Lewicka's two-volume study of language in the comic theater. On the other hand, Bakhtine argues that carnival language (found in the *sottie* as well as in the *mardi gras* celebrations) was a unique type of language, 'impensable en temps normal' (*Rabelais*, p. 19).

32 Robert Garapon includes both enumeration and repetition among the four basic types of 'fantaisie verbale' discussed in *Fantaisie*. Although enumerations and repetitions are frequently gratuitous, and not primarily intended to communicate (see Garapon's criteria, p. 10), nonetheless they are not *fantaisie* (in the sense of the free creation of images by the imagination). They are rather limiting and monotonous, instead of untrammeled and capricious. Moreover, they are basic rhetorical and poetic figures, repeated generation after generation.

33 Lewicka discusses a fifth type in 'Un procédé comique de l'ancienne farce:

La Fausse Compréhension du langage', in *Mélanges de langue et de littérature du Moyen Age et de la Renaissance offerts à Jean Frappier*, 2 vols. (Geneva: Droz, 1970), vol. II, pp. 653–8.

34 See Edmond Faral, *Les Arts poétiques du XIIe et du XIIIe siècles* (Paris: Champion, 1924), pp. 94–6.

35 Other passages built on this procedure are found in *Les Sotz escornez* (ll. 59ff.): 'corner' and derivatives; *La Feste des Roys* (ll. 142–62): 'sot'; *Le Cry de la Bazoche* (ll. 262–5): 'faire' and 'prendre'; and *Folle Bobance* (ll. 5–6 and 10–12) and *Les Vigilles de Triboullet* (ll. 1–11): derivatives of 'fol'.

36 *Caractéristiques*, p. 47.

37 For a discussion of this topic, see Ernst Robert Curtius, *European Literature and the Latin Middle Ages*, trans. Willard R. Trask (New York and Evanston: Harper & Row, 1953), pp. 94–8.

6 THE IMPORTANCE OF FOLLY IN THE *SOTTIE*

1 Foucault, *Histoire de la folie*, pp. 37–8. Much of Foucault's discussion of *folie* in this period is an attempt to explain this fact, that 'à partir du xvème siècle le visage de la folie a hanté l'imagination de l'homme occidental' (p. 27). Cf. Swain, *Fools and Folly*, p. 91: Mother Folly became 'the archetype of fifteenth-century cynicism'.

2 For an amusing verbal portrait of a fool, see the eulogy of Triboullet, where he is celebrated as a formidable drinker and eater, but also as a physician; furthermore, he was frightful to see on his *roussin* and unequaled 'en sotoyant' (*Les Vigilles de Triboullet*, ll. 129ff.).

3 See Porter, 'Farce et sotie', p. 94; Swain, *Fools and Folly*, pp. 64–5 and 112; and Foucault, *Histoire de la folie*, p. 25.

4 Brown, *Music*, pp. 170ff.

5 Other incitements to rejoicing occur in *L'Astrologue*, ll. 3–4; *La Folie des Gorriers*, ll. 203, 206; *Les Maraux*, ll. 356–7; *Le Monde, Abuz*, ll. 1165–6; *Les Premiers*, ll. 277–82; and *Les Troys Galans et un Badin*, ll. 1–28.

6 In *Les Rapporteurs* a *sot* is defined above all as someone who thinks he possesses some quality of which, in reality, he has only the shadow: wise men are fools who think they know something; fops are ridiculous fools who think they are elegant (ll. 49–61).

7 The *commedia dell'arte* developed opposing types similar to those of the *sottie*. The second *zanni* (valet) was *sot*, according to Attinger, while the first one was 'rusé, vif, spirituel et sait tromper son monde' (*L'Esprit de la 'commedia dell'arte'*, pp. 41–2).

8 Mauron's study of the *mauvais fils* who pushes his revolt too far has obvious application to the *sottie*, specifically to the evil-doers. Portraits of this type, according to Mauron, 'constituent des satires politiques, sociales ou morales' (*Psychocritique*, p. 70). The *gens nouveaux* do resemble

such a bad son in revolt against the father figure, Le Monde. However, I am concerned in this study with conscious expressions of class conflict, rather than with unconscious psychological forces, as is Mauron. (Both may of course co-exist in the same work.)

9 *L'Arbaleste*, in Antoine J. V. Le Roux de Lincy and Francisque Michel (eds.), *Recueil de farces, moralités et sermons joyeux* (Paris: Techener, 1837), vol. I. This subject could well be studied in more detail.

10 The evil-doers are obviously aggressive characters. The accuser can be at times no less aggressive, in particular when he becomes one of the manifestations of what Elliott calls the 'railer' (*Satire*, p. 140). The fool who criticizes the great – king or Pope – affords the audience vicarious satisfaction. The best examples of the aggressively wise fool are to be found in *Le Jeu du Prince des Sotz*.

11 *Histoire de la folie*, p. 40.

12 See also *Le Pelerin et le Pelerine*, ll. 323–4: 'Car des fols le premier passage / Est de s'estimer estre sage', and *Le Roy des Sotz*, ll. 287–9.

13 Fletcher, *Allegory*, p. 121.

14 These struggles for power sometimes end, as we have seen, in the conversion of the wicked fools. This is a further characteristic of allegory, according to Fletcher: 'When an arbitrary conversion occurs. . . we must ask if that is not the moment when mimesis gives way to allegory' (*ibid.* p. 150).

15 *Ibid.* p. 73. Fletcher points out that if allegory 'may be intended to reveal, it does so only after veiling a delayed message which it would rather keep from any very ready or facile interpretation' (p. 330). Allegory that involved *sots* was even more opaque than simple allegory.

16 To my knowledge the only modern study devoted to satiric allegory is *Satiric Allegory: Mirror of Man*, by Ellen Douglass Leyburn (New Haven: Yale Univ. Press, 1956).

17 See Fletcher, *Allegory*, p. 346, on allegorical rituals; Elliott, *Satire*, p. 58, on satire and ritual.

18 *Satire*, p. 4.

19 *Allegory*, p. 345.

20 Charles Mauron's study of the comic genre has been helpful in developing my own view of the *sottie*. He studies at length the 'fantaisies de triomphe' which he perceives existing, on an unconscious level, throughout the development of Western comedy. My study of the *sottie* has concentrated on more or less conscious 'triumphs' over recognized if unnamed enemies, which is not to say that an unconscious fantasy may not also exist.

21 It is remarkable that a period of similar economic and social change was occurring at the time of Aristophanes, some of whose satires are not unlike the *sottie*. Mauron points out (*Psychocritique*, pp. 114–15) that Athenian society at the time was concerned with the growing power of money; that the aristocracy was deteriorating and the peasants growing poorer, while merchants and artisans grew richer.

Bibliography

I EDITIONS OF THE PLAYS

A PRINCIPAL MANUSCRIPTS AND EARLY PRINTED BOOKS

Bibliothèque Nationale f. fr. 17527 (ancien Saint-Germain 1556), in-fol. Contains *Les Croniqueurs*, 54v–61v

Bibliothèque Nationale Ye 1317. Rés. Paris, 1512, in-8. Contains *Le Jeu du Prince des Sotz et de Mère Sotte*, A2v–C5v

British Library C.22.a.30, Paris: Jehan Trepperel [?], *c.* 1515, pet. in-8. Contains *Les Sotz nouveaulx farcez couvez*. See description by Droz, in *Recueil Trepperel*, pp. xxxiii–lxiii

Bibliothèque Nationale f. fr. 24341 ('La Vallière' manuscript). 74 plays, written in Normandy about 1575

British Library C.20.e.13. *Le Recueil de Londres*. 64 plays, printed separately in the 16th century, by various printers. Facsimile edition, Geneva: Slatkine, 1970

B COLLECTIONS OF PLAYS, INCLUDING 'SOTTIES', COLLECTIONS AND INDIVIDUAL EDITIONS OF 'SOTTIES'

Bossuat, André and Robert, eds. *Deux moralités inédites composées et représentées en 1426 et 1427 au collège de Navarre*. Paris: Librairie d'Argences, 1955 (Bibliothèque elzévirienne). Edition of the *Moralité faicte en foulois pour le chastiement du Monde*

Caron, P. Siméon, ed. *Collection de différents ouvrages anciens, poésies et facéties*. 3 vols. Paris: 1798–1806

Cohen, Gustave, ed. *Recueil de farces françaises inédites du XVe siècle*. Cambridge, Mass.: Mediaeval Academy of America, 1949

Collerye, Roger de. *Oeuvres*. Ed. Ch. d'Hericault. New edn. Paris: Jannet, 1855 (Bibliothèque elzévirienne)

Droz, Eugénie, ed. *Le Recueil Trepperel*. 2 vols. Paris: Droz, 1935. 1: *Les Sotties* (Bibliothèque de la Société des Historiens du Théâtre, 8)
Le Recueil Trepperel. *Fac-similé des trente-cinq pièces de l'original*. Geneva: Slatkine [1966]

Fournier, Edouard, ed. *Le Théâtre français avant la Renaissance*. Paris: Laplace, Sanchez [1873]

Gringore, Pierre. *Oeuvres complètes*. Eds. Ch. d'Hericault and A. de Montaiglon. 4 vols. Paris: Jannet, 1858–77. I: *Le Jeu du Prince des Sots*

Lacroix, Paul (P. L. Jacob, pseud.), ed. *Recueil de farces, sotties et moralités du XVe siècle*. Paris: Delahaye, 1859

Lecocq, Georges. *Histoire du théâtre en Picardie, depuis son origine jusqu'à la fin du XVIe siècle*. Paris, 1880; repr. Geneva: Slatkine, 1971. Contains *Le Jeu par Jehan Destrées*

Le Roux de Lincy, Antoine J. V. and Francisque Michel, eds. *Recueil de farces, moralités et sermons joyeux*. 4 vols. Paris: Techener, 1837 ('La Vallière' manuscript)

Le Roy, F.-N., ed. *Deux sotties jouées à Genève*. Geneva: Gay, 1868

Mabille, E., ed. *Choix de farces, sotties et moralités des XVe et XVIe siècles*. 2 vols. Nice: Gay, 1872

Montaiglon, A. de, and J. de Rothschild, eds. *Recueil de poésies françoises des XVe et XVIe siècles*. 13 vols. Paris: Jannet, 1855–78 (Bibliothèque elzévirienne)

Pauphilet, A., ed. *Jeux et Sapience du Moyen Age*. Paris: Gallimard, 1951 (Bibliothèque de la Pléiade)

Philipot, Emmanuel, ed. *Six farces normandes du Recueil La Vallière*. Rennes: Plihon, 1939

Picot, Emile, ed. *Recueil général des sotties*. 3 vols. Paris: Firmin-Didot, 1902–12

Picot, Emile, and Christophe Nyrop, eds. *Nouveau Recueil de farces françaises des XVe et XVIe siècles*. Paris: Morgand & Fatout, 1880

Sottie à dix personnages, jouée à Genève, en la Place du Molard, le Dimanche des Bordes, l'an 1523. Lyon: Pierre Rigaud, no date [c. 1750]. British Library G. 17891

Tappan, D. W., and S. M. Carrington. 'Deux pièces comiques inédites du manuscrit BN fr. 904', *Romania*, 91 (1970), 169–88. Edition of *La Croix Faubin*

Viollet-le-Duc, Eugène, ed. *Ancien Théâtre françois ou collection des ouvrages dramatiques les plus remarquables depuis les Mystères jusqu'à Corneille*. 10 vols. Paris: Jannet, 1854–7 (Bibliothèque elzévirienne)

II OTHER MEDIEVAL AND RENAISSANCE WORKS

Ascensius, Badius. *Stultiferae naves*. In *Bibliographie des impressions et des œuvres de Badius Ascensius, imprimeur et humaniste, 1462–1535, avec une notice biographique et 44 reproductions en facsimile*, vol. I. Ed. Philippe Renouard. 3 vols. Paris: Paul et Guillemin, 1908; repr. New York: Burt Franklin, 1967

Bouchet, Jehan. *Epistres morales et familières du Traverseur*. Poitiers: 1545

Brant, Sebastian. *The Ship of Fools*. Trans. Edwin H. Zeydel. New York: Dover, 1962

The Shyp of Folys of the Worlde. Trans. Alexander Barclay. London: Richard Pynson, 1509.

Erasmus, Desiderius. *Eloge de la Folie*. French trans. Pierre de Nolhac. Paris: Garnier-Flammarion, 1964

Gringore, Pierre. *Les Fantaisies de Mère Sotte*. Ed. R. L. Frautschi. Chapel Hill: Univ. of N. Carolina Press, 1962
Oeuvres complètes. Ed. Ch. d'Hericault and A. de Montaiglon. 2 vols. Paris: Jannet, 1858–77

III BIBLIOGRAPHIES AND REPERTORIES

Françon, Marcel. *Guide bibliographique pour servir à l'étude de l'histoire littéraire en France aux XIVe et XVe siècles*. Cambridge, Mass.: Harvard Univ. Press, 1941

Lewicka, Halina. *Bibliographie du théâtre profane français des XVe et XVIe siècles*. Paris: Centre National de la Recherche Scientifique, 1972

Petit de Julleville, L. *Répertoire du théâtre comique en France au Moyen Age*. Paris: Cerf, 1886. (Part 4 of *Histoire du théâtre en France*)

Stratman, Carl Joseph, *Bibliography of Medieval Drama*. 2nd edn, revised and enlarged. New York: Unger, 1972

IV SECONDARY MATERIAL

Alter, Jean V. *Les Origines de la satire anti-bourgeoise en France*. 2 vols. I: *Moyen Age – XVIe siècle*. Geneva: Droz, 1966

Arnaud, Leonard E. *French Nonsense Literature in the Middle Ages: The 'Fatras' and its Later Evolution*. New York: New York Univ. Press, 1942

Attinger, Gustave. *L'Esprit de la 'commedia dell'arte' dans le théâtre français*. Paris: Publications de la Sociéte d'Histoire du Théâtre, 1950

Aubailly, Jean-Claude. *Le Monologue, le dialogue et la sotie*. Paris: Champion, 1976 (Bibliothèque du XVe siècle, 41)
Le Théâtre médiéval profane et comique: La Naissance d'un art. Paris: Larousse, 1975

Bakhtine, Mikhail. *L'Oeuvre de François Rabelais et la culture populaire au Moyen Age et sous la Renaissance*. Trans. Andrée Robel. Paris: Gallimard, 1970

Bergson, Henri. *Le Rire, essai sur la signification du comique*. Paris: PUF, 1969

Bloch, Marc. *La Société féodale*. Paris: Albin Michel, 1968

Bowen, Barbara C. *Les Caractéristiques essentielles de la farce française et leur survivance dans les années 1550–1620*. Urbana: Univ. of Illinois Press, 1964

Brantôme. *Oeuvres complètes de Pierre de Bourdeille, seigneur Brantôme*. Ed. Ludovic Lalanne. 11 vols. Paris: Renouard, 1864–82 (Société de l'Histoire de France)

Brown, Howard Mayer. *Music in the French Secular Theater*. Cambridge, Mass.: Harvard Univ. Press, 1963

Cannings, Barbara (now Barbara C. Bowen). 'Towards a Definition of Farce as a Literary "Genre"', *Modern Language Review*, 56 (1961), 558–60

Carrington, Samuel Macon, Jr. 'The Elements of Humor and Satire in the Medieval Farces and *Sotties*.' Doctoral dissertation, Univ. of North Carolina, 1963. *Dissertation Abstracts*, 26, 3946–7

Chambers, E. K. *The Mediaeval Stage*. 2 vols. London: Oxford Univ. Press, 1903; repr. Oxford: Clarendon Press, 1925

Chatelain, Henri. *Recherches sur le vers français au XVe siècle: Rimes, mètres et strophes*. Paris: Champion, 1908

Cohen, Gustave. *La 'Comédie' latine en France au XIIIe siècle*. 2 vols. Paris: Les Belles Lettres, 1939

'Maître Mouche, farceur et chef de troupe au xve siècle', *Revue d'Histoire du Théâtre*, 6 (1954), 146–9

'Rabelais et le théâtre', *Revue des Etudes rabelaisiennes*, 9 (1911), 1–72

'Le Théâtre à Paris et aux environs à la fin du xive siècle', *Romania*, 38 (1909), 587–95

Le Théâtre comique au XVe siècle et dans la première moitié du XVIe siècle. Paris: Centre de Documentation Universitaire, 1940

Le Théâtre en France au Moyen Age. 2 vols. Paris: Rieder, 1928–31; new edn, PUF, 1947. II: *Le Théâtre profane*

'Triboulet, acteur et auteur comique du dernier quart du xve siècle', *Revue d'Histoire du Théâtre*, 6 (1954), 291–3

Conroy, Peter. 'Old and New in Medieval French Farce', *Romance Notes*, 13 (Winter 1971), 336–43

Darmesteter, A., and Adolphe Hatzfeld. *Le Seizième Siècle en France, tableau de la littérature et de la langue*. 15th edn, revised. Paris: Delagrave, 1928

Defourneaux, Marcelin. *La Vie quotidienne au temps de Jeanne d'Arc*. Paris: Hachette, 1952

Dittmann, Walter. *Pierre Gringore als Dramatiker*. Berlin: Ebering, 1923, repr. Nendeln: Kraus, 1967. Appendix: 'Die pariser Enfants-sans-souci zu Gringores Zeit', 259–333

Douce, Francis. *Illustrations of Shakspeare, and of Ancient Manners: with Dissertations on the Clowns and Fools of Shakspeare*. 2 vols. London: Longman, Hurst, Rees, and Orme, 1807

Doutrepont, Georges. *La Littérature française à la cour des Ducs de Bourgogne*. 1909; repr. Geneva: Slatkine, 1970

Duby, Georges, and Robert Mandrou. *Histoire de la civilisation française*. 2 vols. Paris: Colin, 1958

Elliott, Robert C. *The Power of Satire: Magic, Ritual, Art*. Princeton: Princeton Univ. Press, 1960

'Saturnalia, Satire, and Utopia', *Yale Review*, 55 (1926), 521–36

Fabre, Adolphe. *Les Clercs du Palais*. 2nd edn. Lyon: Scheuring, 1875

Faral, Edmund. *Les Arts poétiques du XIIe et du XIIIe siècles*. Paris: Champion, 1924

Les Jongleurs en France au Moyen Age. Paris: Champion, 1910

Febvre, Lucien. 'Une question mal posée: les origines de la Réforme française et le problème général des causes de la Réforme', *Revue Historique*, 161 (May–Aug. 1929), 1–73

Le Problème de l'incroyance au XVIe siècle; La Religion de Rabelais. Paris: Albin Michel, 1942

Fletcher, Angus. *Allegory: The Theory of a Symbolic Mode.* Ithaca, N.Y.: Cornell, 1966

Foucault, Michel. *Histoire de la folie.* Paris: Plon, 1971 (Collection 10/18)

Françon, Marcel. *Notes sur l'esthétique de la femme au XVIe siècle.* Cambridge, Mass.: Harvard Univ. Press, 1939

Frank, Grace. *The Medieval French Drama.* Oxford: Clarendon Press, 1954

Frappier, Jean. 'Sur Jean du Pont-Alais'. in *Mélanges d'histoire du théâtre du Moyen Age et de la Renaissance offerts à Gustave Cohen*, pp. 133–46, Paris: Nizet, 1950

Frye, Northrop. 'The Nature of Satire', *University of Toronto Quarterly*, 14 (Oct. 1944), 74–89

Gaiffe, Félix. *Le Rire et la scène française.* Paris: Boivin, 1931

Garapon, Robert. *La Fantaisie verbale et le comique dans le théâtre français du Moyen Age à la fin du XVIIe siècle.* Paris: Armand Colin, 1957

Goth, Barbara. *Untersuchungen zur Gattungsgeschichte der Sottie.* Munich: Fink, 1967. Review in *Zeitschrift für romanische Philologie*, 88 (1972), 233–5

Graus, F. 'The Late Medieval Poor in Town and Countryside', in *Change in Medieval Society*. Ed. Sylvia L. Thrupp, 314–24. New York: Appleton-Century-Crofts, 1964

Hallays-Dabot, Victor. *Histoire de la censure théâtrale en France.* Paris: Dentu, 1862

Harvey, Howard Graham. *The Theatre of the Basoche.* Cambridge, Mass.: Harvard Univ. Press, 1941

Heers, Jacques. *Fêtes, jeux et joûtes dans les sociétés d'Occident à la fin du Moyen Age.* Montreal: Institut d'Etudes Médiévales, 1971

Huizinga, Johan. *Le Déclin du Moyen Age.* French trans. J. Bastin. Paris: Payot, 1961

Jauss, Hans-Robert. 'Littérature médiévale' et théorie des genres', *Poétique*, 1 (1970), 79–101.

Jeffery Brian, ed. *Chanson Verse of the Early Renaissance.* 2 vols. London: Brian Jeffery, 1971–6.

Journal d'un bourgeois de Paris sous Charles VI et Charles VII. Ed. Alexandre Tuetey. Paris: Champion, 1881

Journal d'un bourgeois de Paris sous le règne de François Ier. Ed. V.-L. Bourrilly. New edn. Paris: Picard, 1910

Journal d'un bourgeois de Paris sous le règne de François Ier (1515–36). Ed. Ludovic Lalanne. Paris: Renouard, 1854 (Société de l'Histoire de France, 75)

Kaiser, Walter. *Praisers of Folly; Erasmus, Rabelais, Shakespeare.* London: Gollancz, 1964

Kilgour, Raymond Lincoln. *The Decline of Chivalry as shown in the French Literature of the Late Middle Ages*. Cambridge, Mass.: Harvard Univ. Press, 1937 (Harvard Studies in Romance Languages, 12)

Knight, Alan E. 'The Medieval Theater of the Absurd', *PMLA*, 86: 2 (March 1971), 183–9

Laborde, Léon de. *Les Ducs de Bourgogne; Etudes sur les lettres, les arts et l'industrie pendant le XVe siècle*. 3 vols. Paris: Plon, 1849–53

Lacy, Norris J., ed. *Medieval French Miscellany*. Papers of the 1970 Kansas Conference on Medieval French Literature. Lawrence: Univ. of Kansas, 1972 (Univ. of Kansas Humanistic Studies, 42)

Langlois, Ernest. *Recueil d'arts de seconde rhétorique*. Paris: Leroux, 1902

Lefebvre, Joël. *Les Fols et la folie; Etude sur les genres du comique et la création littéraire en Allemagne pendant la Renaissance*. Paris: Klincksieck, 1968

Lenient, C. *La Satire en France au Moyen Age*. 4th edn. Paris: Hachette, 1893
La Satire en France ou la littérature militante au XVIe siècle. 3rd edn. 2 vols. Paris: Hachette, 1886

Lewicka, Halina. *La Langue et le style du théâtre comique français des XVe et XVIe siècles*. 2 vols. Paris: Klincksieck, 1960
'Les plus récentes datations d'anciennes farces françaises', *Bulletin d'Humanisme et Renaissance*, 25 (1963), 325–36
'Notes sur quelques pièces du *Recueil de farces inédites*', *Romania*, 76 (1955), 342–73
'Un Procédé comique de l'ancienne farce: La Fausse Compréhension du langage', in *Mélanges de langue et de littérature du Moyen Age et de la Renaissance offerts à Jean Frappier par ses collègues, ses élèves et ses amis*. 2 vols. II, 653–8. Geneva: Droz, 1970

Leyburn, Ellen Douglass. *Satiric Allegory: Mirror of Man*. New Haven: Yale Univ. Press, 1956

Lintilhac, Eugène F. L. *Histoire générale du théâtre en France*. 5 vols. Paris: Flammarion, 1904–10. II. *La Comédie: Moyen Age et Renaissance*

Lot, Ferdinand. *L'Art militaire et les armées au Moyen Age en Europe et dans le Proche Orient*. 2 vols. Paris: Payot, 1946

Lucki, Emil. *History of the Renaissance*. Salt Lake City: Univ. of Utah Press, 1963. Book I: *Economy and Society*

Magnin, Charles. 'Ancien Théâtre françois', *Journal des Savant* (1858), 201–11, 265–88, 406–27

Malherbe, François de. *Oeuvres*. Ed. Ludovic Lalanne. 5 vols. Paris: Hachette, 1862–9

Mauron, Charles. *Psychocritique du genre comique*. Paris: Corti, 1964

Maxwell, Ian Colin Marfrey. *French Farce and John Heywood*. Melbourne & London: Melbourne Univ. Press in association with Oxford Univ. Press, 1946

Miraulmont, Pierre de. *Les Mémoires de Pierre de Miraulmont escuyer*. Paris: Claude La Tour, 1612

Mohl, Ruth. *The Three Estates in Medieval and Renaissance Literature.* New York: Columbia Univ. Press, 1933 (Columbia Univ. Studies in English and Comparative Literature)

Nelson, Ida. *La Sottie: Jeu du gay vouloir.* Paris: Champion, 1974

Oulmont, Charles. *La Poésie morale, politique et dramatique à la veille de la Renaissance; Pierre Gringore.* Paris: Champion, 1911

Parfaict, François and Claude. *Histoire du théâtre françois, depuis son origine jusqu'à présent.* 15 vols. Paris: Mercier & Saillant, 1745

Paris, Gaston. *La Poésie du Moyen Age.* 3rd edn. 2 vols. Paris: Hachette, 1895
La Poésie du XVe siècle. Paris: Lanier, 1886

Petit de Julleville, L. *Histoire du théâtre en France.*
Part 1: *Les Mystères.* 2 vols. Paris: Hachette, 1880
Part 2: *Les Comédiens en France au Moyen Age.* Paris: Cerf, 1885
Part 3: *La Comédie et les mœurs en France au Moyen Age.* 1886. 4th edn. Paris: Cerf, 1897; repr. Geneva: Slatkine, 1968

Picot, Emile. *La Sottie en France.* Nogent-le-Rotrou: Impr. Daupeley-Gouverneur, 1878

Pirenne, Henri, A. Renaudet, E. Perroy, M. Handelsman, and L. Halphen. *La Fin du Moyen Age.* Vol. VII of *Peuples et Civilisations; Histoire générale.* Paris: Alcan, 1929; repr. 1931. Ch. 7: 'Les Nouvelles Tendences économiques' (by Pirenne)

Porter, Lambert C. 'La Farce et la sotie'. *Zeitschrift für romanische Philologie,* 75 (1959), 89–123
La Fatrasie et le fatras; Essai sur la poésie irrationnelle en France au Moyen Age. Geneva: Droz, 1960

Quicherat, J. E. S. *Histoire du costume en France depuis les temps les plus reculés jusqu'à la fin du XVIIIe siècle.* Paris: Hachette, 1875

Renaudet, Augustin. *Préréforme et humanisme à Paris, 1494–1517.* 2nd edn. Paris: Champion, 1953

Rice, Eugene F., Jr. *The Foundations of Early Modern Europe (1460–1559).* New York: Norton, 1970

Rigollot, M.-J. *Monnaies inconnues des Evêques des Innocens, des Fous et de quelques autres associations singulières du même temps.* Paris: J.-S. Merlin, 1837

Roaten, Darnell. *Structural Forms in the French Theater. 1500–1700.* Philadelphia: Univ. of Pennsylvania Press, 1960

Schenck, Mary Jane. 'Functions and Roles in the Fabliau', *Comparative Literature,* 30: 1 (Winter 1978), 22–34

Stetcher, J. 'La Sottie française et la sotternie flamande', *Bulletins de l'Académie royale des Sciences, des Lettres et des Beaux-arts de Belgique,* 2nd series, 43 (1877), 388–432

Swain, Barbara. *Fools and Folly during the Middle Ages and the Renaissance.* New York: Columbia Univ. Press, 1932

Tunison, Joseph S. *Dramatic Traditions of the Dark Ages.* 1907; repr. New York: Burt Franklin, 1970

Welsford, Enid. *The Fool; His Social and Literary History*. London: Faber & Faber, 1935; repr. Garden City, N.J.: Anchor Books, 1961

Wilmotte, Maurice. *Etudes critiques sur la tradition littéraire*. Paris: Champion, 1909

Young, Karl. *The Drama of the Medieval Church*. Oxford: Clarendon Press, 1933

Zeller, Gaston. *Les Institutions de la France au XVIe siècle*. Paris: PUF, 1948

'Louis XI, la noblesse et la marchandise', *Annales: Economies, Sociétés, Civilisations*, 1 (1946), 331–41

Zumthor, Paul. 'Classes and Genres in Medieval Literature', in *Medieval French Miscellany*. Ed. Norris J. Lacy, pp. 27–36. Lawrence: Univ. of Kansas Press, 1972 (Univ. of Kansas Humanistic Studies, 42)

'Essai d'analyse des procédés fatrasiques', *Romania*, 84 (1963), 145–70

Essai de poétique médiévale. Paris: Seuil, 1972

'Fatrasie et coq-à-l'âne', in *La Fin du Moyen Age et Renaissance, mélanges de philologie offerts à Robert Guiette*, 5–18. Antwerp: Nederlandsche boekhandel, 1961

Index